PRAISE FOR STRENGTHS-BASI RECRUITMENT AND DEVELOPMENT

'Higher productivity is the key to rising living standards but it will not happen just by relying on new technology and skill training. It needs good personnel management to get the right people in the right jobs. Sally Bibb explains convincingly that traditional recruitment based on technical competence too often produces square pegs in round holes. Her advocacy of strengths-based recruitment, identifying what recruits actually want to do and how to liberate their strengths, is supported by evidence which I found compelling. Several NHS Trusts, Saga, the AA, Starbucks and others depend on their staff's ability to deal well with patients or customers and this can only happen if staff are contented and highly motivated: all have successfully used the methodology described in the book.' **Vince Cable, former UK Secretary of State for Business, Innovation and Skills**

'For an HR professional, this is a must-read. The strengths approach challenges the way many of us have thought about and done talent development and management for years. In this book, Sally Bibb puts that challenge to us in a compelling, practical and evidence-based way.' **Kristina T S Vestbø, Vice President, People and Organization, Technology, Projects and Drilling, Statoil**

'Successful people are good at what they do. So why not build the talent in your organization by putting your people in positions they excel at, and give them jobs they enjoy doing? *Strengths Based Recruitment and Development* shows you how to do just this and how to avoid the common pitfalls that exist developing talent in many organizations today. Sally Bibb provides practical and real-life examples from organizations, both large and small, who have successfully implemented the approach.

Superbly practical and accessible, this book takes you step by step through what you need to do to adopt this new approach, which is easy to implement and will significantly improve your bottom line. A must-read for business leaders, HR professionals and academics alike.' **David Buckley, Chairman, SIN Capital International Limited, and former CEO, Morgan Stanley Bank International Limited**

'As a learning and development professional, I'm always looking for more effective ways of enhancing performance and improving productivity. This book provides compelling evidence as to why using a strengths-based approach to recruitment and development helps to achieve this.' **Jo Kelly, Head of Executive Progression, John Lewis Partnership**

'This book is a must-read for anyone involved in talent management, in recruiting the next generation of managers. Making sure that we identify the personality of the candidate and of the role, and ensuring a good fit, is a strengths-based approach, but it is rarely done. This book highlights the how and why... excellent read.' **Professor Sir Cary L Cooper, CBE, 50th Anniversary Professor of Organizational Psychology and Health, Manchester Business School, University of Manchester, UK, and President of the CIPD, the British Academy of Management, RELATE, and the Institute of Welfare**

'"Go with your strengths!" How many times have I heard this advice and how often have I used the phrase in my own coaching of talent? Sally Bibb provides the means, the methods and the rationale for executives and organizations in her new book. She demonstrates successful strengths-based talent selection, development and management for the 21st century. Her advice is holistic, systematic, and both rational and practical. It's hard to imagine leaders not following her approach and integrating it into their agendas.' **John Hofmeister, former President, Shell Oil Company, and former HR Director, Royal Dutch Shell**

'This is the most refreshing book I have read about recruiting and retaining talent. It encapsulates everything a leader needs in order to fully appreciate the value of strengths-based recruiting. With the millennial and centennial generations entering our workforce, we need, more than ever before, a step change in ensuring we embrace, nurture and challenge high-potential talent.' **Emy Rumble-Mettle, Director of Talent and Development, GroupM, a WPP Company**

'I found this book extremely interesting and, more importantly, useful and practical. Strengths-based talent management is becoming a critical tool when developing a team or organization which will both believe in and execute a strategy – not because they "have" to but because they "want" to. This makes for a truly high-performing and motivated team!' **Ian Carter, President, Global Development, Hilton Worldwide**

'Strengths-based recruitment is rightly here to stay and any serious recruiter can no longer ignore the benefits. Sally Bibb is the preeminent expert and has given us an interesting, practical and inspiring guide to everything we need to know. This is the perfect guide for beginners and experts alike and gives you everything you need to know.' **James Darley, Executive Director, Graduate Recruitment, Teach First**

'This book contains important lessons for anyone involved in recruiting and managing people across all sectors, at all levels, and in organizations of every size. Its messages resonate with my 35 years' experience in retailing, healthcare, strategy consultancy across a wide range of industries, as an entrepreneur, on NHS boards and in the third sector. Great careers and great performance result from playing to strengths and ensuring you have "round pegs in round holes". Sally Bibb explains what strengths-based talent management is all about, offers guidance on how to do it, and provides plenty of ammunition for leaders needing to persuade sceptical colleagues of the case for change.' **Tom Hayhoe, Chairman, West London Mental Health NHS Trust**

'With solid intellectual foundations in positive psychology, Sally Bibb's *Strengths-Based Recruitment and Development* is a timely and welcome challenge to the current and outdated orthodoxies that bedevil how people in organizations are managed. Sally's highly compelling book offers us a convincing case for how the strengths-based approach can make a positive difference and bring about meaningful change in organizations; moreover, with the aplomb of a highly skilled practitioner of the strengths-based approach herself, she shows us how we can all become more effective and fulfilled in our professional and personal lives.' **Eugene Sadler-Smith, Professor of Organizational Behaviour, Surrey Business School, University of Surrey, UK**

'Sally Bibb has articulated the themes in strengths-based recruitment with such simplicity, clarity and conciseness in this book. This is definitely a must-read for the organizations looking to implement an understandable and effective strategy for their talent management and resourcing.' **Sam Kumar, Director of International Sales, *Washington Post***

'This book is thought provoking and inspirational. Strengths-based talent management has the potential to transform the recruitment and performance management of an organization. Sally Bibb's new book shows us how to get it right – it describes a tried and tested approach that means we can know with more certainty that we are choosing a person who will not only be appropriate for their role but will be energized and motivated to do it well.

The insights presented by leaders and senior managers into how strengths-based talent management has impacted on their organizations are eye-opening.

If you want to make a profound change to the performance and well-being of your staff and organization, then this book is for you.' **Dame Jill Macleod Clark, DBE, PhD, RGN, FRCN, Emeritus Professor and former Dean of the Faculty of Health Sciences, University of Southampton, UK**

'HR is besotted with the pursuit of the latest big idea, irrespective of the needs of the recipient organization and the veracity of the bought-in solution. Strengths-based recruitment is at the other end of the spectrum. It is based on analysis of needs and proven technologies, which unusually for "HR products" can generate substantial and tangible benefits. Sally Bibb's book describes this brilliantly.' **Mike Haffenden, Founder of Corporate Research Forum and Strategic Dimensions**

'Imagine the competitive advantage that your organization would enjoy if you could maximize the potential of *all* your staff. In this book Sally Bibb makes the business case for applying strengths-based practice in

the workplace. This book is the first of its kind to provide evidence-based guidance, insightful case studies and practical tools, tips and strategies to make strengths-based recruitment and development work for your organization. Are you ready to join the strengths-based revolution?'
Bridget Grenville-Cleave, MAPP, MBA, FCCA, Positive Psychology Consultant, Workmad Ltd, and Visiting Lecturer at the University of East London, UK, Anglia Ruskin University, UK, and Masaryk University, Czech Republic

'A very powerful and impactful book with practical application for any organization compelled to create sustainable performance in the 21st century, beginning with the recruitment process! In a very crowded marketplace of academic approaches to the challenges of talent acquisition, this book captures precisely what is now demanded for successful recruitment and onboarding. A must-read for any HR practitioner who wants a seat at the strategic table!' **Charlie Walsh, President, HOPS International LLC, and Managing Director, International Center for Organizational and Leadership Excellence**

'Recruiting the right staff can seem like a "dark art" at times but this excellent book will inspire you to undertake strengths-based recruitment in your organization. This book is an essential guide for all senior nursing and HR leaders who want to recruit the best using a tested and endorsed methodology. I can highly recommend it.' **Sarah Rushbrooke, Deputy Chief Nurse, The Royal Marsden NHS Foundation Trust**

'Sally Bibb has been a keen observer of the development of management talent throughout her career. She knows what works!

Her superb knowledge is encapsulated in *Strengths-Based Recruitment and Development*. This book is a toolkit for managers and corporate coaches to motivate and get the best out of current and future employees. If you want to build a great team and make sure that your company is a winner, this is the book you need.' **Dr Karen Otazo, President, Global Leadership Network**

'Whether you're looking to improve the efficiency and profitability of your business or you're an ambitious graduate looking for a job that's the right fit, Sally Bibb's book makes compelling reading.' **Susan Debnam, Visiting Lecturer, CASS Business School, City University London, UK**

'Motivating, energizing, in a virtuous circle… the positive difference for both employee and employer of being "a round peg in a round hole" is massive. Having worked in many companies where annual appraisals focused far more on weaknesses by constantly comparing us with the (theoretical) "perfect" employee who excelled at everything, it is really refreshing to read about organizations focusing on their employees' real strengths.' **Neil Munz-Jones, Founder and Director, mdj2 associates, and author of** *The Reluctant Networker*

'As a marketing professional, it's fascinating to apply the concept of taking your best customers and analyzing them to find others who look like them to your working team. Sally Bibb advocates the use of this concept to use the knowledge of what strengths makes a team member excel and apply this in the recruitment process.

   The real-life insights and stories set this book apart from other business books. This section provides interviews that allow you to start from a more knowledgeable starting point and take advantage of learning from other companies who successfully implemented SBR.' **Soo Son, Marketing Director, US pharmaceutical company**

'Packed with real examples, this book shows how strengths-based recruitment can help organizations to achieve ongoing success. It is a must for everybody who cares about helping their organization to shape a successful future.' **Mike Pegg, author of** *The Art of Strengths Coaching*

Strengths-Based Recruitment and Development

A practical guide to transforming talent management strategy for business results

Sally Bibb

Giles

May you always go from strength to strength!

All the best

Sally.

Kogan Page

LONDON PHILADELPHIA NEW DELHI

First published in Great Britain and the United States in 2016 by Kogan Page Limited

2nd Floor, 45 Gee Street
London
EC1V 3RS
United Kingdom

1518 Walnut Street, Suite 900
Philadelphia PA 19102
USA

4737/23 Ansari Road
Daryaganj
New Delhi 110002
India

www.koganpage.com

© Sally Bibb, 2016

The right of Sally Bibb to be identified as the author of this work has been asserted by her in accordance with the Copyright, Designs and Patents Act 1988.

ISBN   978 0 7494 7697 7
E-ISBN 978 0 7494 7698 4

British Library Cataloguing-in-Publication Data

A CIP record for this book is available from the British Library.

Library of Congress Cataloging-in-Publication Data

Names: Bibb, Sally, 1963– author.
Title: Strengths-based recruitment and development : a practical guide to
   transforming talent management strategy for business results / Sally Bibb.
Description: London ; Philadelphia : Kogan Page, 2016.
Identifiers: LCCN 2015051169 (print) | LCCN 2016007012 (ebook) | ISBN
   9780749476977 (paperback) | ISBN 9780749476984 (ebook)
Subjects: LCSH: Employees–Recruiting. | Employee retention. | Personnel
   management. | Manpower planning. | BISAC: BUSINESS & ECONOMICS / Human
   Resources & Personnel Management. | BUSINESS & ECONOMICS / Management. |
   BUSINESS & ECONOMICS / Leadership.
Classification: LCC HF5549.5.R44 B5165 2016 (print) | LCC HF5549.5.R44
   (ebook) | DDC 658.3/1–dc23
LC record available at http://lccn.loc.gov/2015051169

Typeset by SPi Global
Print production managed by Jellyfish
Printed and bound by CPI Group (UK) Ltd, Croydon, CR0 4YY

CONTENTS

**11   Interviews with people who transitioned from the
wrong job to the right job** 216

ABOUT THE AUTHOR

Sally Bibb is the Founding Director of Engaging Minds, a specialist strengths consultancy. Her background is in international organizational change and development in Europe, the United States, Latin America and Asia. In the corporate world she held senior roles at The Economist Group and in the telecommunications and media sectors.

She is an award-winning author of several business books, including *The Right Thing: An Everyday Guide to Ethics in Business* (2010, John Wiley and Sons), *The Rookie's Guide to Generation Y* (2009, Marshall Cavendish), *Management F/Laws* (with Russ Ackoff and Herb Addison, 2006, Triarchy Press), *The Stone Age Company* (2005, Cyan Books) and *Trust Matters* (with Jeremy Kourdi, 2004, Palgrave Macmillan).

Sally serves on the Steering Committee of The Daedalus Trust, a charity founded by Lord David Owen to promote research hubris syndrome in business. She also works in schools and colleges to bring strengths-based thinking into their careers support for young people. She has an MSc in Change Agent Skills and Strategies from the University of Surrey and is a Fellow of the Royal Society of Arts.

FOREWORD

Over the last 5 to 10 years, we've lived through dramatic times. The financial crisis of 2007–08 has had a significant impact on workplaces and employee engagement: large scale lay-offs, atypical working relationships, including the rise of zero-hours contracts, employee perceptions that they are working harder than ever, and so on.

With this backdrop, I sense that many human resources professionals have turned inwards and their roles are focused heavily on productivity by cost reduction and 'doing more with less'. Who could blame them? But there are other ways to enhance organizational performance, whether it be retention of your best employees, improving quality and reducing error rates, and improving productivity by ensuring you have the best people in your critical roles. Based on my professional experience and the case studies in this book, strengths-based human resources practices have the power to transform organizational performance.

The idea of harnessing employees' strengths in human resources management, whether it be recruitment or development, are not new. They have been around some time. But many organizations have not yet gone down this path. Sally Bibb's book comes at the right time and I am hoping it provides the call to action that has long been needed.

Grounded in positive psychology, a 'strength' is the innate way we each think, feel and respond to stimuli around us. And we're all different. What excites one person won't necessarily excite the next. Take top-performing sales people. Given equal product knowledge and skills, such as negotiating and overcoming objections, why do some excel whilst others struggle? Having studied sales professionals over the years, one strength that accounts for this performance difference is competitiveness. The best love to compete, they strive to be at the top of their sales league, they constantly measure achievement against their own targets – and they are usually bad losers! But if you're not naturally competitive, going into a 'head-to-head' with others is likely to fill you with dread.

Sadly, few organizations have woken up to this fact. Many are still taking a 'remedial' approach to people management, trying to 'train in' certain strengths that the employee may be missing. This is not only misguided but a waste of resources. Why? Strengths are more or less hard-wired as a result of how synaptic connections in our brains communicate with one another, through nurture or neglect as a child. This means we can't develop these innate talents later on in life. Take empathy, for example. If you don't naturally 'tune in' to others or feel what they are feeling, you can't learn to do it. I can change my behaviours to give the impression of being more empathetic, such as making encouraging noises to people ('uh huh'), using expressions like 'I see', using non-verbal clues, such as good eye contact and nodding. But these will be learned behaviours and won't appear natural or sincere.

So why haven't more organizations gone down the strengths path? Prior to the economic crisis, the best human resources professionals were focused on building differentiating capabilities to deliver performance and competitive advantage. Along came the downturn and a change of focus – cost-cutting, risk avoidance, sticking to the old ways of doing things. Who would want to put their head over the parapet by suggesting more enlightened ways to boost bottom line performance than merely cost-cutting?

However, my main hypothesis is that until Sally's book, there has been little practical and readily accessible literature on the subject. *Strengths-Based Recruitment and Development* is the first book on the market that provides real practical insights and guidance on how to embed strengths practice, particularly the unique methodology she describes on developing strengths and motivations profiles of top performers as a basis for recruitment and selection.

This book also provides inspiring insights from leaders across different sectors who've adopted strengths-based recruitment and documents the transformational impact it has had. We hear from employees who've been in the wrong career and the impact it has had on their lives. The stories of people who have been a 'square peg in a round hole', who discovered their passions and are now doing something they love, are uplifting.

Reading through some of these interviews reminded me of how 'playing to strengths' had a fundamental impact on my life. Yet prior to June 2000 I was blissfully unaware of the concept. I vividly remember that all changed when a new Human Resources Director joined Standard Chartered Bank, where I was working at the time. I was Head of Human Resources (HR) for our European business and not really enjoying myself at all. On paper, it was a classic HR role and the next logical career step for me. But did I get a buzz out of it? Not at all. Was I brilliant at it? Competent, but not brilliant. I couldn't work out what was wrong. I was on the verge of leaving and would have probably made the mistake of going into a similar role, but just changing environment.

On his second day, the new HR Director took me off to the local Starbucks and sat with me for an hour or so. Not talking about the issues at work or his vision for HR. The conversation was simply about what I loved doing at work, what drove me, what gave me a real buzz. And within that hour it became clear that I was in the wrong job – and more critically, why.

What we quickly worked out was that I was not using my natural strengths at work. The stuff I'm really good at – developing and implementing new ideas, acting as a change agent – was not being used at all. Although I had tried to get the business to do things differently, the whole HR machine at the bank at that time was not geared up for it.

The new HR Director changed that. He had a very different vision and needed someone to lead the thinking on it. And what was the change brief? Part of it was to embed a strengths-based approach to people management. That was right up my street. I moved role and never looked back.

I believe Standard Chartered was truly pioneering at that time in adopting a holistic strengths-based approach to recruitment, development and employee engagement. And it was one factor in helping transform the bank's perform-ance. From 2002 to 2011 it had 10 years of increasing annual profits year on year, even after the crisis hit.

We started with strengths-based selection and development of our leaders. Counter-intuitively, we have the greatest potential for performance growth in our areas of natural strength. So we had a complete change of development strategy. Leaders got to understand their strengths and how to use them, rather than getting the usual focus on what was missing. We then percolated this down the organization. This was hugely liberating for our people. And they started talking a new but shared language. They appreciated each other's differences and could see who had complementary strengths.

Sally and I first met many years ago at a conference whose key theme was building HR strategic practices on positive psychology – or 'playing to strengths'. That was pre-financial crisis, of course. I was one of the speakers, sharing the work my colleagues and I had done at Standard Chartered Bank to im-plement strengths-based recruitment and development. Sally happened to be one of the delegates. It was then we struck up a lasting professional relation-ship based on our mutual passion to spread strengths practices.

I've since had the privilege of working with Sally on strengths-based recruit-ment in the National Health Service (NHS). Reading Katherine Fenton's interview in this book is proof positive that strengths-based approaches are having as much of an impact in certain parts of the NHS as they did on my career.

Working with strengths has been Sally's driving focus for the last 15 years. There is no one better to write this book.

The HR Directors and NHS leaders featured in this book share some-thing in common. They think big and have had the courage to be bold and sponsor what they believe in. They have all made a huge difference to the success of their organizations and the people working there. They have all left a legacy they should be proud of.

This book makes 'playing to strength' much more accessible to leaders, providing clear 'how tos' as well as concepts. Sally takes something that is rigorous and makes it highly practical to implement. For this reason, I hope it stimulates HR professionals to stop their fixation with weaknesses: a strategy focused on trying to develop an innate strength in someone that doesn't have it simply does not work. It may get them to mediocre performance, but no further. It's also highly demoralizing for the employee and undermines confidence.

Imagine a workplace where we all use our strengths much of our time at work. That means doing work we are naturally good at, getting out of bed with a sense of excitement about what the day will hold, being more productive and engaged as we are doing things that resonate with us, and being on top of our game. This has not characterized the world of work in recent times. It's time for a change.

If you are thinking about adopting a high-performance strategy, give strengths a try. Take the first step. Study what strengths make for top performance in your key roles. Recruit rigorously to ensure a great match between critical strengths and motivators for the job and those the candidate possesses. It has the power to transform people and organizational performance.

Debbie Whitaker
former Group Head of HR Strategy and People Product Management,
Standard Chartered Bank, HR commentator and consultant

ACKNOWLEDGEMENTS

The author is only one of many people who create a book. In the case of this one, it wouldn't have been possible without a good number of people.

The people and organizations I am proud to call clients have been the pioneers that have put their trust in my team and I and given us the chance to work with them. Some of them feature in this book. Many others don't. I'm grateful to you all for giving us the opportunity to work with, and make a difference to, your organizations.

To everyone who has been interviewed and shared their stories for the book, thank you for your generosity of time and your openness. The book is a lot richer for your contribution.

My team at Engaging Minds have supported, commented on, reviewed and contributed to this book in many ways. They all put their heart and soul into the work we do, without which there would be no book. I'm grateful to work with such smart, committed and caring people. Particular thanks to David North for your research, review and comment on the manuscript and your valued partnership from day one.

My thanks too to all the reviewers of the early drafts, some I know and some I don't. Your critique, comments and suggestions have improved it no end.

Sally Blake has been there from the beginning, is a valued collaborator, and stalwart supporter of all I do. This book is no exception. Your many talents as writer, story-teller, web wizard, critic and person who knows what it's like to follow your heart, has helped me make this book a solid one as well as an inspiring one.

I am lucky to have known many people who are 'round pegs in round holes' in their chosen fields and whom I admire. My late mentor Gerard Fairtlough, former boss David Laird, colleagues at the Daedalus Trust, poet David Whyte and the nurses I have worked alongside in the NHS have been particularly significant. In their own ways they make the world a better place.

Thanks also to the people who tell me straight, give me feedback, challenge me to keep raising my game and are always on my side; Judie Bibb, Mark Cooper, Fiona Davis, Mike Haffenden, Jan Hammond, Fiona Hickman-Taylor, Andy Maslen, Shaun Orpen, David Robertson, Yannis Roussos and Kate Saunders.

Writing a book whilst also running a business is a stretch. If it wasn't for Charlie Haynes's Urban Writers' Retreats I don't know how I would have produced 95,000 words on time. Thanks Charlie for the space and hospitality.

Thank you too to my wonderful assistant Janet Dunkley who kept the wheels on the bus while I retreated to write for several days at a time.

Thank you Debbie Whitaker for your incisive and galvanizing foreword and for your inspiration and insight over the years. Also huge thanks to Lucy Carter, my Development Editor at Kogan Page. You have been fantastic to work with and have helped me to produce a book that I'm proud of. And thanks to Melody Dawes, Katy Hamilton, Megan Mondi, Arthur Thompson and their colleagues at Kogan Page for commissioning the book and for all you have done. It's a real pleasure to work with you.

Last but not least, a massive thank you to my family and friends for encouraging me in my work and for your enthusiasm for this book. And for the fun and good times we've had amidst all the work!

Introduction

It doesn't matter where you look, every day you see people in organizations who are desperately unhappy and who are longing to do something more fulfilling, more real and that makes them feel more alive. Some of them are trapped in a perpetually sad state of questioning how they've ended up in a job that they are so unhappy in and that feels so wrong for them. Some feel regret that they never had the guidance, insight or encouragement to find a career that was right for them.

This is not a new phenomenon. Seven hundred years ago Dante began his epic poem the *Commedia* with the words, 'In the middle of the road of my life I awoke in a dark wood where the true way was wholly lost.' Of those that find their right path, or their calling, some find it by accident. Others never do and find themselves in mid-life or older dwelling on the regret of wasted potential and lack of fulfillment in their working lives.

Of course, finding fulfillment in our work is a somewhat modern notion. Probably the majority of people of our grandparents' generation and further back worked just to put food on the table and a roof over their families' heads. They had little or no expectation of feeling fulfilled or happy. But to live a full and vibrant life we need to do work that we love. If we don't, then we're spending our days watching the clock. If we don't feel passionate about what we're working at, each day feels like an ordeal to tolerate until the relief of the weekend comes. A symptom of this widespread dissatisfaction with modern work is that one of the most Googled questions is: 'What shall I do with my life?'

We all know when we encounter someone who is doing what they *really* want to do with their life. It's obvious. There is a contentment and a vibrancy about them. We feel inspired in their presence, irrespective of whether they are a shop worker or a surgeon. And if we're unhappy in our work the contrast between them and us feels painful and we look at them with envy. We all seek that feeling – the one of being on the right path. We all want to be able to announce 'I love my job' and mean it. And we all want to work in an organization that values us for who we are.

My own journey into the strengths-based field of work has its seeds in my early twenties when I found myself as a so-called HIPO (high-potential) in BT International, as it was then. One of my first jobs was such a great fit for me and I loved it. The job was crewing BT Marine cable-ships. When we got a call that a cable had gone down and needed repairing we had to get one of the ships to sea within 24 hours, or a huge financial penalty was incurred. My job was to ensure the right number of people with the requisite skills and experience were on the ship. It was fast-paced, took a lot of organization and problem solving, and meant I connected with people all day, every day. My office was on the quayside, so I could connect easily with people coming on and off the ships. I loved it and was very good at it. So they promoted me! The new job couldn't have been a worse fit. It involved doing desk research in preparation for my bosses' negotiations with the trades unions. I sat in a quiet office with my manager. People rarely came in and I rarely went out. They sent me on a data analysis course and I became competent enough with figures and spreadsheets but I found the work draining, whereas my previous job had been so energizing for me. My confidence dropped and neither I nor my boss could really understand how it was that I was so vibrant and successful in my previous role but not in my new one. I had ticked all the boxes in the interview but it didn't occur to any of us to ask whether it was actually a good fit for me.

BT did celebrate what I did well when I was doing it. But as soon as I got into a position where I was not doing well their approach was to try and fix my weaknesses by sending me on various training courses. The same weaknesses were discussed at each appraisal discussion and didn't improve much over time. It was unintentionally demotivating. And it was wrong-headed.

All too often organizations make it their business *not* to celebrate what's right with their people but instead they try to identify what's wrong with them and set about trying to fix them. So even those who are stars and doing fantastically well in their jobs feel demoralized because they are not valued for their strengths. The message instead is, 'We want you to become this "ideal" person who fits our competency framework.' There is no logic to this. It's dehumanizing and over time this mindset chips away at people and undermines their ability to do a great job.

Customers can't love an organization unless those who are working in it love what they do. If work is more pain than pleasure then we're constantly stifling and inhibiting the potential of each person and therefore the entire organization in which they work. A revolution is needed in the way we think about work and the way we value people and release them to do their work as *themselves* and not as some stylized 'ideal' described in flat and uninspiring ways.

The revolution that is needed is so easily within our grasp. It's simple and, for those who experience it, it's a great relief.

Few organizations are full of vibrant people doing what they love every day. And the difference between what they have/do and what they strive for is simply a small but distinct shift in thinking.

There's a desperate need to guide people – from students who are just starting out to middle managers who are worn out from the daily grind of trying to bend themselves into a shape other than that which they are – into their rightful work where their natural strengths and talents are best mined, and where they are doing what matters and means something to them.

The revolution that I am talking about is one that focuses on what is right with people in organizations. One that selects people based on who they are and whether they will thrive in their work. It's a strengths-based revolution and, as I write, it has already started. Some leaders have had the vision, foresight and intuition that this is the way to go. Their organizations are now using strengths-based approaches to talent management and it has transformed not only their results but also their mindset.

This book is about the strengths revolution and the organizations that are leading it.

These organizations have discovered how to find and keep employees who are in their element doing their job. They have adopted a strengths-based approach to recruitment and talent management that is based on selecting and managing people on the basis of their *strengths* (what they are really good at and love to do) as well as just competencies (what they *can* do).

Given the results that these organizations are experiencing – both quantitative and qualitative – my prediction is that over the next decade or so there will be a shift from prevailing ways of recruiting and selecting to a strengths-based approach.

The usually elusive connection between intervention and return on investment is not elusive with strengths-based recruitment (SBR). I have worked in the field of human resources (HR) and development for many years and have never come across anything else that so obviously and quickly demonstrates a return on investment as SBR does. With the rise in so-called 'evidence-based HR', it seems inevitable that an approach for which the evidence of effectiveness is so clear and fast occurring will become a must-do.

Finally, though, this approach is felt by some to be controversial. The reason? Because the premise behind the strengths approach is that if someone hasn't got a natural strength they cannot acquire it. We are who we are by the time we are about 15 years old. Fundamentally we don't change unless something drastic or dramatic happens to us. You can't learn to be someone you are not. All you can learn is skills or knowledge.

So the strengths approach challenges decades of practice where organizations have tried to get people to fit their competency model. It says, for example, if you're not a competitive person you can never become one. So if you are in sales and not a competitive person you will always lack a necessary strength for that job no matter how much training or coaching you receive.

This is a controversial idea for some organizations whose approach to recruitment and development has been based on the premise that, essentially, anyone can learn anything.

But then, controversy is quite often the basis for revolution!

The structure of this book

The book is made up of two parts. Part One: A practical guide to implementing strengths-based recruitment and development; and Part Two: Real-life insights and stories.

Part One explains the what, why and how. It is intended to be a resource guide for those who want to know about the rationale and benefits as well as the essentials of how to implement strengths-based talent management. Part Two contains interview transcripts with three groups of people from organizations as diverse as Gap, the NHS, SABMiller and Starbucks UK. There are eight interviews with executive board level people who have commissioned strengths-based recruitment/development for their organizations; six interviews with managers and recruiters who have been involved in implementation; and six interviews with individuals who, at one time, were in the wrong job and are now in jobs where they are 'round pegs in round holes'.

PART ONE

A practical guide to implementing strengths-based recruitment and development

An introduction to strengths-based recruitment

01

This chapter answers these questions:

- What is strengths-based recruitment (SBR)?
- How is SBR different from other recruitment approaches?
- What are the different SBR methodologies?

The old man knew he was dying, and so did the ward sister. He had had no visitors and no friends or family to sit with him in his last days. But he had a beloved dog at home. So the ward sister arranged to have his dog brought in to the hospital. It was obviously against hospital rules, but the need to do the right thing by the old man and make a difference to him in his dying days was more important to her, so she went ahead and broke them. She didn't put anyone else at risk in any way but she got into serious trouble for it. Nevertheless, she said she'd do it again if it were the right thing for her patient.

This true story illustrates why strengths-based recruitment is now being embraced by visionary leaders in organizations. These leaders want their organizations to be full of people who are great at, and committed to, their jobs. They want people who go the extra mile for their customers. And they realize that their people are their brand. It's all about finding employees who are the right kind of people, and that means delving down and looking beyond the surface. It's about understanding the strengths, values and motivations that are behind a person's behaviour.

The ward sister who smuggled the dog into the hospital could have been seen to be risk-taking. And indeed, if that behaviour were borne of the wrong intentions, it would have been. However, there were three strengths at work in this situation that meant that this ward sister was exactly the type of person that this National Health Service (NHS) Trust's Chief Nurse said she wanted in her team. Three of the thirteen strengths that this ward sister, and all other great ward sisters, has are 'doing the right thing', 'making a difference' and 'having very high standards'. This story tells you how the NHS is now able to identify nurses with the potential to become great ward sisters. It's not simply a tactical HR issue to improve recruitment processes; this is a strategic issue for the NHS. By appointing the right people in the first place and improving patient outcomes, they can fulfil their primary duty and restore public faith in the nursing profession and, by extension, the NHS.

Katherine Fenton, Chief Nurse at University College London Hospitals NHS Foundation Trust, in an article in the *Health Service Journal* in February 2014 said, 'Strengths-based recruitment is about changing the selection processes of an organization, yes. But it's about more than that. It's a strategic intervention that transforms organizational culture, service and performance.'

This chapter defines strengths and how they are developed, explains what strengths-based recruitment is and explores its origins. It also looks briefly at the alternatives to SBR and explains how SBR is different. Finally, the different SBR methodologies are examined.

By the end of this chapter you will clearly understand SBR, how it works and how it compares to other methods of recruitment.

What is strengths-based recruitment (SBR)?

Strengths-based recruitment is attracting, selecting and promoting people with the right innate strengths and motivators for the job. It's about finding people who are a great fit for the role, really want to do it and will thrive in it versus hiring those who just *can* do it. In a nutshell, it's about finding 'round pegs' for 'round holes'. Despite the huge amount of effort organizations make to attract and hire the right people there are a surprising number who are 'square pegs' in 'round holes'.

As Steve Jobs, the late Chief Executive Officer (CEO) of Apple, once said, 'Your work is going to fill a large part of your life, and the only way to be truly satisfied is to do what you believe is great work. And the only way to do great work is to love what you do.' Steve Jobs was right when he said this. If you've ever been in the wrong job you will probably relate to this. It's hard to be great if you don't like or aren't very good at your job. It saps your energy and enthusiasm and is a confidence killer. Identifying people who will do great work because they are a natural fit is the essence of SBR.

What is a strength?

A strength is defined as something that someone is innately good at, loves doing and is energized by. Organizations that adopt SBR do so because they want to select people whose innate strengths match the requirements of the job they want them to do.

Starbucks UK make a clear link between employees who love their jobs and customer satisfaction. They wanted to identify the strengths and motivators of their best baristas, the goal being to understand the 'formula' so that they could recruit more of the best. Sandra Porter, who was the HR Director of Starbucks UK and Ireland and introduced strengths-based recruitment into the company, said, 'I felt that there was a huge opportunity to improve the effectiveness of our recruitment if we could tap into what someone is genuinely good at and has a passion for.' If a person's strengths don't meet the needs of the job it is easy for them to understand why, yet still feel good about themselves. They can become great ambassadors for the company, too, because the selection process feels very positive and they walk away understanding why that job is not for them instead of feeling rejected.

Where do strengths come from?

A person's strengths are created by synapses, or connections, in the brain. A synapse is a connection between two brain cells than enables the cells (neurons) to communicate with one another. These synapses are your threads – and behaviour depends on the formation of appropriate interconnections among neurons in the brain. Crudely, your synapses create your strengths.

On day 42 after conception your brain creates its first neuron; 120 days later you have 100 billion – or 9,500 neurons every second. Sixty days before birth your neurons start to communicate with each other and make connections (synapses). By the age of 3 years old each of the 100 billion neurons have formed 15 thousand synaptic connections with other neurons. That's 15 thousand connections for each of your 100 billion neurons. But then things take a strange turn. Nature now prompts you to ignore a lot of your woven threads, and as these get neglected they fall into disuse and connections start to break. Between the ages of 3 and 15 you lose billions of these synaptic connections. By the age of 16 ½ the network is gone. And you can't rebuild it. Your genetic inheritance and early childhood experiences assist you in finding some connections smoother and easier to use than others, for example the caring connections, or the strategic or relating connection. Through use or nurture some of these dwindle and some of them are used and honed so that they become very well established. By puberty these synaptic connections are formed and we don't really change that much after that. The neuroscientist and paediatric neurologist Dr Peter Huttenlocher (2002), in his studies of neuroplasticity and neural connections, found that the typical pattern for a child's cognitive development is that an overabundance of synaptic connections are formed early on, only later to be refined on the basis of which are used most often, that is, which are most consistently fired in response to environmental stimulus.

Our strengths are like a four-lane super-highway of the brain – the connections that are fast and efficient are those that are used often and are well trodden. The connections (or synapses) that are used less often are like a minor road that is unfamiliar, more difficult to navigate and not an enjoyable experience. Dr Harry Chugani, Professor of Paediatrics, Neurology and Radiology at Wayne State University School of Medicine put it this way, 'Roads with the most traffic get widened. The ones that are rarely used fall into disrepair' (Coffman and Gonzalez-Molina, 2002: 21).

This does not mean that people cannot change, but it implies that people are who they are by puberty and don't change significantly. We may modify our behaviour, but what thrills us or drains us stays fairly constant over time. For example, if you end up with a super-highway for competitiveness, when you see numbers you can't help but use them to compare your performance with other people's. Or if you have no connection with strategy you understand that thinking strategically is important but you just can't seem to think like that. It means we all filter information or respond to situations naturally in different ways.

What are the origins of SBR?

The strengths-based approach to recruitment and development has its roots in the Positive Psychology and Appreciative Inquiry (AI) movements. Positive Psychology is a branch of psychology that is primarily concerned with the positive, adaptive, creative and emotionally fulfilling aspects of human behaviour. The humanistic psychology movement, with its emphasis on the growth of the human, which has its origins in the 1950s, was the most obvious predecessor of Positive Psychology. The most notable of humanist psychologists were Carl Rogers who introduced the notion of the fully functioning human being and Abraham Maslow who was the first psychologist to use the term Positive Psychology, and whose work emphasized self-actualization. Appreciate inquiry is a term coined by David L. Cooperrider in 1986 to describe the discipline of looking for what works in a system or individual.

Martin Seligman from the University of Pennsylvania noted back in 2000 that psychologists know a lot about what is wrong with people but very little about what is right. Indeed, until the 2000s psychological research was predominantly focused on disorders, suffering and dysfunction. Seligman consequently believed that the time had come for things to change: 'the time has arrived for a positive psychology ... to remind our field that psychology is not just the study of pathology, weakness, and damage; it is also the study of strength and virtue. Treatment is not just fixing what is broken; it is nurturing what is best' (Seligman and Csikszentmihalyi, 2000).

From a cultural and organizational perspective this can present something of a challenge. Discovering what is wrong and attempting to fix it is a dominant mode of operating in Western cultures and in many organizations. Indeed this approach is necessary and has led to amazing discoveries, inventions and innovations. However, the problem comes when that is the only way of working or looking at the world. When there is a lack of attention to what is good, what is working and what is right about something, it is tantamount to ignoring why something works so well. Think of it this way. You wouldn't raise a child by constantly focusing on, and pointing out, what it couldn't do. If you did you would end up with a shrunken, limited person lacking in the confidence and ability to reach their potential. In a way, though, that is what organizations do when they focus solely on training and developing people to fix their weaknesses (or 'gaps' as weaknesses have sometimes been re-labelled by companies wishing not to sound negative about their employees).

Appreciative Inquiry (AI) has provided a questioning-based methodology for discovering what energizes and makes systems capable and effective. It is a search for insight into what works well about an organization, a system and its people. It can be applied to economic, organizational, ecological and human systems and it involves a method of inquiry using positive questioning. The assumption behind AI is that every system has untapped positive potential, and by focusing on the strengths of a system (or individual) positive change can occur. So AI is a very important approach in the field of Positive Psychology and, as such, has made a crucial contribution to the field of strengths-based approaches to organizations.

The first, and most famous, case study of the use of Appreciative Inquiry in an organization is that of the Cleveland Clinic in 1980. David Cooperrider was a doctoral student working helping Al Jensen in his research on physician leadership at one of the Cleveland Clinics. They asked research participants about their biggest failures and successes. Cooperrider's attention was caught by what made the clinic work well, the successes and positive elements. They decided to look at the data in terms of the positives, that is all the elements that energized and made the system and people effective, successful and engaged. The report to the Board of the Cleveland Clinic was so well received that they asked that AI be used at all levels of the 8,000 employee organization to facilitate change. In 1986 Cooperrider wrote his dissertation on the process of AI and created the academic grounding for this new form of research.

Another well-documented example of the use of Appreciative Inquiry in business was that of the Green Mountain Coffee Roasters (GMCR). In the late 1990s GMCR achieved a 7 per cent reduction in gross costs by implementing AI. Its CEO, Bob Stiller, said, 'When you focus on what works and you dream of the possibilities, it's very inspiring to people.' Stiller believed too much attention was placed on trying to fix what is wrong in business and illustrated the point with an example of a company that has 99 per cent customer satisfaction rate but focuses on the 1 per cent that is wrong rather than understanding why the 99 per cent are happy. An article in *Harvard Business Update* in 2003 describes how Stiller introduced AI into his business to discover and make the most of the organization's best attributes and practices (Kinni, 2003). The author makes the point that AI is often thought of as a 'soft strategy' but the measurable differences to GMCR's bottom line were far from soft!

> [My] dissertation was defended on August 19th, 1985. But curiously, every month for the last several months, students and others have asked me about that early writing... And the seed vision continues, in my view, to be enormously relevant as vast opportunities for Appreciative Inquiry are emerging everywhere.
>
> *(Cooperrider, 2013)*

One of the opportunities that Cooperrider refers to in this statement is that which exists in organizations. AI is gaining in popularity in organizations. The application of strengths-based recruitment can be seen as a sub-set of AI in that it is all about understanding what it is about people that makes them great at what they do.

It's clear from the response that Seligman, Cooperrider and others have received about their work that appreciative and strengths approaches to organizations resonate with people. Indeed, that is my experience too when working with people at all levels of organizations. However, despite the appeal of the strengths-based approach it's taking a while to permeate large organizations in meaningful ways that make a difference. Arguably, Standard Chartered Bank (SCB) is one of the few organizations to have taken a holistic approach to the application of strengths across its people and organizational development approaches.

SCB is a global financial services firm, and in 2000 it pioneered a strengths-based approach to selecting and managing people. The move came because the bank's HR Director thought it could create a step change for them. He was interested in approaches to people management that could transform the bank's performance from 'very good' to 'world-class'. With its bias towards evidence-based methods, the strengths movement seemed an attractive option.

They started with implementing strengths profiling of the managers who had excellent customer relationship skills. They discovered what made them so great at their job. That was their first foray into what now would be classed as a strengths-based talent management intervention. The strengths profiling was successful in that the bank now clearly understood what made a great performance. So they applied the approach more widely to staff whose role meant they could have a positive and measureable impact on revenue. They found that people they selected based on their strengths generated 40 per cent more revenue on average after only three to six months.

The effect of a move to a strengths-based approach has created great energy in the organization, as well as delivering superior performance. People have found the focus on strengths – and changing what was already good to world-class – inspiring. People showed a real appetite for this approach, as if something very natural was being tapped into. It was also very liberating for people, as individuals no longer needed to hide their weaknesses. The focus was now on bringing out the best in them. In a financial services environment, where results are key, it is telling that after more than ten years the organization is still committed to strengths-based approaches.

Perhaps the earliest proponent of a strengths approach to organizational leadership, though, was Peter Drucker, the American writer, educator and management consultant. In the 1950s he argued that organizations built on strengths offer the greatest potential for performance, growth and individual fulfilment. He suggested that the effective executive makes strengths productive, and that one cannot build on weakness – strengths are the true opportunities (Drucker, 1967).

It's taken some time for strengths-based approaches to talent management to create any kind of practical impact on organizations. But that has started and is gaining momentum fast, as you will see from the case studies in this book.

How is SBR different?

SBR is different from most other selection methods in the following ways:

- The underlying assumption of SBR is that people are who they are and can't change their innate strengths, values and motivators.
- The prime goal is to find out what people are naturally good at, love doing and are energized by, rather than just their past experience and skill.
- It focuses more on what the person is like rather than how they behave.
- Potential applicants are usually able to tell from strengths-based job adverts whether they are likely to be a good fit for the job, thus screening themselves in or out.
- The strengths-based selection process is usually an invigorating and affirming one for candidates, who often report that they learn a lot about themselves.
- The candidate cannot study or learn how to 'pass' a strengths-based interview, as they can for other forms of interview.
- If a candidate is unsuccessful they usually come away realizing that for themselves.
- Unsuccessful candidates don't leave the process feeling deficient in some way. Instead they realize that they would be a poor fit for the particular job.
- Interviewers and candidates both feel that the interviewers really get to know them as people.

SBR feels like a very human process for all concerned, because the end result is a candidate being seen for who they are. If they are appointed they realize that it's because they are a round peg in a round hole. If not, they understand that it's because they would be a bad fit for the job and therefore wouldn't be happy in it. So to that extent it has put the humanity back into what, very often, has become a mechanistic and soulless approach to recruitment.

A brief history of recruitment

The activity of recruiting people for paid work in organizations goes back a long way. Selection based on 'subjective', albeit often sensible, criteria such as connections with the boss was much more common in the early days of paid employment.

From the latter half of the nineteenth century, technological advances resulted in economic development in so-called developed economies. The Industrial Revolution heralded the first industrial giants. As companies got larger and demand for products grew, so did the number of workers needed. And with that growth in need came an increasing complexity in the process of hiring paid labour.

This was the beginning of modern mass recruitment and the start of the challenge to identify people who were going to be good workers. Recruitment advertising began as a method of finding large numbers of people, and companies tried to find ways of assessing whether they were the right people as they could no longer rely on word-of-mouth recommendation or nepotism.

Figure 1.1 illustrates the changing approach to recruitment from the, frequently, subjective recruitment of the 1950s, to the other extreme of 'scientific' recruitment in the 1980s, and finally swinging back to achieve the 'best of both worlds' of strengths-based recruitment, which is where an increasing number of organizations are today. In the 1950s selection was more often a highly subjective process but the positive thing about it was that the person was central to the process and could be seen and distinguished from other candidates.

In the 1980s organizations that introduced competency-based interviewing did so because they were attempting to introduce more objectivity and structure into the interview process. They wanted to replace unstructured interview approaches that meant interviewers asked their own questions and used their gut reaction or feelings about a candidate to judge whether they offered them a job. With competency-based interviewing the employer could in theory be more confident that bias was eliminated and defensible selection decisions were being made. Having a standard approach that all interviewers used gave them consistency across their organizations.

The strengths-based approach blends the best of both worlds, ie the person can clearly be seen for all that they are whilst having a large degree of rigour that comes with an evidence-based selection approach.

Competency-based interviews are sometimes also referred to as behavioural interviews, situational interviews or structured interviews. The most usual questioning method used in competency interviews is where the interviewer asks a series of questions designed to determine whether the candidate has the required competencies. They use probing questions to try to elicit evidence of required competencies in the candidate. However, the method gives candidates much less opportunity to express themselves and can feel very rigid. There is a bigger problem with the competency approach, though.

FIGURE 1.1 The 'art' of recruitment

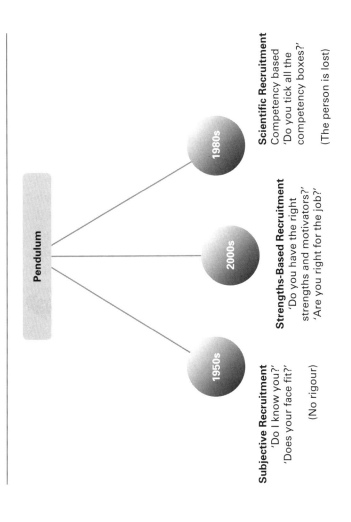

Pendulum

1950s

2000s

1980s

Subjective Recruitment
'Do I know you?'
'Does your face fit?'

(No rigour)

Strengths-Based Recruitment
'Do you have the right
strengths and motivators?'
'Are you right for the job?'

Scientific Recruitment
Competency based
'Do you tick all the
competency boxes?'

(The person is lost)

Richard Boyatzis, an American organizational theorist and Professor of Organizational Behavior at Case Western University defined a competency as 'a capacity that exists in a person that leads to behavior that meets a job's demands within the parameters of the organizational environment and that, in turn, brings about desired results' (Boyatzis, 1982). Boyatzis published research in 1982 using critical incident technique to explore what made managers competent. Critical incident technique is a procedure for gaining information about behaviour that leads to successful performance. It is commonly used for job analysis purposes. There is nothing inherently wrong with the above definition of a competency. The problem comes when the interviewers focus just on the behaviours and skills that a person has, or says they have. This is a problem for two reasons. First, a behaviour or skill could be learned, which means it is unlikely to be consistent. For example, a person can go on a course to learn how to improve their listening skills. But when they are stressed or busy they will tend to revert to their natural way of being. The second problem is that a behaviour can sometimes result from a number of deeper motivations or values. Think back to the opening story of this chapter. You could argue that the behaviour of the ward sister was 'risk-taking'. In fact risk-taking was not a natural behaviour of this person. But she behaved in that way in that situation because a deeper driver was at work, ie her desire to do the right thing.

Competency-based interviewing has gradually been adopted by most large organizations and many medium-sized and small ones, but its efficacy as a selection tool is increasingly being questioned.

What are the alternatives to SBR?

There are many approaches to selection, often even within the same organization. Sometimes the HR department determines the approach and policy, sometimes managers are allowed to decide for themselves which approach to use. However, most selection processes consist of some or all of the following stages:

1 Creation of a job description and person specification.

2 Attraction phase – where potential candidates are either approached directly or a job is advertised and candidates are invited to apply.

3 Application (can be online), where candidate submits an application form or CV.

4 Aptitude testing, eg testing for numerical or verbal reasoning.

5 Psychometric testing.

6 Assessment, which can be one or all of the following:

   a Interviews – there are two categories of interview – one that checks whether a person has the right technical skills and experience to do the job and one that checks whether they are the right sort of person. Sometimes both of these elements are covered in one interview. Sometimes they are conducted separately. Sometimes interviews are done face-to-face and sometimes virtually by phone, Skype (or similar technology).

   b Exercises.

   c Role plays.

7 Job offer.

8 Reference checking.

9 Induction/orientation.

A strengths-based approach to recruitment affects all stages of this process except stage 4 (aptitude testing). We will look at how each stage is affected below.

First, let's look at the most common approach to selection (and main alternative to a strengths-based approach), the competency approach.

The competency-based approach to selection

The UK Chartered Institute of Personnel and Development (CIPD) defines a competency framework as follows:

> A 'competency framework' is a structure that sets out and defines each individual competency (such as problem-solving or people management) required by individuals working in an organization or part of an organization.

There are two categories of competency – behavioural and technical. Examples of behavioural competencies found in most competency frameworks are teamwork, problem-solving and communication skills. Technical competencies would include things like 'ability to administer an injection' (for nurses), ability to use a spreadsheet package (for accountants) and other such elements that are about the skill and knowledge needed to do a particular job.

The CIPD has found that most competency frameworks are designed in-house but use generic competencies from pre-existing frameworks.

Some organizations do their own internal research using methods like a repertory grid, which is designed to determine the competencies of their high performers. However, this seems to be fairly rare, with most organizations drawing on and adapting existing frameworks.

Different authors and commentators have cited the benefits of competency frameworks as:

- Giving clarity to employees as to what is expected of them.

- Helping managers to know what to look for in new recruits and what to expect in their existing people.

- Creating a standard for training programmes to be geared towards.

There can be significant downsides to some competency frameworks, though. Here are some common criticisms that are levelled at the types of competency frameworks used in organizations:

- If the organization has not done rigorous research into what competencies their high-performers have, the framework becomes a wish-list or profile of an ideal person, which means that no real person can ever match the competencies. It's effectively an 'ideal' or composite profile that does not take account of individual differences.

- Some competency frameworks are based not on what makes people high performers, but on what the organization says it wants.

- Time, effort and money are spent trying to get people to fit the framework, which is unrealistic and can be demotivating.

- The competencies are usually articulated in an unspecific way using terms that are too broad or hard to relate to, eg 'communication skills'.

- Competency frameworks can be far too detailed with different levels of behavioural indicators. This makes them complex and unworkable, and busy managers don't have time to make sense of them.

- The language can be distant and jargon-laden, which means that it is impossible to recognize a real person in the description.

- People spend a lot of time trying to fit the competency framework and year after year the same conversations come up in performance reviews, with people focusing on the competencies that they are not reaching.

- Most competency frameworks focus on behaviours, not the underlying values and motivators that create those behaviours.

How does a CBR interview work?

The goal of a competency-based recruitment interview is to seek evidence that establishes whether or not a candidate has the required competencies. That is done by asking questions about previous behaviour, the assumption being that past behaviour is the best predictor of future behaviour.

The questioning technique typically follows the following format:

Tell me about a time when you... [or] Give me an example of...

(the interviewer describes a situation or scenario)

What was the situation?

What was involved?

What actions did you take?

What part did you personally play?

Why did you take the actions you did?

What was the outcome?

What might you have done differently?

The scenarios that the interviewer poses to the interviewee are based around the competencies in the organization's competency framework. They could include things like:

1 Tell me about a time when you had to deliver bad news.

2 Tell me about a time when you had to deal with a challenging customer.

3 Give me an example of a time when you led a group of people to deliver a particularly difficult task.

4 Give me an example of where you had to influence a group of people to do something.

Aside from whether or not the approach is effective, one of the problems is that people can prepare for a competency-based interview and practise giving answers that the assessors want rather than what they actually did. It is relatively easy for a candidate to find out what questions will be asked in interviews. Websites like Glassdoor allow contributors to post their experiences of selection processes with different organizations.

Indeed, there are websites and consultants that coach people in how to pass a competency-based interview. The following is the kind of advice that is given on websites.

Providing examples is essential when answering competency questions. Think of these examples in advance. Then you will be able to attend the interview with this information fresh in your mind. That will help you to answer their questions clearly and succinctly. The interviewer wants you to provide evidence that you can do the job better than any other candidate. To do that you need to give a strong, confident, relevant example which demonstrates each competency required.

Contributors to the Glassdoor website made the following comments on interviews they have had:

'Standard competency questions, followed by a surprise question to catch you off guard (changes all the time).'

'They asked questions like these – competencies and attributes: 1) commitment to teamwork; 2) ability to lead and inspire; 3) respectability and responsibility – are you how the company would like to be perceived by clients?'

'Competency questions, eg Tell me about a time when you had to deal with a difficult customer.'

'It was a one-to-one, face-to-face interview which lasted for an hour and was all related to past experiences in customer-facing role involving competency-based questions.'

'A lot of scenario-based questions and the interview is awfully long. For example, tell me about a time when you held a minority viewpoint in a group.'

In a strengths-based interview (SBI), on the other hand, trained interviewers ask a series of simple, open-ended questions. They assess whether the candidate has the strengths and motivators required to be great in the role. Unlike competency-based interviews (CBIs), SBIs don't rely on set scenarios. This makes it impossible for candidates to rehearse ideal answers. The only way to prepare for an SBI is to be yourself. This makes it much more likely that the real person will shine through.

Most companies hire on competencies alone. The problem with that is that just because someone *can* do something doesn't mean that they really *want* to do it. So hiring on competencies never produces consistently high performance. When people *love* what they do they perform better, have more energy for their work, are more engaged and stay in the job longer.

Hiring on the basis of strengths makes sense and has been proven to be successful. The financial sector is probably ahead of the game. Standard Chartered Bank, Aviva and Norwich Union have all been using strengths-based approaches to recruitment for several years. There are some companies in the retail and services sector too that are reaping the benefits and that others could learn from. Having employees who love what they do and have natural strengths in the role has such a direct and immediate impact on customers.

How is each stage of the recruitment process affected by SBR?

As mentioned above, a strengths approach changes, or has an impact upon, how each stage of the recruitment process is done. Here's how:

1 Creation of a job description and person specification – once you know the strengths profile of someone who is great at a role, the person specification part of the job description must reflect that. In essence that means that the ideal person is described in terms of their strengths; other essential requirements, such as qualifications, skills and experience, are also added, but behavioural competencies are usually entirely replaced by the strengths profile.

2 Attraction phase – where potential candidates are either approached directly or a job is advertised and candidates are invited to apply. The advert is written in a way that it describes a person with the strengths that you know are needed to be successful in the role. The idea is that a person reads a strengths-based job advert and can either recognize themselves in it or not. People can then select themselves in or out of the recruitment process.

3 Application (can be online) – where a candidate submits an application form or CV. Sometimes strengths-based questions can be included in this stage of the selection process as a sifting mechanism, ie those who answer it in a way that suggests they have one or more of the required strengths are put forward.

4 Aptitude testing, eg testing for numerical or verbal reasoning. This stage of the process is not about checking for someone's strengths, so it is not affected.

5 Psychometric testing – a large number of different psychometric tests are available that are designed to measure personality, interests or aptitude or ability to carry out certain tasks. Depending on what

is being sought, and why psychometric tests are being used, sometimes this type of testing can be dropped entirely when SBR is introduced.

6 Assessment – which can be one or all of the following:

   a Interviews. There are two categories of interview – one that checks whether a person has the right technical skills (or competencies) and experience to do the job and one that checks whether they are the right sort of person. Sometimes both of these elements are covered in one interview. Sometimes they are conducted separately. Sometimes interviews are done face-to-face and sometimes virtually by phone, Skype (or similar technology). The strengths-based interview replaces all but the technical competency style of interview because it tells you whether the person is right for the job or not.

   b Exercises and role plays. More often than not exercises that are designed to test for behavioural competences are no longer needed because a strengths-based interview goes beyond assessing behaviour and actually assesses the strengths that underlie behaviour.

7 Job offer. Having interviewed the person using a strengths-based interview you can give them specific feedback about why you selected them for the job. This makes the job offer process more personal and engaging.

8 Reference checking. Understanding people's strengths means that you can direct your reference checking questions towards understanding more about how that person's strengths played out in practice.

9 Induction/orientation. The induction process can be tailored to appeal more to new recruits because you understand their strengths (including their motivators). So the induction/orientation process becomes more engaging for people, getting them off to a flying start.

In summary, a strengths assessment adds to the selection decision by telling us whether a person is the right kind of person for a job. The technical competency interview tells us whether a person has the necessary skills and knowledge. Combined, these approaches give you all the information you need (Figure 1.2).

FIGURE 1.2 What is the crux of a strengths-based recruitment approach?

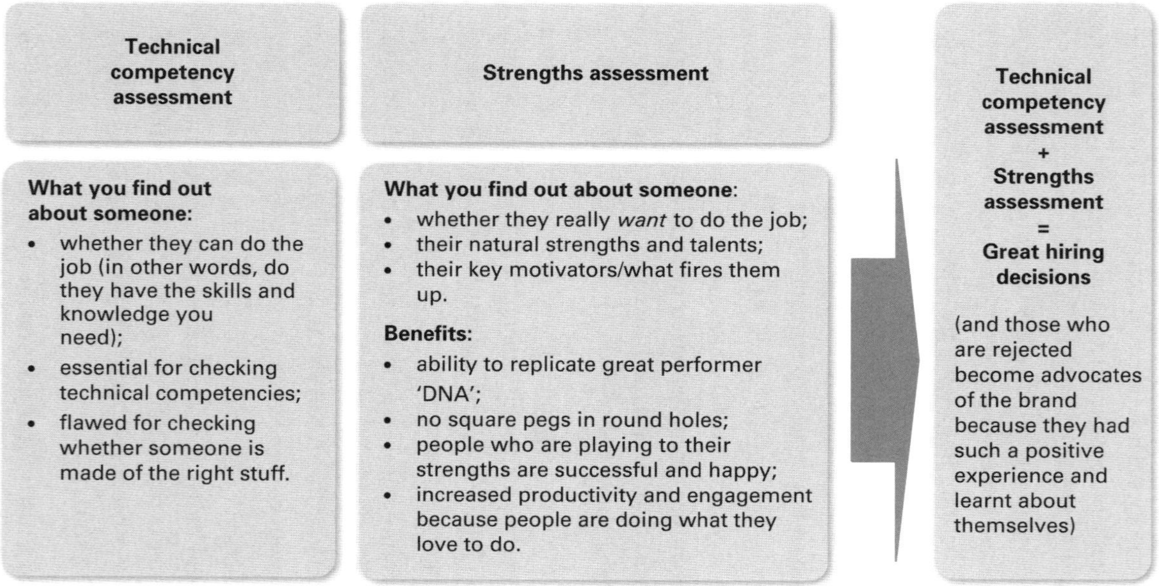

Technical competency assessment

What you find out about someone:

- whether they can do the job (in other words, do they have the skills and knowledge you need);
- essential for checking technical competencies;
- flawed for checking whether someone is made of the right stuff.

Strengths assessment

What you find out about someone:

- whether they really *want* to do the job;
- their natural strengths and talents;
- their key motivators/what fires them up.

Benefits:

- ability to replicate great performer 'DNA';
- no square pegs in round holes;
- people who are playing to their strengths are successful and happy;
- increased productivity and engagement because people are doing what they love to do.

Technical competency assessment + Strengths assessment = Great hiring decisions

(and those who are rejected become advocates of the brand because they had such a positive experience and learnt about themselves)

The different SBR methodologies

There are two main SBR methodologies – profiling methodology, and the database or dictionary approach.

Profiling methodology uses workplace observation and structured conversational interviewing to elicit the strengths (including motivators and values) that all great performers in a particular role have. A 'strengths and motivator profile' is created and interviewers are taught how to conduct a strengths-based interview that determines whether a candidate has the strengths in the profile.

The database approach usually involves interviews or focus groups with high performers where they are asked about what they find engaging, what they are good at and what they enjoy. Their strengths are then established from a database or dictionary of strengths, and a report is produced that identifies the strengths that are believed to be the ones needed to succeed in the given role.

The pros and cons of each methodology are outlined below.

Strengths profiling methodology

Pros

- **The approach takes account of the fact that people tend not to know or recognize their own strengths**
  The profiling methodology works on the assumption that people tend not to know themselves or their strengths very well. Even when they do, they tend to take them for granted so they may overlook them in a conversation or interview.

  The methodology is based on careful observation and analysis of top performers, which means the resultant profile describes what they are actually like versus what they or others think they are like.

- **Profiles have high face-validity and credibility**
  The profiling methodology recognizes that accurate profiling is an art as well as a science. There is a qualitative element as well as a quantitative one, and the qualitative part allows and encourages the profilers to use their intuition and experience to really get under the skin of what the high performers are like. The result is a profile that speaks to people, because it is in their language and describes real people in a way that database-driven approaches can't. Done well, profiles have high face-validity; that is, they appear to people to accurately describe what they purport to describe. An example of someone's reaction when a profile has high face-validity is a comment by Debbie Hutchinson, who led the introduction of SBR at King's College

Hospital. She said, 'When I started learning about strengths-based recruitment and saw the Band 7 Ward Sister profile I realized that the elements it described are what we had not been able to pinpoint before and they are the things that people can't be taught. It helped us to understand why some wards struggle and others don't.'

- **The profiles are specific to the organizational context**
  The strengths and motivator profiles are not a list of pre-written strengths from a database or strengths dictionary, they are specific to each organization. This means that they are more relevant and credible and achieve the buy-in of stakeholders.

Cons

- **Time taken**
  It can be time-consuming to undertake the profiling because it involves spending time with high performers in their workplace, observing them at work, and interviewing them and others that know them well.

- **Cost**
  It generally costs more than database or dictionary-based approaches because of the time needed to do the workplace observations and interviews. (However, the cost is usually offset quickly by cost-savings and performance improvement.)

Database or dictionary methodology

Pros

- **Cost**
  It is quicker and therefore often less expensive than the profiling methodology.

Cons

- **The methodology inherently compromises accuracy and quality of outcome**
  The methodology is based on what people think high performers are great at (those people themselves and others) which of course may not be true. So it could miss some key elements of what makes a great person great. The result could be appointing people who are not actually cut out for the job and/or missing out on people who are.

- Potential waste of time and money
  If the resultant list of strengths is not accurate and the wrong people are appointed, the credibility of strengths-based recruitment is compromised. And the time and money spent on the process will have been wasted.

Useful questions

- To what extent are high-quality employees important to delivering your customer proposition and differentiating you from the competition?

- How well equipped are your current people to develop and grow the business?

- Do you know what makes your great performers great?

- How important is it to you currently to attract high-calibre job applicants?

- Do you have a high volume of applicants for any of your roles and, if so, do you struggle to separate the best from the rest?

- Could you make savings by reducing staff turnover and associated recruitment costs?

Tips for the practitioner

If you think SBR is right for your organization and want to sell the idea to colleagues:

- Make the case by appealing to the heart as well as the head, ie this is common sense (round pegs in round holes), and the return-on-investment data shows its impact.

- Use the NHS story from the beginning of this chapter as an example case study – most people have experience of hospitals and will relate to the story. Stories are a powerful way to communicate.

- Be clear about why you think the switch to SBR is the right one for your organization (use the diagnostic questions above to help you).

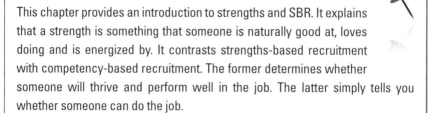

Two-minute chapter summary

This chapter provides an introduction to strengths and SBR. It explains that a strength is something that someone is naturally good at, loves doing and is energized by. It contrasts strengths-based recruitment with competency-based recruitment. The former determines whether someone will thrive and perform well in the job. The latter simply tells you whether someone can do the job.

Key facts to remember

- A strength is something that someone is innately good at, loves doing and is energized by.

- A person's strengths are established by the time they are about 16 years old. We pretty much are who we are by then.

- Strengths approaches to organizations and leadership have their origins in Positive Psychology and Appreciative Inquiry (AI).

- The competency-based approach to recruitment establishes whether someone has the skills to do the job, but it provides a flawed understanding of whether they are the right kind of person and will thrive in the job.

- A key figure in Positive Psychology is Martin Seligman.

- A key figure in Appreciative Inquiry, and inventor of the term, is David Cooperrider.

- The first large organization to use strengths-based recruitment/selection and development widely was Standard Chartered Bank.

- There are two main types of strengths-based recruitment methodologies – the profiling approach and the dictionary or database approach.

The full transcripts of interviews carried out for this book can be found in Part Two.

References

Boyatzis, RE (1982) *The Competent Manager*, Wiley, Oxford

Chartered Institute of Personnel and Development (CIPD) (2014) *Competence and Competency Frameworks (revised August)*, CIPD Factsheet

Coffman, C and Gonzalez-Molina, G (2002) *Follow This Path: How the world's greatest organizations drive growth by unleashing human potential*, Warner Books, New York

Cooperrider, DL (1986) Appreciative inquiry: Toward a methodology for utilising and enhancing organizational innovation, Doctoral Thesis, Case Western University

Cooperrider, D (2013) Rare Admiration: Appreciative Inquiry's contribution and impact on Obama and Romney, June 18. Available from: www.davidcooperrider.com (accessed 21 July 2015)

Drucker, P (1967) *The Effective Executive*, Harper and Row, New York

Fenton, K (2014) Transform nursing with strengths based recruitment, *Health Service Journal*, February. Available from: www.hsj.co.uk/topics/technology-and-innovation/transform-nursing-with-strengths-based-recruitment/5067109.fullarticle (accessed 1 September 2015)

Huttenlocher, PR (2002) *Neural Plasticity: The effects of the environment on the devlelopment of the cerebral cortex*, Harvard University Press, Cambridge, MA

Jobs, S (2005) Commencement address at Stanford University, 12 June

Kinni, T (2003) Exploit what you do best, *Harvard Management Update*, 8 (6)

Seligman, MEP and Csikszentmihalyi, M (2000) Positive psychology: An introduction, *American Psychologist*, 55 (1), pp 5–14

Why do organizations implement strengths-based recruitment?

02

This chapter answers these questions:

- What is the qualitative and quantitative evidence that SBR works?
- What have been the benefits of SBR to organizations that have implemented SBR?

This chapter describes the quantitative and qualitative benefits that organizations are experiencing as a result of implementing SBR. It features case studies and results from organizations in the public and private sector. And it describes the impact of SBR on candidate attraction, candidate experience, retention, performance, interviewer experience, employee engagement and customer service.

The benefits cited are ones that are reported frequently by organizations that implement SBR. Much of the data cited in this chapter are drawn from a study of five market-leading businesses that have implemented SBR and whose findings were reported in the report 'Welcome to the strengths revolution' (North, 2013) for which 20 key stakeholders were interviewed and 80 employees were surveyed.

American science-fiction writer Robert Heinlein once said, 'Never try to teach a pig to sing; it wastes your time, and it annoys the pig.' This quote vividly describes what, at its worst, the competency approach to selection and development attempts to do. At its worst it attempts to knock round pegs into square holes such that people who are not a natural fit for a particular role keep trying to become good at it. It's normally done with the best intentions, and employers often provide training or coaching, but if a person is fundamentally unsuited for a particular role no amount of development activity will change that. This chapter is about what has been achieved by organizations that have moved away from that thinking.

The benefits, in a nutshell

Organizations that adopt strengths-based recruitment report clear quantitative and qualitative benefits. Usually both sets of benefits occur very quickly, often within weeks. The benefits cited in this chapter are from two main sources. One is directly from organizations that have implemented SBR, and the other source is research studies by a variety of bodies.

As we saw in Chapter 1, SBR makes a lot of sense to people and they understand its potential value very quickly. The face validity (people's subjective impression of whether it measures what it purports to measure) is high, because people view it as common sense – it's about selecting people into jobs where they are round pegs in round holes. And one of the reasons that it has taken off is that actual quantitative and qualitative benefits come about quickly and confirm people's initial view that it is a sensible and effective approach.

Being the right person for the job positively affects performance in the job and therefore the organization's performance. This has a ripple effect in that managers spend less time and energy dealing with under-performance. Having the right person in the job is far reaching in its consequences. Lynda Greenshields, who was HR Director of the company that owned the AA, Saga and Allied Healthcare, spoke of the impact on the organization of implementing SBR:

> You know, we used to actually have to drop the targets for people when they came out of training so that they could have a chance of achieving them. We don't have to do that post-SBR, some now come out of training and beat the targets!

For manager's in this organization, a whole raft of employee 'problems' had completely fallen away and they were able to fill their working hours with positively focused activities and proactive projects. They are less stressed, enjoying their own jobs and achieving far more. This is another example of SBR being the nucleus. You might start by recruiting the right people for your front-line roles based on their strengths, but the effects are wide-reaching and impact the whole operation for the better.

The experience that Lynda shares is a common one. In summary, the reported benefits to organizations that implement SBR are:

- Individual and organizational performance improvement from having the right people in the job.
- Increased employee engagement because people are happier, leading to increased customer satisfaction.
- Improvement in the organization's reputation through positive candidate experience.
- Cost savings because less time and money is wasted recruiting people who don't stay or who are wrong for the job.
- Less need for expensive training and development to fix weaknesses.
- Reduced frustration of managers having to deal with job-holders who are unsuited to their roles.
- Improved rigour and efficiency of recruitment processes.
- Fairer treatment of young job applicants who lack experience and may therefore be disadvantaged by traditional job interviews.
- Increase in candidate advocacy because rejected candidates understand and accept why the job is not right for them.
- Renewed energy and enthusiasm is generated throughout the organization.
- A positive shift in company culture that has the potential to be lasting.

One organization in the social care sector implemented SBR because it was struggling to attract and keep the right calibre of carers. It was experiencing high levels of staff turnover, which was costing a lot of money as well as damaging performance and sometimes having a negative impact on the care it was providing to clients. The impact of SBR was outlined by the SBR Project Lead a year into implementation:

> Strengths-based recruitment has totally transformed the way we attract and recruit and it will have a huge impact on the future growth and reputation of our business in terms of quality. We now know what great looks like and the results are showing us that it's working.

Such results are fairly typical, and the impact on one aspect of organizational performance has a ripple effect on others. For example, in this care company engagement increased amongst trainers because the quality of the new recruits that they were training rose markedly.

The importance of insight

The underpinning factor that drives these benefits is the insight into what exactly a great employee is like. If an organization has that insight as well as knowing what it wants to improve the benefits are clear and easy to see.

The discipline of marketing invests a huge amount in gaining customer insight. They seek to understand in detail who their consumers and customers are, what motivates them and what they care about. It is this insight that allows them to make effective decisions about selling and communicating with them. No such discipline exists in the world of HR. Relatively little effort is made to truly understand employees and potential employees in the way that marketeers are obsessed with understanding their consumers. SBR redresses that because at its core is a rigorous and detailed insight into employees – who they are, what they care about and what they are motivated by.

The evidence

In 2013 Engaging Minds undertook a study into the results experienced by five organizations in a range of sectors: financial services, healthcare, restaurant, retail and travel. The study found clear financial benefits as evidenced in a number of areas including attraction, performance, attrition and customer service. Most of the examples of quantitative and qualitative improvements are from this survey and were reported by individuals or a number of the participating companies. Other evidence in this section is derived from interviews conducted specially for this book. Other sources are referenced appropriately.

The quantitative evidence

Engagement and performance

There is a strong, and growing, body of research evidence that points to the performance benefits of focusing on strengths in the workplace. Some of this evidence can be seen in the 2002 Performance Management Survey of 34 companies in 29 countries that the Corporate Leadership Council conducted. The study found a 36 per cent improvement in performance when managers' formal feedback focused on the positive, ie the strengths. One of their conclusions was 'emphasising performance strengths during performance reviews draws better performance from people'.

It seems like common sense that people who love what they do will be more engrossed and engaged. Indeed this is backed up by Gallup, which has carried out research over many years into engagement at work. Susan Sorensen reported that people who use their strengths every day are six times as likely to be engaged in their work (Sorensen, 2014).

Further research evidence is provided by Harter et al (2002), who found that 'the opportunity to do what you do best each day', that is, using our strengths, is a core predictor of workplace engagement, which in turn is a core predictor of a range of business outcomes. Similarly, Minhas (2010) found that work engagement increased when people developed either their realized or unrealized strengths.

Standard Chartered Bank introduced strengths-based techniques in 2000 and was one of the first large organizations to do so. Initially it focused on employee engagement. The managers with the highest engagement scores in their departments were studied and profiled in order to understand what they were doing that was working so well. Then they introduced strengths-based recruitment for sales roles. The results were impressive. Between three and six months after starting in the job, employees hired using SBR were on average bringing in 40 per cent more revenue than those hired using the previous approach. Debbie Whittaker, who led the project at Standard Chartered, reported in an article in *HR Magazine* (Gray, 2014), 'Perhaps counterintuitively, the greatest growth potential you have is in the areas where you are already strong. It's a bit like polishing a gem.'

Starbucks UK also adopted SBR because they wanted to improve barista engagement and the customer experience as well as reduce staff turnover. Turnover was a problem particularly in large cities where people in this sector generally change jobs frequently. They wanted to improve and maintain a high level of staff engagement, because engaged staff tend to provide great customer service. Sandra Porter, who was the HR Director who introduced SBR into Starbucks UK, reported,

> We knew from our customer data and from what store managers were telling us, that we needed to change the recruitment mindset. I knew I had to respond with something bold that would make a difference, tinkering with what we had was not going to be good enough. And I knew I had to do it fast... The difference began to show in the data. You can't attribute all the changes to one thing but the shift was significant and we started to see changes come through in store manager, barista and customer feedback.

Attrition and retention

Improving sales staff retention was a big issue for most of the five companies in the study. All five saw improvements when they introduced SBR, disproving a commonly held belief that the only way to reduce staff turnover in sales is to increase pay. One organization reported a 50 per cent reduction in customer service employee turnover. Another reported an overall 66 per cent reduction in sales person employee turnover and a 37.5 per cent reduction in first three months sales person employee turnover. The HR manager of that company said, 'We've been trying unsuccessfully to tackle high turnover for many years... we didn't think it was possible to achieve a reduction.'

An HR Director whose organization had experienced a reduction in attrition as a result of implementing SBR reported, 'The improvement in results is very predictable. When one branch lost six of the eight people they'd recruited in a month I knew they had stopped using the SBR approach... and I was right.'

Charlotte Henderson was a Team Leader at a financial services firm in the first couple of years following their implementation of SBR. In an interview for this book she commented that attrition improved greatly.

> We also didn't lose many people during induction training. They 'got' what customer service was and we didn't have to train them on how to listen to customers because it was natural to them. People enjoyed themselves in their jobs. They were better performers and they were doing better than people who had been there two or three years because they were thriving in what they were doing.

She said that the company was saving a significant amount of money because of the drop in attrition.

One company had a chronic staff retention problem when they decided to try out the new strengths approach. Once they had introduced SBR they started seeing the positive effects almost immediately. Staff turnover figures during 2012 were 57 per cent for sales agents recruited using CBR, and only 19.3 per cent for agents recruited via SBR.

Another company experienced a similar improvement for new call centre agents and this drop in attrition saved the company GBP 352,000 at one of their sites in one month.

In one company's largest and most important call centres, against a forecast for 2012 of 25 per cent, attrition was 30.4 per cent for CBR recruits and 10.5 per cent for SBR recruits. At the same call centre, sales agent turnover in the first three months fell from 24 per cent in 2011 to 15 per cent in 2012.

This improvement was particularly significant given that the first three months included the induction training period, with all its associated costs.

Induction training for sales agents in one company in the study lasts six weeks. Attrition can be a problem during this period, and it dropped from 7.5 per cent to 2.9 per cent when they introduced SBR.

Like many organizations that implement SBR, Saga was drawn to it because of the prospect of reducing attrition rates and therefore cost. Nick Corbo, their Director of Customer Experience and Agent Development, was a key stakeholder in the SBR implementation. Attrition and cost were the drivers for Saga: 'We are a strongly performance-driven culture and improving performance was the strategic driver behind introducing SBR.'

Attrition was also one of the key measures that Starbucks UK used to judge the effectiveness of SBR. They piloted SBR initially and their 90-day attrition rate, which was a key measure for them, started to fall. Lisa Robbins, who succeeded Sandra Porter as HR Director of Starbucks UK and Ireland, stated in an interview with *HR Magazine* in 2014: 'Staff turnover among our new apprentices has reduced by a third and we anticipate that, by applying these recruitment strategies, we can continue to reduce this rate and retain future leaders in our business' (Gray, 2014).

Lynda Greenshields of Acromas Group also reported a pleasing impact on attrition: 'One year after we began the project, one of the businesses reported that the turnover rate in the first three months of employment had fallen from 22 per cent to 10.8 per cent. An incredible result.'

An important point to make about the effect of SBR is that those people recruited using SBR leave for different reasons than those not recruited by SBR. SBR recruits don't leave because the job is not a good fit for them. Keith Jones, a Recruitment Manager in a financial services company, said his organization has had exactly that experience: 'Reasons for leaving changed – people were leaving for what I would call good reasons, not because they were dissatisfied with the job.'

Candidate attraction

One organization that participated in the study had struggled to attract applicants to its call centre. After introducing SBR it had a 25 per cent increase in the number of applicants.

Another organization had the opposite problem, in that their recruitment adverts attracted too many of the wrong people. They found that the number of applicants reduced once they started using SBR but their conversion rate from interview to appointment went up.

Strengths-based interviewers' experience

A total of 97 per cent of trained interviewers in the organizations that participated in the study said SBR would help them find the right people, improve performance and enhance their brand.

Training

In one organization 48 trainers were surveyed and 100 per cent agreed with the statement 'SBR has had a good impact on training', with one of the group going so far as to say, 'SBR is the best thing that has happened to the business by far; trainee quality has improved significantly.'

Performance

One of the participating organizations reported the following results in their sales team:

- 20 per cent increase in productivity after three months.
- 2 per cent increase in commission earnings after three months.
- 6 per cent reduction in sickness absence after three months.

Performance improvements are clear very soon after the introduction of SBR. One manager in a call centre said, 'My new group of customer service recruits is more focused and determined to succeed. Their productivity is 4 per cent above the department average, and their handling time almost 10 per cent above team average.'

Customer service and brand advocacy

One of the companies that participated in the study reported a 12 per cent increase in customer satisfaction, and another stated there had been an impressive 80 per cent reduction in customer complaints.

It is clear that SBR recruits have a positive impact on the quality of customer service being provided by their companies, too. In one company the impact of recruiting all new staff for a brand new store was highlighted by mystery shopper visits that rated the staff as excellent.

Nick Corbo, Director of Customer Experience and Agent Development at Saga, found a marked improvement in the service they provided to their customers when they implemented SBR 'because the SBR recruits connect well and are naturals with our customers'.

An SBR team in another company quickly achieved the highest ever customer service scores in key areas such as answering questions and resolving difficulties.

The qualitative evidence

Clearly, qualitative benefits and quantitative benefits are closely connected. If staff turnover drops in a coffee shop, for example, regular customers are going to have the benefit of building a relationship with the same staff every time they come in and those staff will be more experienced. To take another example, if the volume of job applications is reduced because the job advert is more effective at attracting only the right people, less time is wasted and the company gets to interview a great number of suitable candidates, thus making the process more efficient.

Here are some of the benefits that organizations have reported as a result of introducing SBR, together with comments from leaders in those organizations.

Candidate attraction

A key feature of SBR is the rewriting of recruitment adverts so that the right candidates instantly recognize themselves in the adverts and are drawn to apply. The following examples demonstrate the effectiveness of SBR in relation to candidate attraction.

When a manager asked new recruits why they had applied to his company they said the advert had 'shone out' to them.

New starters were surveyed in a financial services company, some of whom had been recruited using CBR and some using SBR. A total of 27.5 per cent of those recruited using SBR said they felt that 'the role was exactly suited for me and appealed to me'. Only 17.5 per cent of those appointed using CBR felt the same.

A recruitment manager in a healthcare company said, 'We're now interviewing people who would have been rejected before through lack of relevant experience, and not selecting people simply because they have relevant experience.' This was for a role where they realized people could learn the necessary skills, but couldn't be taught to be the type of person who would be great in the role. This recruitment manager's view was supported by a team leader in the same business who said, 'We're attracting a far broader range of candidates now... from different age groups, backgrounds and work histories... we have been very narrow in the past.'

In another company an HR Manager highlighted the increase in retention as a result of the shift to SBR: 'We've moved away from call centre job hoppers.' A recruiter in the same company said that SBR was allowing them to home in on more suitable candidates: 'I'm confident that the people I am taking on with strengths-based recruitment are the right people for us.'

A Regional Manager in a restaurant company summarized the contribution of SBR to candidate attraction: 'We are finding the right people through this process and from a range of diverse backgrounds... Ph.D.s, language students, even store managers who want to drop a level. We're recruiting them because they want to work here.'

Lisa Robbins, HR Director of Starbucks UK, which introduced SBR in 2010, reported in *HR Magazine* in May 2014: 'a significant benefit of this process is not relying on a potential employee's work experience at interview stage – the strengths and motivator profile allows candidates to share more examples from their life experience, which is very relevant for our apprentice candidates who are usually coming to us straight out of school or college.'

Candidate interview experience

The strengths-based interview approach is markedly different from other forms of interview. Organizations that adopt SBR often report that candidates, both internal and external, are pleasantly surprised by the approach.

According to a Regional Manager in one company the interviews are 'unlike anything they've experienced before. [They're] more enjoyable, and flow more naturally'.

Keith Jones, Recruitment Manager at a financial services company, reported: 'Candidates love the strengths interview. We do workshops with them afterwards about their recruitment experience with us. They tell us they've loved it and feel energized by it. They don't realize how much they have talked and relayed to you in the interview. We've never had any negative feedback.'

A project manager in another organization reported some feedback she had received from a newly appointed recruit who had been selected by the SBR process: 'Great feedback about the interview, her training and her journey so far.'

These views were further endorsed by a comparative questionnaire of 80 competency-based and strengths-based recruits in one of the five companies in the study. They were asked what their overall impression was of the interview they had experienced compared to previous interviews they had. Some 84 per cent of those who had a strengths interview gave it a positive rating compared with 43 per cent of those who had a competency-based interview. The ones who had a strengths interview reported that it felt very personal and relaxed and that the interviewers really got to know them.

Even unsuccessful candidates were positive about their strengths-based interview experience. An HR manager in one company told us, '[Candidates] say they understand why the job isn't right for them, they enjoyed the interview (often saying that they found out things they didn't know about themselves) and they feel clearer about what kind of job they would be well suited to.'

Starbucks UK asked their new recruits about their experience of the strengths-based interview. The feedback was that they appreciated the process and felt that the store managers who interviewed them were genuinely interested in them. Sandra Porter, HR Director of Starbucks UK and Ireland at the time, commented, 'It was the start of a relationship with their store manager which is *so* important because, as the old saying goes, "people leave managers not organizations".'

Recruiters' experience of SBR

Recruiting managers usually love SBR. The majority really like doing strengths-based interviewing and once they are trained and become involved they normally become great advocates of SBR. Elisabeth Pullar of Guy's and St Thomas' NHS Foundation Trust reported that 'People are very fired up and word is spreading. They're espousing the benefits of SBR and telling people how excited they are. People are now asking to join in rather than being forced to attend training.'

HR managers repeatedly reported that they were rejecting people that they might not have rejected using a competency-based interview. They said the strengths-based interview allowed them to really get to the heart of what the people were like and whether they were well suited to the job.

One HR director described the positive impact of SBR on the professional development of some of her team, and the credibility of the HR function. Before the introduction of SBR, she worried that some business partners were little more than 'process jockeys': 'The effect upon a number of my key HR leaders has been transformational. They now see the potential of the approach, and how its principles reach beyond simply amending the recruitment process.'

The introduction of SBR has transformed the experience of all the interviewers in the study. It has overcome the interview fatigue that many who had been using the competency-based approach had reported.

The positive impact begins when they are introduced to a strengths and motivator profile as part of their strengths-based interviewing profile. One recruitment manager described this as an 'aha' moment: 'For the first time we understood what a great person looked like, and [we realized] that we already had some of these people working in our stores.' Helen Lamont, Nursing and Patient Services Director at Newcastle upon Tyne Hospitals NHS Foundation

Trust, said, 'When I first read the ward sister profile, which was clear and written in plain English, it resonated with me, and I immediately wanted to share it with my senior team and engage people in implementation of SBR.'

Many respondents talked about how SBR shifts the focus of attention away from the process to the person in front of you:

'SBR helps you get to know the candidate, not just their experience.' (Interviewer)

'Candidates are more relaxed, and seem to enjoy the chance to talk… which means fewer of the short answers you get when people are nervous.' (Team leader)

They also liked the simple, uncomplicated nature of the interview process. Here's what two managers in the companies that participated in the study said:

'It's easy to use… it's quick and efficient, which is key when everything is timed… our store managers love it.' (Regional manager)

'Before SBR, the recruiters dreaded interviewing. Newly trained SB recruiters now can't wait to get started.' (HR manager)

This kind of feedback is common amongst people who have made the shift from competency-based to strengths-based interviewing. They are excited about the people they hire, feeling accountable for their success and taking more of an interest in them and how they are doing once they start. As one team manager said, 'You remember the candidates as people'.

The quality of strengths-based recruits

Hilary Chapman, Chief Nurse at Sheffield Teaching Hospitals, told me in an interview for this book:

We've made some very good appointments. Some of the people we appointed have been real surprises. They are showing huge strength in their very challenging ward leader roles. They are succeeding in their jobs and leading their clinical areas well. We wouldn't have made some of these appointments without SBR. Before you would sometimes have a gut feeling about someone that you didn't think they were the right person, you had nagging doubts, yet they met all the criteria in the person specifications. Now we know whether they are definitely the right person.

The companies in the study also talked about the positive impression that strengths-based recruits have made within their businesses.

Responses were more or less the same from recruiters, trainers and managers. They said the new hires were 'different' and 'better' than candidates that they had recruited previously. On the whole they said that the recruits hired using strengths-based interviewing were more positive, flexible and engaged, and how this was benefiting customers and colleagues alike. As the following comments show, each company was very positive about the quality of people they were recruiting using SBR:

'We have a different calibre of person now… when I walk in a store I think wow!' (Regional manager)

'SBR enables us to recruit wonderful people.' (Project manager)

'The quality of the candidates is a definite improvement. The recruitment process enables the genuinely strong candidate to shine.' (Recruitment manager)

Attracting people from new talent pools

One of the benefits of SBR for organizations that have roles for which people don't need any previous experience in that type of job is that it opens up new talent pools to recruit from. One example was the financial services company call centre for which Keith Jones is a Recruitment Manager. When I interviewed him for this book he told me, 'We're also now fishing from different and bigger pools. We're attracting people of different ages, backgrounds and walks of life. It's brought us a good mix, including a 50-year-old landscape gardener and ex-military personnel.'

Performance

Aside from quantitative improvement, companies in the survey reported that SBR recruits give a better customer experience and are more engaged colleagues: 'We're seeing improvements in sickness absence, productivity and a willingness to take live calls earlier' (HR manager).

Those closest to the recruits are particularly encouraged:

'I expect three of my new SB recruits to be in the top five of my 13 team members within six months. They're driven to sell, engaged in everything we do, they quickly want to take live calls on their own, they have a pride in themselves and their work, and they ask for help from me rather than wait. A couple of these have been my highest performers in recent weeks, beating people who've been here six or seven years.' (Team leader)

'You can tell SBR employees when you walk into a store. They are quicker to engage with customers, they smile more, they take the initiative.' (Regional manager)

Janice Sigsworth, Director of Nursing at Imperial College Healthcare NHS Trust, said in an interview for this book:

I feel we have a strong set of ward sisters in place now. We have seen the patients' experience of care improve as measured by the National Patient

Survey. For five to six years we were behind our peer teaching hospital Trusts, now we're not. It's because we've now got ward leaders who are able to lead in a way that means the patient experience is good. Some of our consultants have also commented on what tremendous senior nurses we have.

Progress in training

In the study, all five companies reported that SB recruits have been highly engaged in their induction training and, as the comments from this trainer illustrate, they have also been eager to apply their learning on the job:

'They ask more questions, and are more proactive when they don't understand something.'

'They are thirsty for knowledge and master the system quicker.'

'They are positive about getting on the phones and show less fear than agents we used to recruit using competency-based recruitment.'

Nick Corbo, Director of Customer Experience and Agent Development at Saga, reported that historically new recruits in their call centres had been reluctant to go live and take calls. However, people that they recruited using SBR commonly are eager to start taking live calls, and that was unheard of. When they implemented SBR they got early positive feedback from the trainers who ran their induction training, who were saying the recruits are brilliant because they are the right people and have an innate ability to talk to customers. Nick said he told one of the teams they would be able to spot which were the SBR teams and which weren't. And they said they could and they saw the difference immediately. That early positive feedback helped Saga build momentum for SBR.

The impact of SBR on unsuccessful candidates

Managers in the study also valued the way that the SBR interview process helps them to feed back to unsuccessful candidates. Charlotte Henderson, Team Leader in a financial services company, said, 'The people who we rejected were fine too because it's easy to explain to them why they weren't a good fit for the job.' And an operations manager in one of the five companies in the study said, 'It's easier to ring people to say they haven't got the job... you can be honest... you can say, "there's nothing worse than being in the wrong job".'

More often than not the interviewees learn about themselves and their strengths at the interview. If the outcome is that they do not get appointed, they understand and accept the reasons. And they also go away with a better idea of what kind of job would be a good fit for them.

Karen Coles, who was on the team who led the implementation of SBR at Newcastle upon Tyne NHS Foundation Trust, commented:

> For people who don't fit the profile I have found that they recognize themselves during the strengths interview that they don't have the strengths. In the past sometimes the only feedback that was possible to offer them was that there was a better candidate on the day. Now we can give them feedback about their strengths. Selection panels now have much more powerful information about candidates.

Sandra Porter of Starbucks UK told me about what some of their successful and unsuccessful candidates had said:

> Some people said that they hadn't thought about what they liked doing before their interview with Starbucks and they actually started to give that some thought. The interview helped them think about when they were at their happiest, what made them feel satisfied and which environments they would love... and hate. Before their experience with Starbucks some of them were just looking for any job rather than something that they knew they would be really suited to.

Engagement and job satisfaction

Research consistently tells us that highly engaged employees can make a meaningful difference to their organization's success. The opportunity to do what they do best every day drives increased productivity, performance, innovation and, ultimately, shareholder value.

The study revealed that leaders in each of the five companies consistently commented on the positive attitude of their new recruits, and its impact on others:

> 'Our best strengths-based recruits are fully engaged in everything we do and are always looking for extra responsibility.' (Team leader)

> 'These people are smart, heads up and eyes forward, and start great conversations. They're confident, proud of who they are and they're clearly engaged. Most important, they're living the brand values.' (Regional manager)

> 'These people are amazing!' (HR manager after seeing SBR recruits in their induction training)

The SBR recruits in the study further endorsed the managers' views that they are a very engaged group:

> 'I love my job.'

> 'This job completely suits me.'

> 'I can't believe I get paid to do this.'

Charlotte Henderson, who managed a team of contact centre agents at a financial services company, talked about the benefits to her as a manager of SBR: 'As a manager, walking away from my day-to-day work was so much better because I could see my people were energized. I didn't have to spend a lot of time on performance management and disciplinaries. I was coaching and developing people instead. So it saved a lot of my time.'

Contribution to leadership development

With its emphasis on open questions, listening and observing for non-verbal cues, SB interviewing has an added advantage of developing leaders' communication skills. These are capabilities they can then take with them into other settings, such as performance conversations and team meetings.

Some people described how the training has influenced their whole attitude towards people management. They now appreciate that everyone is unique and requires slightly different leadership to maximize their strengths.

Charlotte Henderson talked about how the introduction of SBR helped her to become a better leader:

> I drew up a matrix of all my team and their different strengths. I tried to help them play to their strengths. I knew what motivated them now because of the profiles so was able to keep them very motivated. The profile gave us an understanding of the people. It was quite obvious once I had [the profile]. It was as if in your head you have a character and you understand them. You tune in with people because you 'get' them and can connect with them. And you become a great leader because you're leading and developing them in the right way.

Customer service and brand advocacy

Lynda Greenshields explained the connection between SBR and company brand:

> Your employees, your brand, your employer brand, your employee brand, your customer experience of your brand – words that people so often use to describe what they see as separate things – I believe they're all one and the same, your brand... your business. I placed SBR at the heart of our HR strategy because I knew it could impact our brand reputation and business results.

Because SBR recruits are more engaged and excited about what they do, they become great advocates for their brands. This was the case irrespective of their role. Whether they're providing care to an elderly person, making a cup of coffee, or handling an insurance policy query, their passion shines through: 'We now use SBR for all our stores; this represents a 110 per cent commitment to putting customers at the centre of our business' (recruitment manager).

Charlotte Henderson talked of customer service and quality scores improving when they started to recruit people based on their strengths: '[The SBR recruits] were really listening to the customers. Lots of customer commendations started coming through and senior management were really impressed.'

Company culture

The attitude displayed by SBR recruits tends to be quickly visible, and when a number of them are working in one team the positive impact on that team's culture can be quickly seen. When recruited in groups, SB recruits often demonstrate a strong togetherness and desire to help each other succeed. Their positive modelling role has a ripple effect, encouraging other employees to improve their standards:

> 'We're hiring quality people who are positively impacting the call centre culture.' (HR manager)

> 'SB recruits seem to be having a positive impact on existing staff, challenging them to raise their standards.' (Recruitment manager)

> 'There's a buzz when a group of new recruits finishes their training and comes to work in a contact centre... everybody notices the difference.' (HR manager)

Keith Jones commented on the difference SBR has made to the 'buzz' in the calls centres in his company:

> Because they are all positive about their work they tend to keep an eye on each other and keep each other in line too. They have the right attitude. Heads of department notice it and say that they are great, they're not afraid to speak up and ask questions. They have much more energy. Sometimes it's challenging for longer-serving people that they are sitting next to. It's raised everyone's game. I think it feels different in the contact centres now because of this. There's a much better buzz.

One of the reasons SBR has such an impact on organizational culture is that it introduces the notion of focusing on the positive as a way of understanding and augmenting high performance. This creates a shift in thinking that has a big ripple effect. As Nick Corbo from Saga observed, 'SBR is a complete mindset shift, it's not just a different way of recruiting.'

CASE STUDY

In this section we tell the story of one company that wanted to improve performance and cut cost by reducing employee turnover across several of its diverse businesses. In the words of their HR director: 'We'd been trying unsuccessfully to tackle high turnover for many years… we'd tried everything, and people had started to think it was impossible to achieve a reduction.'

The HR Director was clear about the problem to be fixed: 'Reducing our employee turnover rates was the immediate on-the-ground problem being faced by the business, and I had hard numbers to share… people already knew there was a problem, but the numbers clarified the severity of the situation.'

They wanted to replace their failing competency-based recruitment process with a new strategy based on recruiting for strengths. They knew they needed to revamp the entire recruitment process, from attraction to orientation, emphasizing the importance of natural strengths, values and motivators.

This organization's goal was more fundamental to the core business strategy than simply reducing employee turnover. They wanted to recruit and retain great people – people whose strengths meant that they could easily achieve the promise made to customers. They made a clear connection between recruiting the right people, reducing staff turnover and improving customer satisfaction.

The performance and customer satisfaction data available within the business meant that the HR team knew who the great employees were. The HR director's hypothesis was as follows: 'If the business clearly understood the strengths and motivators of their star performers, and were able to attract and select more like them turnover should reduce and performance levels would increase.'

SBR was piloted in the parts of the business whose performance was the worst and staff turnover was the highest. The organization tracked a wide range of performance metrics so the impact of SBR was easy to see. The results were extremely positive and some highlights were:

- A 25 per cent increase in applications for roles where candidate attraction had always been difficult.

- A 13 per cent increase in attendance of people invited for first interview.

- An 8 per cent increase in people starting work (they had previously had a problem with people accepting jobs but then getting a better offer from a competitor company).

- A 50 per cent year-on-year reduction in staff turnover.

- A 60 per cent reduction in staff turnover during the critical induction training period.

- A 20 per cent increase in productivity.

- A 12 per cent increase in customer satisfaction.

This placed the HR director in an excellent position when reporting back to her fellow executives, and opened opportunities to build out from the pilot. Her peers on the executive team were impressed. They didn't think improvements of this scale would be possible.

Armed with internal evidence of the benefits of SBR, not only in tackling staff turnover but also in reducing other costs and improving performance, the HR director was able to extend SBR to other parts of the business, and build a case for strengths-based leader development and performance reviews: 'We made some big changes… [strengths] became the central principle of our People Strategy.'

The HR director recognized that the success of the new recruitment process meant that new, high-quality recruits would need to be properly supported by their team leaders, or they might leave. That is why she then decided to focus on leadership development.

This combination of organizational and individual benefits of SBR results in a win–win where the organizational performance increases and people are engaged, happy and giving their best.

Checklist

In considering the potential benefits to your organization of implementing SBR, it's useful to think in terms of what problems its introduction might help you to solve (see Figure 2.1).

Useful questions

These questions help you consider how you measure performance in your organization and whether the data is indicating that there is a problem that could be fixed by using SBR. If that is the case, refer to the section 'Tips for the practitioner' (below) which gives recommendations for how you might implement an SBR pilot.

- Which metrics give the most useful insight into the performance of your organization and people?

- Do you have the data you need to enable you to clearly understand what is working well and not working in your organization?

FIGURE 2.1 Checklist: what problems might SBR help you solve?

You don't know why your great performers in key roles are great

You have high staff turnover that is costing you time and money

You struggle to attract excellent people into key roles

Your people are not highly engaged and this is affecting customer service (and therefore potentially sales and reputation)

You are worried that your people can't deliver the performance and reputation that you want your organization to have

You need to find a way to substantially improve performance very quickly

Your competitors are performing better than you

- How do you know whether your recruitment process is working well? What key measures do you track?

- Are you happy with your current employee attrition rate?

- How much does your current attrition cost your organization?

- What are your current levels of employee engagement?

- Is your customer service as good as it could be?

- What percentage of your current employees are great? What would the impact be on performance if a larger percentage of them were truly great?

Tips for the practitioner

In order to clearly see the benefits of implementing SBR follow these simple steps and implement a pilot in an area of your business that most requires improvement and/or amongst a group of employees who make the biggest difference to your organization's performance.

1 **Understand the issue to be fixed**
   What is the challenge you need to address, and what data is available to help you define and understand the issue? For example, if you believe that sales are too low in your business, do you have data to show which sales people are the highest performing, what revenue and profit they generate compared to their peers, and their customer retention rates?

2 **Develop your hypothesis**
   How do you explain the current problems, and how do you imagine SBR will positively impact these key measures of business performance? To continue the example, are you currently rewarding your sales team for numbers of deals made rather than size of business they win, or the quality of their long-term relationships with clients? Are some of your sales people not right for the job?

3 **Run a pilot**
   Trial SBR in one part of your organization, while continuing with the old approach elsewhere, so that you can compare the results. For example, choose an area of the business where you need big improvement quickly and appoint sales people that you know are great (having profiled the strengths and motivators of the great ones). Track the numbers to see what difference it makes. Make sure you

have decided, at the beginning of the pilot, how you will evaluate its success. For example, will you measure revenue and profitability growth per sales person, customer retention rates, number of sales made?

4 Analyse the results

What are the findings of the pilot study telling you? How is the new process affecting key operational measures and business results? What is the evidence? In sales it's usually very easy to see the impact. What follow-up action is needed to sustain any improvements in performance? Where else in the business could benefit from the findings?

Two-minute chapter summary

Quantitative and qualitative research shows that SBR is having a significant impact on performance, engagement, customer service and cost.

The evidence for SBR is strong and, with each new organization that adopts the approach, the body of evidence is growing. This chapter gives examples of qualitative and quantitative benefits, case studies and comments from organizations that have implemented SBR, including the NHS, Starbucks UK and Saga.

Key facts to remember

- There is a large and growing body of quantitative and qualitative evidence that demonstrates the efficacy of SBR.

- Key areas where a clear return on investment can be seen in organizations that have adopted SBR are attraction, retention, performance, customer service and engagement.

- Standard Chartered Bank, one of the first major organizations to adopt SBR, found that employees hired using SBR were on average bringing in 40 per cent more revenue than those hired using the previous approach.

- Organizations in the following sectors have experienced qualitative and quantitative benefits of introducing SBR: financial services, health, retail, restaurant and travel. All of these sectors are characterized by their close tracking of quantitative performance metrics.

The full transcripts of interviews carried out for this book can be found in Part Two.

References

Corporate Leadership Council (2002) Performance management survey. Available from: www.teams-and-leadership.com/pdfs/better-performance-management.pdf (accessed 21 July 2015)

Gray, R (2014) The rise of strengths-based recruitment (13 May), *HR Magazine*. Available from: www.hrmagazine.co.uk/hro/features/1144017/rise-strengths-recruitment#sthash.SFZbh6cN.dpuf (accessed 21 July 2015)

Harter, JK, Schmidt, FL and Hayes, TL (2002) Business-unit-level relationship between employee satisfaction, employee engagement, and business outcomes: A meta-analysis, *Journal of Applied Psychology*, **87**, pp 268–79

Minhas, G. (2010) Developing realised and unrealised strengths: Implications for engagement, self-esteem, life satisfaction and well-being, *Assessment and Development Matters*, **2**, pp 12–16

North, D (2013) Welcome to the strengths revolution: An in-depth study into the benefits of strengths-based recruitment. Available from: www.engagingminds.co.uk (accessed 21 July 2015) [A study of the impact of SBR in five well-known organizations from the following sectors: financial services, restaurant, retail, social care and travel. Findings were based on interviews with 20 key stakeholders and a survey of 80 employees.]

Sorensen, S (2014) How employees' strengths make your company stronger, *Gallup Business Journal*, February. Available from: www.gallup.com/businessjournal/167462/employees-strengths-company-stronger.aspx (accessed 21 July 2015)

Notes on organizations referenced in this chapter

The **AA** is a British company that provides car insurance, driving lessons, breakdown cover, loans and other related services. It is a FTSE 250 company and has more than 14 million customers in the UK.

Acromas Group was established in 2007 to acquire and hold investments in the Saga and AA group of companies. Saga and AA were listed on the London Stock Exchange in May 2014 and June 2015, respectively.

Guy's and St Thomas' NHS Foundation Trust comprises two of London's best-known teaching hospitals: Guy's Hospital and St Thomas' Hospital. It also includes Evelina London Children's Hospital and both adult and children's community services in

Lambeth and Southwark. It also provides specialist services for patients from further afield, including cancer, cardiothoracic, women's and children's services, kidney care and orthopaedics. It has approximately 13,650 employees.

Imperial College Healthcare NHS Trust is in London and comprises five hospitals: Charing Cross Hospital, Hammersmith Hospital, Queen Charlotte's and Chelsea Hospital, St Mary's Hospital and the Western Eye Hospital. The Trust employs approximately 10,000 people.

King's College NHS Foundation Trust is one of London's largest teaching hospitals and comprises: King's College Hospital, Princess Royal University Hospital, Orpington Hospital and additional services at Beckenham Beacon, Sevenoaks Hospital and Queen Mary's Hospital in Sidcup. The Trust employs over 6,000 people.

The **Newcastle upon Tyne Hospitals NHS Foundation Trust** provides healthcare to the communities of the North East of England. It comprises the following: Freeman Hospital, Royal Victoria Infirmary, Campus for Ageing and Vitality, Newcastle Dental Hospital, Newcastle Fertility Centre and Northern Genetics Service. The Trust employs approximately 13,500 people.

Saga is a UK company that is focused on serving the needs of customers aged 50 and over. It is listed on the London Stock Exchange and is a FTSE 250 company. It has more than 2.5 million customers and provides a wide range of insurance products, personal finance and package holidays including cruises.

Sheffield Teaching Hospitals NHS Foundation Trust is one of the UK's busiest and most successful Trusts. It comprises five of Yorkshire's best-known teaching hospitals: the Royal Hallamshire, the Northern General, Charles Clifford Dental Hospital, Weston Park Cancer Hospital and Jessop Wing Maternity Hospital. It provides a full range of local hospital and community-based care. It has approximately 15,000 employees.

Standard Chartered Bank is a British multinational banking and financial services company and is listed in the FTSE 100. It operates in more than 70 countries.

Starbucks is an American coffee company. It is listed on the NASDAQ and operates in more than 60 countries.

How does strengths-based recruitment work in practice?

03

This chapter answers these questions:

- How does SBR work in practice?
- What are the pros and cons of the different approaches to SBR?
- What are the different types of strengths-based interviewing?

There are different approaches to strengths-based recruitment, which can be confusing for those wanting to understand and implement a strengths approach to recruitment. This chapter explains and clarifies the different practices that are used under the titles 'strengths-based recruitment' and 'strengths-based interviewing'. It describes the different SBR methodologies and the different types of strengths interview. It also describes how SBR methods work in practice in the workplace.

Definitions and approaches

Strengths-based recruitment is still a relatively new kid on the block. Inevitably, as with any new approach that is in its infancy, a range of different approaches and practices are emerging. Some are evidence-based and rigorous, some are not. The savvy practitioner will need to be able to unravel which is which, understand the pros and cons and the risks and benefits of their chosen approach. Ultimately they need to decide what is most likely to meet their organization's needs and succeed in achieving their goals.

First let's look at definitions and labels:

- Strengths-based recruitment (SBR) – This is the term that is normally used to define an entire strengths-based approach to selection, including attraction and induction. A core element of an SBR approach is the analysis of what strengths high performers have in any given role. There are two main approaches to doing this analysis – the profiling approach and the database or dictionary approach (see pages 25–26 for definitions of these approaches).

- Strengths-based interviewing (SBI) – This is just one part, albeit a crucial part, of the selection process. There are two main types of strengths-based interview. One type is used to assess a candidate against a set of strengths that has been established using either a profiling or a database/dictionary methodology. The other type is used as a stand-alone activity that does not assess a candidate against a set of strengths that has been elicited as a result of one of the two main methodologies.

- SBR profiling methodology – The SBR profiling methodology uses workplace observation and structured conversational interviewing to elicit the strengths (including motivators and values) that all great performers in a particular role have. A Strengths and Motivator Profile is created and interviewers are taught how to conduct a strengths-based interview that determines whether a candidate has the strengths in the profile. In addition, attraction and induction are tailored according to the strengths in the profile.

- SBR database or dictionary methodology – This approach usually involves interviews or focus groups with high performers where they are asked about what they find engaging, what they are good at and what they enjoy. Strengths are then chosen from a database or dictionary of strengths and a report produced that identifies the strengths believed to be the ones needed to succeed in the given role.

Selecting out or selecting in?

Most selection processes appear to have the implicit goal of selecting out the wrong people rather than attracting the right ones. In practice this means that people are gradually eliminated from the different parts of the selection process until a shortlist is reached. The 'selecting out' approach is particularly prevalent where an organization receives high volumes of applications for certain jobs and wants to reduce the number of applicants. The big down-side of this approach is that it means that people who could be right for the role might not realize this and don't apply. At worst, this approach of screening out rather than screening in leaves you with average or mediocre new recruits rather than great ones.

The question is, why do people end up applying for jobs for which they are unlikely to be suited? There are a number of reasons. They may be desperate for a job. In the UK, unemployed people are required to prove that they are actively submitting a certain number of job applications in order to receive their benefits payments from the social security system. So some people apply for jobs simply to meet that criterion. There will also be a proportion of candidates who apply for jobs for which they are not suited because it is hard for them to know from the job advert whether they are likely to be a good fit. Where employment agencies are used, they often do not understand what kind of person would be a great fit for the role so it is hard for them to draw up a good shortlist of candidates. A key question is whether the recruiting organization knows exactly what they are looking for and can they express that well in a person specification or job advert.

An approach that selects in the right candidates as opposed to selecting out the wrong ones is much more effective and energizing for candidates and recruiters. It is also better for the organization's reputation, because when people don't succeed it is clearer to them why that is the case.

So, how to move more towards a 'select-in' approach? The first step is to focus on how to attract the right kind of people and give enough quality time to the selection process so that recruiters can be certain that they are making the right selection decisions.

All too often selection has been reduced to just a process where the focus is on the process itself, including volume of applicants and time taken for interviewing or assessment, instead of the quality of both applicants and selection decisions.

Selecting in requires a different mindset from selecting out. It's a positive mindset that says 'we are going to find the right people' rather than 'we are going to make sure we cut out the wrong ones'. There are some key principles involved in a select-in approach:

- Consciously choosing 'select-in' rather than 'select-out' and regularly challenging yourself that you are doing so.
- Understanding what kind of person will be a great fit for the role, which means knowing what great performers are like.

- Steering clear of vague, unspecific and jargon-laden descriptions of people in person specifications and job adverts.
- Creating job adverts that accurately describe the kind of person who excels in the role.

Jonathan Gunson was a Project Manager at an engineering company for many years. Reflecting on the use of competency-based recruitment, he spoke vividly of the downsides of what he referred to as the 'sifting out' method of candidate shortlisting:

> Traditional competency recruitment starts by reducing a pile of CVs to those who have those basic competencies to do the task in hand. The next stage will be to look for reasons to reduce the number of potential candidates. The great risk here is that the remaining candidate may well be capable of doing the task in hand, but he or she is unlikely to be much else other than inoffensive.

'Inoffensive' candidates, as Jonathan puts it, can plod along doing an adequate job. They are neither bad nor great, but simply competent. There is a great difference between people who can do the job and those who are a great fit and thrive in it. In order to attract the great ones you need to know a lot about those who are round pegs in round holes. And then you need to be able to articulate that in a job advert or person specification that is going to attract them.

Despite the sophistication of the discipline of marketing advertising today, the art of appealing copy-writing has not, on the whole, reached person specifications and job adverts. Few stand out as appealing and effective forms of communication.

An example of a select-out job advert is this advert for a care worker in the UK:

> In these vital roles, life experience is more important than work experience. You'll have an empathy with the needs of older people and understand the importance of treating our residents with dignity and respect.
>
> We'll give you all the support, training and development you'll need to help you enjoy an extremely satisfying career in social care. The work can be challenging, but the rewards are beyond measure.
>
> If you feel you can help to make our care home a place that our residents can really call home, we'd love to hear from you.
>
> You'll be required to work evenings, weekends and bank holidays on a rota basis.

There are several problems with this advert. There is very little information on the type of person who would do well in this job other than vague statements like 'you'll have empathy with the needs of older people' and 'understand the importance of treating our residents with dignity and respect'. Some people may fit this description but it doesn't mean to say they would be great at the job. The advert is not inspiring, it is simply descriptive. This organization could receive a lot of applications from people who either don't really know what it entails and/or have no idea whether they would be the sort of person who would be right for it.

Here's an excerpt from a job advert for a sales manager in a well-known American retail store:

> The role of the sales manager is to acquire and develop sales and service professionals who exemplify the brand in their interpersonal skills. The SM creates associates who feel empowered to take care of the customer. SMs are responsible for leading, supporting, and inspiring their sellers each and every day to provide an outstanding service experience for their customers.
>
> The successful candidate will be resourceful, open-minded, inspired by challenges, a self-starter and flexible. They will have the ability to insert self intentionally into teachable moments and be able to demonstrate a positive attitude with a leadership presence.
>
> They will also be able to work collaboratively across functional areas to achieve results and preferably have a four-year college degree.

In the first paragraph the advert gives information about what they want the successful candidate to do. The second paragraph describes what kind of person they want, but most of the words used are vague and open to interpretation. 'Resourceful', 'open-minded', 'self-starter' and 'flexible' can be defined in different ways. And the phrase 'will have the ability to insert self intentionally into teachable moments' is wonderfully intriguing and obscure but tells the candidate nothing about what they will actually have to do and how! At best the advert will attract people who have experience in sales management and a degree and who think they fit the description. Whether or not they do fit it depends on whether the organization is clear what each descriptor means.

Contrast the adverts above with the following strengths-based one – an advert for a nurse – whose aim it is actively to attract the right kind of people:

Is making a difference what drives you most? Are you a caring, fair person who sees everyone as equal?

Is it really important to you to do the right thing, and are you the type of person who speaks up if you think something is wrong?

Are you a very reliable, hard-working person who has high standards and likes to do an excellent job? And are you known for always going the extra mile?

If this sounds like you and you love the responsibility and accountability of being a nurse, we'd love to hear from you.

Here's what one of our nurses says about the job: 'For me the job is simply about caring about everything – patients, colleagues, doing a good job… and maintaining your high professional standards.'

The advert clearly, and in plain English, describes the type of person who excels as a nurse. If you read the advert you know whether it is the job for you or not. The quotation from a nurse gives some insight into what motivates her so that the person reading the advert can ask themselves, 'does that sound like me?'

Of course there will be some people who are not sure whether they fit the description, or just hope that they do. But giving a clear description of the type of person who thrives in the job will encourage applications from the right kind of person and discourages applications from those who are not a good fit. With more of the right people applying, the 'select-out' method becomes unnecessary. The recruiters are looking to see how people fit the person specification instead of looking for ways in which they don't.

Selecting without compromise

I don't know about you, but I have recruited people in the past who I have known weren't quite right but, for whatever reason, I was desperate to recruit someone for the position. It's never a good idea and usually leads to an unhappy time for all concerned. My worst mistake was recruiting a senior person for a position onboard a ship. My boss and I did the interviews and we both knew he was not a good candidate. But we were under pressure from senior management to fill the position so we hired him. A few weeks later I was at London Heathrow Airport meeting the newly dismissed recruit who had been repatriated after an unsuccessful few weeks in employment!

As Seth Godin, entrepreneur, blogger and bestselling author, said in his blog post of 18 August 2015, 'We say we intend to hire and train great people, but in the interim, we'll have to settle for cheap and available… The interim is forever, so perhaps it makes sense to act in the interim as we expect to act in the long haul.'

My example above wasn't a case of 'cheap and available', but it was a case of 'qualified and available'. The worst thing was we knew we were making the wrong decision. The cost of that decision in time, money and stress was great. And it wasn't a kind thing to do to a person who was clearly going to be a square peg in a round hole.

Famously, Dan Jacobs, Head of Talent at Apple, said, 'I'd rather have a hole than an arse-hole.' For sure, hiring the wrong person in a role can have repercussions in terms of time, performance and stress (of the person, their boss who is trying to performance manage them and the rest of the team). It's simply not worth it.

I'm sure I'm not alone in having learnt the hard way that compromising on recruitment decisions is a mistake. Even if we can't pinpoint exactly why the person isn't right for a job, we usually know that they are not. With SBR there is no escaping the evidence – they are either cut out for the job or they are not. It discourages recruiters from appointing people that aren't a good fit. And it also discourages candidates themselves from taking the job. If they didn't already know, the interview itself shines a light on their strengths and it becomes clear whether or not they are a good fit. And it leaves their pride intact, because they don't walk away feeling that they were deficient in some way. As we saw from some of the examples in Chapter 2, they often leave with more insight into themselves and an understanding of why the job is not right for them. So the SBR approach not only discourages employers from compromising on selection decisions, it discourages candidates from doing so too. In that way it really does feel like an equal and fair process in contrast with other approaches, which can feel like the employer holds all the cards.

Strengths-based interviewing

Why people like it

Proponents of strengths-based interviewing like it for the following reasons:

- It is an engaging process for the interviewee and interviewer as it feels more natural and less wooden.

- Candidates cannot prepare in the same way for a strengths interview as they can for a competency-based interview so interviewers are more likely to get a realistic picture of them and see the real person.
- Candidates enjoy the interview and often learn things about themselves.
- Unsuccessful candidates have more of an understanding of why they have been unsuccessful.

It's good for the reputation of the organization because candidates generally have a very positive experience.

See the section 'Strengths-based interviews – FAQs' on page 67 to discover more about strengths-based interviewing and strengths-based interviews.

Questions asked in stand-alone strengths interviews

Here are some examples of the sort of questions asked at stand-alone strengths interviews:

What do you enjoy doing the most at work?

Why do you think you enjoy this the most?

What energizes you?

What makes a good day for you?

What activities come naturally to you?

What are your greatest strengths?

What do you really dislike doing?

What gets done on your 'to do' list? What never gets done?

How do you stay motivated?

How do you make sure you always do your best?

What makes you feel you've had a rewarding and successful day?

What has been your most significant achievement?

Questions like these are also sometimes used in the strengths interviews that are associated with database or dictionary SBR approaches.

These questions are not asked in strengths interviews that are associated with the strengths profiling SBR approach. When you have a strengths profile that has been elicited through workplace observations and interviews you know exactly what the strengths are that high performers share. This means that you ask the candidate about the strengths that are in the relevant profile and the interviewers' job is to assess whether the candidate does indeed have each of the strengths.

No probing!

A characteristic of all strengths-based interviews is that, unlike competency based interviews, they don't involve probing. The interviewers ask the questions and take notes of the responses. Probing is not done because pushing for information, which the candidate may well have prepared, means you can lead candidates and thus this can turn a poor candidate into an average one.

The danger of stand-alone strengths interviews

In theory it sounds easy and exciting to introduce strengths-based interviewing as a stand-alone part of the selection process. Organizations that want to re-energize and improve their interview method may be tempted by a new, fresh and promising approach.

The obvious downside of introducing strengths-based interviewing without using either profiling or database/dictionary methodologies is that there is no rigorous method of knowing whether the strengths they are looking for in a strengths interview are indeed strengths that high performers possess. They may be inadvertently creating a 'wish list' of strengths that no one person has. It could be argued that without knowing what strengths a person needs to be good at to thrive in a particular role, a strengths interview is no more effective for selecting the right candidate than a behavioural competency interview is.

The two main SBR approaches and how they work

As we have seen, the two main SBR approaches at the time of writing this book are profiling methodology and database or dictionary methodology. Each of these approaches have been used in large organizations, and their use has been established over a number of years so there is a track record associated with them both. They are different from each other in a number of ways, and each has its pros and cons, as we saw in Chapter 1. Here we will look at how each method is implemented in practice.

SBR database or dictionary methodology

A typical process used in this methodology is as follows:

1 An analysis is done of great performers in a role, typically in a focus group format, by asking them questions about what they enjoy and what they are good at.

2 The output is a job description, the elements of which are drawn from a pre-existing dictionary or database of strengths.

3 A selection process is then designed whose objective is to identify the strengths in the job description.

4 The first step of the process is sometimes a situational judgement test (SJT) followed by a strengths interview and possibly an assessment centre. A situational judgement test poses hypothetical scenarios to the candidate, who has to choose what they believe is the best answer from a number of options. This test is done online and its purpose is to eliminate candidates at this stage of the selection process. Critics of SJTs say that they are questionable as a means of assessment for a number of reasons: the scenarios are necessarily brief and therefore unrealistic; they can be faked as it is often obvious what the correct answer is; candidates who fail could actually be good recruits and just need to be educated into the particular context. Also, it is impossible to judge whether someone has particular strengths based on their answers to an online test.

5 The next step of the process is a strengths interview, which uses the types of questions listed above. This is the most important part of the overall selection process.

6 An assessment centre is the final stage of the process and involves the candidate being set challenges and tasks that are designed to reveal their strengths. Assessment centres are commonly used in the SBR database/dictionary methodology but not in the profiling methodology because the interview approach means that all the necessary strengths are assessed so there is no need also to run an assessment centre.

SBR profiling methodology

The SBR profiling methodology has at its heart evidence of what makes great performers great in a specific role and context. The process that is used is as follows:

1   Establishing the criteria to use to identify the great performers in a role.

2   Once a pool of great people has been identified they are closely observed in their workplace. Then structured interviews with the great performers and those that know them well (including customers where appropriate) are carried out.

3   The quantitative and qualitative data collected during the observations and interviews are analysed using a grounded theory methodology, which is a research methodology involving the construction of a theory through the analysis of data.

4   A strengths and motivator profile is created, which describes the strengths (including values and motivators) that the great performers have been found to have.

5   Recruiters are trained how to conduct a strengths-based interview, which enables them to assess whether a candidate has the strengths and motivators described in the profile.

6   The overall selection process is reviewed so that decisions can be made about which other elements will be replaced by the strengths interview and which need to be retained.

No more behavioural competency assessments

Behavioural competency interviews and exercises are almost always unnecessary once you introduce strengths interviewing because once you know a candidate's strengths you don't need to assess their behavioural competences. The reason for this is that our strengths (including our values and motivators) drive our behaviours and are more consistent and predictable than our behaviours. To explain what this means, here is an example. Engaging Minds profiled ward sisters (also called ward managers) for the top ten UK NHS Trusts. One of the beliefs about great ward sisters up until that point was that they were naturally assertive. In fact, it was discovered that none of them were naturally assertive. However, we did witness a lot of assertive behaviour in these ward sisters. One example was an incident where a senior doctor came onto a ward wearing a watch. The policy, for infection control reasons, on this ward was that all staff had to be bare below the elbow. The ward sister asked the doctor to remove the watch and he refused. The ward sister stood her ground and, after a heated conversation, the doctor eventually removed his watch. The ward sister's behaviour in this situation was most definitely assertive but it was very difficult for her to challenge the doctor, and she said afterwards in the structured interview that she hated doing it. The reason she couldn't *not* do it was because she really cared about doing the right thing for her patients and she had high standards, so was not going to run any risk of infection. So, what we can see from this example is that an unnatural behaviour can occur if someone's strengths kick in. This ward sister was not the naturally assertive type who would, say, send food back in a restaurant if there were something wrong with it. But she would challenge anyone who was putting high standards at risk and where it was the right thing to do. However, if an assessment centre were (in this case mistakenly) looking for assertive behaviour in candidates they would have ruled this person out.

Some organizations focus solely on recruiting and developing behaviours. You can see from the above why this approach is flawed – it is not looking deeply enough. Another example that is easy to relate to is people who are not naturally good at customer service but who receive training at 'smile school' that teaches them to display certain behaviour, such as smiling. If you have ever been served by such a person in a restaurant or shop it is obvious that their smile is not natural or authentic.

Where does the strengths interview fit?

A decision has to be made at which stage in the selection process the strengths interview is conducted. There is no one right answer to this. It depends on the role and on what else needs to be assessed. Below are some examples of which stage the strengths interview fits within the selection process of some organizations.

Care assistant

Stage 1: Strengths-based job advert based on the strengths and motivator profile.

Stage 2: Online application including one values-based question.

Stage 3: Literacy and numeracy test.

Stage 4: Strengths interview to assess the strengths and motivators in the profile.

Sales manager

Stage 1: Strengths-based job advert based on the strengths and motivator profile.

Stage 2: Submission of CV.

Stage 3: Strengths interview.

The key question to ask when deciding at what stage of the selection process the strengths interview should take place is whether the appointee needs particular technical skills, competency or experience without which they could not be appointed. If the answer is yes then you will need to assess for those first. However, if the most important thing is that they are the right sort of person then conducting the strengths interview first is the best thing to do. Clearly, the type of role determines this. For example, if you are recruiting, say, an architect, an airline pilot or a doctor you will definitely want to know that they have the right qualifications and experience first because if they don't you won't recruit them. If they do then you can go on to assess whether they are a good fit for the job in terms of the type of person they are.

Useful questions

Here are some questions that will help you ascertain whether your current recruitment approach is working as well as it might and, if not, whether SBR could help you:

- What works about your current approach(es) to recruitment?
- Does your current selection approach select out or select in?
- What elements of your current approach do you want to change and why?
- What benefits do you see SBR potentially bringing?
- Is the database/dictionary approach or the SBR profiling methodology best for you?

Tips for the practitioner

- Be clear about what your goals are in introducing strengths-based recruitment.
- Understand your starting point and what assumptions (explicit or implicit) are at play. For example, does your approach select in or select out?
- Write down the names of some of your best performers in any given role – do you understand why they are great?
- Now write down all the benefits to the organization and individuals of knowing why great performers are great.

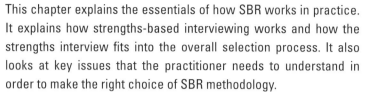
Two-minute chapter summary

This chapter explains the essentials of how SBR works in practice. It explains how strengths-based interviewing works and how the strengths interview fits into the overall selection process. It also looks at key issues that the practitioner needs to understand in order to make the right choice of SBR methodology.

Key facts to remember

- Strengths-based recruitment (SBR) is the term that is normally used to define an entire strengths-based approach to selection. It involves profiling an organization's best performers and introducing strengths-based attraction, interviewing, selection and induction.

- Every selection approach is either select in or select out. The latter has serious downsides in terms of the quality of recruits you hire because it is about eliminating people from the process who don't fit, versus attracting and finding those who fit very well.

- Strengths-based interviewing (SBI) is just one part, albeit a crucial part, of the selection process. It can be limited in its effectiveness if it's used in isolation and not as part of an integrated SBR approach.

- Implementing strengths interviewing normally means there is no need for behavioural competency assessments in the form of interviews or assessment centres.

Strengths-based interviews – FAQs

What is a strengths-based interview (SBI)?

The goal of a strengths-based interview is to ascertain whether the candidate has the natural strengths needed for the job. The interviewers seek to discover whether the candidate would be naturally good at the role, love doing it and be energized by it.

Is there more than one type of strengths-based interview?

Yes there is more than one type. Strengths-based interviews vary depending upon the approach that the prospective employer takes to strengths-based recruitment.

There are two most commonly used types of strengths-based interview. The first is where the questions are based on a strengths profile that has been developed specifically for the role in question (so the interviewers know exactly what strengths great performers in the role actually have). The second is where interviewers are trying to discover generally what strengths a candidate has and whether they are the same as the ones they judge are needed for the job in question.

In both cases interviewers are seeking to discover whether someone possesses the innate strengths for the job, will love it and will thrive in it (as opposed to just being able to do it, which is what interviewers discover in a competency based interview).

What do interviewers look for in a strengths-based interview?

Interviewers are looking for evidence that a candidate has the strengths needed for the role they are being interviewed for. They are trained to gain insight into each candidate as an individual. They take notice of *how* each candidate answers the questions, not just *what they say*.

Is it true that interviewers favour candidates that answer quickly and are expressive?

There are some misunderstandings about what interviewers are looking for in an interviewee. Good interviewers do not mark people on whether they answer quickly and are expressive. They are trained to seek evidence on whether a person has the strengths they are looking for. They treat each candidate on their merit as an individual. Two candidates may have the strengths but behave in different ways. One might answer quickly, one might not; one might be very expressive, one might not. The important thing is whether they have the strengths. The best advice to interviewees is to act as naturally as possible – if you try to 'fake' certain types of behaviour the interviewers will notice.

Can anyone conduct a strengths-based interview?

Strengths-based interviewers are specially trained. The training teaches them how to judge whether a person has particular strengths. Like all good interviewers, they are also good at building rapport, relaxing the candidate, listening and observing.

Is it possible to prepare for a strengths-based interview?

A candidate cannot prepare for a strengths interview in the same way as they might for a behavioural competency-based interview. The best way to get ready for a strengths-based interview is to relax, be open in your answers and be yourself. You might also want to think about what you love most and least in your work life.

People who are used to preparing examples of particular competencies for competency-based interviews sometimes worry about having a strengths-based interview because they cannot prepare in the same way. It's best not to worry. Just be yourself and answer the questions as best you can. Good strengths interviewers can discern whether or not an individual has the strengths needed for a role. It's not possible to 'fake' strengths like you could, if you wanted to, 'fake' competencies by preparing well. With strengths-based recruitment it means you're much less likely to end up in a job that is not right for you.

How long does a strengths-based interview take?

Normally between 45 minutes and an hour.

How does a strengths-based interview differ from a behavioural competency-based interview?

In a strengths interview the interviewers are assessing whether someone has the natural strengths for the job and whether they are likely to *love the job and be energized by it*. In a behavioural competency-based interview the interviewers are simply assessing whether, based on past performance, a candidate *can* do the job.

Interviewers in strengths interviews are assessing how someone answers the question as well as what they say. As well as listening to the interviewee's responses they pay attention to body language, choice of words and tone.

Why are more and more organizations adopting strengths-based interviewing?

Organizations that adopt strengths-based recruitment do so because of the evidence of its effectiveness. Those who have implemented it have found huge benefits in terms of a reduction in staff attrition rates, increase in engagement and performance, improvement in customer service ratings and a positive impact on their culture.

References

Godin, S (2015) The interim strategy (18 August). Available at: sethgodin.typepad.com (accessed 18 August 2015)

Jacobs, D (nd) Quote. Available at: startups.co.uk/richard-reed-shares-his-5-golden-rules-for-running-a-business/ (accessed 26 November 2015)

Successfully implementing strengths-based recruitment

04

Key success factors and pitfalls to avoid

This chapter answers these questions:

- What are the lessons from organizations that have successfully implemented SBR?
- What are the pitfalls to avoid when implementing SBR?
- What advice do senior leaders who have led the introduction of SBR offer to those who are considering it?

As with any organizational transformation, there are factors that will help you make the change effectively and there are also pitfalls to avoid. This chapter describes how to make a successful transition to strengths-based recruitment. The insight, advice and lessons learned in this chapter are all based on the real-world experience of organizations that have successfully implemented SBR.

The factors for successfully implementing SBR

There are a number of steps that organizations that have successfully implemented SBR have gone through.

They establish a clear need

They know exactly why they want to implement SBR. They have specific, and sometimes urgent, problems that they need to solve. Usually they don't know what it takes to be a great performer in one or more of the key jobs in their organization. Some organizations also have high staff turnover that is costing time and money. As a result of one or both of these issues they encounter the following problems:

- They struggle to attract and retain really excellent people in key roles.

- Their staff are not highly engaged and that is affecting customer service.

- They are worried that their people can't deliver the performance and reputation that they want their organization to have.

Irrespective of the type of organization, these issues affect the financials (profitability in the case of private organizations, efficiency and waste in the case of public sector) as well as performance, service and reputation in the case of all types of organizations.

The Shelford Group (comprising the NHS's top ten teaching hospitals) introduced SBR in 2013 at a time when the NHS was under a huge amount of criticism about poor quality of patient care. This was in the context of the public enquiry into the Mid Staffordshire NHS Foundation Trust (resulting in the Francis Report) and the desire of chief nurses in the Shelford Group to ensure the best possible quality of patient care was delivered. Katherine Fenton, Chief Nurse at University College London Hospitals NHS Foundation Trust at the time and Chair of the Shelford Group Chief Nurses, said:

> One of the key roles with great potential to influence the quality of patient care in UK nursing is the ward sister. If you have a great ward sister in place, you get a happy ward, low staff turnover and, most importantly, great outcomes for patients. We intuitively knew who our best ward sisters were and we knew their qualifications and competencies, but we couldn't articulate their strengths, qualities and attributes to be sure we were recruiting the best people for the role. It was a time when circumstance had handed us the freedom to do something new and radical. We were able to try something quite different, to see if we could really make a difference to the quality of patient care.

Katherine Fenton and her senior colleagues in the Shelford Group had established a clear need – they wanted to be certain that they were recruiting the right people into these key roles. Not doing so carried a high risk for the NHS.

Whilst the risk of getting it wrong does not have such a potentially devastating impact in other organizations as it can in the NHS, the urgency can be great. When Lynda Greenshields was HR Director of the Saga and AA brands she needed to tackle a problem that had been causing both organizations difficulties for years – namely staff turnover and customer service:

> At the time, we were facing a huge challenge with call-centre staff turnover rates, and it was felt to be a problem with no answer. Both sales and HR managers felt that they had 'tried everything' and were at the point of resigning themselves to the view that 'it's like this across the whole industry'. And on the other side of that, with respect to our customers, our AA and Saga brands were all about customer service. But, we realized, how can you hope to deliver amazing customer service when you have such high levels of turnover in your customer-facing people? Whenever a customer called us or we called them or visited them, I wanted to make sure that our employee on the phone or in the customer's home would be living our brand and that our customers would experience that as great customer service, every single time. Saga and the AA look after their customers. It's what they are known for. It's what they do.

Lynda Greenshields made the connection between how engaged their people were and the standards of performance with the service that customers were experiencing. It sounds obvious, but all too often initiatives like training programmes and new technologies are implemented to improve customer service when something as simple as recruiting people who are naturals with customers is the most effective thing that can be done.

They have the right senior leader

The senior leader who decides on SBR as an approach is usually also the one who approves the budget and is responsible for successful implementation. My observations of these leaders are that they tend to be people who are courageous. They intuitively know what is right and they are not afraid to make a decision to change, even in the face of opposition. They are also the kinds of people who strive to do the right thing and push hard to achieve what they think is right for their organization. They tend to be straightforward types who say it as it is. One of these people told me about a conversation she had with a headhunter who was talking about wanting a senior person who had a track record in organizational performance improvement. Her response was, 'I'm not interested in a role where that's all they want. Anyone can improve performance. I'm interested in transforming organizations.' That quote just about sums up the leaders that we have met who drive change in their organizations by introducing a switch to strengths. Lynda Greenshields, HR Director for the AA and Saga brands, Hilary Chapman, Chief Nurse at Sheffield Teaching Hospitals, Katherine Fenton, former Chief Nurse at University College London Hospitals, Tim Miller former Group Head of Human Resources at Standard Chartered Bank, Sandra Porter, former Head of HR at Starbucks UK and Ireland, all of them were determined to bring big and positive change about in their organizations. They are role models of leaders who can bring people with them and create a legacy of lasting performance improvement and engagement. A lot can be learned from them about how to present a vision of something different and inspire people to want the change.

In an article for the *Health Services Journal* (2014) Katherine Fenton, former Chief Nurse at University College London Foundation Trust, described her vision as follows:

> Whenever you run a major project such as the great ward sisters profile, there is a risk that some people will see it as a discrete entity, something that can be done, reported on and then parked while everyone gets on with business as usual.
>
> But the nursing profession, the NHS, the public at large and their elected representatives do not have any appetite for business as usual.
>
> They want us to change. We want to change. These profiles are just the first step in a journey that has the potential to transform care in the NHS.
>
> If we want to transform care then we have to make sure that we have the right people to do it.

These leaders tend also be those who are not afraid of going against the prevailing norms. They only do something if they are convinced it will help. Sandra Porter of Starbucks UK said, 'I have never been someone that is keen to roll out a plan of off-the-shelf initiatives, as often the challenges and environments are so different that one size does not fit all.'

Some senior leaders talk about the need to be brave. This includes Hilary Chapman, Chief Nurse at Sheffield Teaching Hospitals, who commented, 'Bravery is crucial because if a candidate is everyone's favourite and the SBR process means that you appoint someone else you have to be brave.'

Eva Sage-Gavin of Gap Inc agrees: '[It takes] Courage! Growing up I was encouraged to take risks and push for the things that I believed in.'

They elicit the support of the right people

Organizations that have implemented SBR successfully and sustainably have done so in large part because senior executives were keen (sometimes desperate) to resolve some or all of the problems listed above that led them to consider introducing SBR in the first place.

Evidence of results experienced by other organizations helped them to understand what was possible and how it could help their organizations. The commitment and interest of senior people in the five organizations featured in the 'Welcome to the strengths revolution' study (North, 2013) made a huge difference to the speed with which SBR was implemented and its effectiveness.

The person who initiates the implementation of SBR is usually either a very senior person, or an influential less senior person, whose attention has been caught by its impact on other organizations. They then set about gaining the support of senior colleagues and key stakeholders.

Hilary Chapman, Chief Nurse at Sheffield Teaching Hospitals, said that the first step for her was to get the right people and resource behind SBR:

> The first step was gaining the support of my executive colleagues, the most important of which in this context was the director of HR. He is responsible for recruitment overall and I needed to know that the strengths-based approach was going to become how Sheffield does things. He already understood the concept of SBR as he had implemented it outside the NHS. Equally I wanted my nine senior nurse directors across the organization to want to do it as much as I did. It was a case of presenting to them, answering their questions and a lot of ground work talking to people. I didn't have a lot of push-back, to be honest.

When asked how she got the support of her senior colleagues, Lynda Greenshields said:

> I had hard numbers to show that, amongst other things, we were not holding on to our best people and what that was costing us. People already knew there was a problem, but the numbers clarified the severity of the situation. Now they wanted to understand what had happened and try to put things right. They were up for it. And that was great, because to effect a massive change like this you need leaders who are ready and willing to move from a point of feeling that nothing can ever make a difference. In this case though, there wasn't the need for a hard sell… the logic was there in the numbers. Something needed to change and we all wanted to make it happen.

Often when talking about how to sell change to senior people, data and numbers are mentioned. These are crucial in presenting a logical case for change that senior people can commit to. They need to be convinced of the return on investment that change can bring, especially change that moves the organization away from something they have been doing for a long time. There is a huge amount of evidence that SBR works and has a positive impact on the bottom line – sometimes to the tune of millions in year one! So you could assume that senior people only need to know about the evidence. However, that is sometimes not enough. We know from Antonio Damasio's Somatic Marker Theory (SMT) that it's emotion that causes people to act, not information. According to this theory the limbic system plays a crucial role in determining a person's behaviour, especially decision making. Somatic markers are physiological states such as anxiety, marked by increased heart rate, feelings of fear, sweating and joy, which is associated with the release of the hormone serotonin. We rely on these markers to help us decide which option will be the most beneficial to us. Damasio and other neuroscientists argue that all decisions are emotionally driven, even if we think our decision is based on logic. The point is that, when seeking to influence someone, it seems wise to appeal to their emotions even when they are a rational kind of person who demands all the logical evidence. It's not about manipulating people, it's about them feeling that something is a good idea as well as thinking that it is. You've probably heard the phrase 'winning hearts and minds'. It's important to do this if people are going to be committed to doing something new. You can only win hearts and minds when you engage people emotionally.

So how do you do that? Indeed, how did the leaders we have quoted in this chapter do it, when it came to bringing their senior colleagues onboard, including the chief executive (and all of the people cited so far reported to the chief executive)? There were a few things that were common to these people and others we know of who have successfully won the hearts and minds of their CEO and boards to switch to SBR.

Of course, they had the data to show that things needed to change and that SBR is a robust and evidence-based approach. So that is the logical part sorted. In terms of winning hearts, here's what else they did:

- They pointed out that the approach is common sense. They often used the phrase 'square pegs in round holes' as shorthand to describe people who were in the wrong job. Everyone knew what they meant. Some people, indeed, had had that personal experience of being a square peg in a round hole and knew how awful it can be. They talked about when people like doing something then they are more likely to do it well, and if they don't like doing something it stresses them out and they can't be as effective. They pointed out the obviousness of the approach.

- They sometimes asked whether senior colleagues had children or other family who were struggling because they were in the wrong job or didn't know what career path to follow. By doing this they related it to their lives and made it very real.

- Some talked of the legacy they wanted to leave. Katherine Fenton, former Chief Nurse at University College London Hospitals, said, 'It would be wonderful if it could help us recruit the right people for all nursing roles from the start. If we knew we were choosing the best people to be student nurses every single time it would be amazing. The overall resulting impact on patient care, experience and outcome would be a tremendous legacy to leave.' She was due to retire a couple of years after introducing SBR and its legacy was an important factor for her. Other leaders who want to make a big change fast have talked in similar terms about being interested in transformation.

Katherine Fenton, when talking about selling the idea of SBR to her colleagues, said, 'SBR is such common sense. We all sensed the possibility.'

Other leaders have talked about intuition and sensing SBR was right for them. Indeed, the leaders cited in this book who have championed SBR are amongst the pioneers. Most of them had relatively little return-on-investment data to go on when they commissioned the work. Some actually said they didn't really need the data, because it felt like the right thing to do.

They appoint the right SBR leads

It's always a good idea to appoint one or two people to take the lead on the implementation of SBR. Some organizations appoint someone from HR and someone from an operational part of the business. It helps to have people who are senior and who are able to engage with and influence others. It's not necessary to appoint someone full time, although some organizations do. What is necessary is that they are committed to doing a good job and that they believe in SBR.

Implementation of SBR went well at Sheffield Teaching Hospitals and Hilary Chapman, the Chief Nurse, puts that down, in part, to her choice of SBR leads. When asked how she selected the two people for the role she replied:

I trust them. They're professional. They understood SBR and could articulate the benefits. They had done the training and understood everything forensically including the outcomes and benefits. I knew they would question things and that they would want to be absolutely happy with everything before implementation. They are strong enough to keep people within the golden rules (ie sticking to the correct interview process and not appointing someone who doesn't have all the strengths), too. Over time I have observed a huge energy and commitment in them. And when they came back to me to discuss things they would challenge me and hold me to how it needed to be done properly. That lovely thing as a senior leader to be challenged on things – they did that to me and pulled me back into line at times! They really believe in it.

Great SBR leads are the key to effective implementation of SBR. These people have a can-do attitude and are the types who make things happen.

When Guy's and St Thomas' NHS Foundation Trust decided to introduce SBR Elisabeth Pullar was appointed as the lead. She was chosen because of her track record of successful implementation of other new innovations. About her appointment as SBR lead, she said:

I have a can-do attitude and my approach is always 'how can we make this happen' rather than to see only the problems with something. I'm a doer. I consider it a necessity to role-model positive and proactive behaviour. I think the chief nurse asked me to lead on SBR because she sees me as a dynamic person with the ability to engage others and I'm not afraid of new things.

On occasion someone appoints themselves as an SBR lead just because they feel so strongly about it that they decide to take on the mantle. Keith Jones from a financial services company was such a person. He said:

Being introduced to SBR was a light-bulb moment for me. I really saw the potential of the approach and found it exciting so took it on as my own. This involved explaining the approach to people, making sure that colleagues were being compliant in the way they did the strengths interviews, helping colleagues on other sites to implement it well and getting support and buy-in.

They know what makes a great champion and they encourage and support them

When an organization implements SBR, advocates, or 'strengths champions', emerge naturally. They are people whose hearts and minds are captured – for some of them this happens early on. Others may have been sceptical, but once they have completed the training they become convinced of the value of SBR.

Many, if not most, of those who are trained in strengths interviewing become strengths champions. Delegates find the training motivating and stimulating and this is part of why they become enthusiastic and go on to become advocates and, in some cases, evangelists. Nick Corbo from Saga, in an interview for this book, knew that the training usually convinced people who were not sure about SBR. He said, 'If there were any sceptics I say to them, "go on the training and then come back and tell me it doesn't work!"'

Being introduced to strengths generally has a powerful impact and a natural reaction is to want to 'spread the word'.

Charlotte was one such strengths champion. When her company introduced SBR she was a team leader in a busy call centre. She enjoyed her job and was good at it. Charlotte trained in strengths-based interviewing and loved it. She saw its potential and couldn't wait to start using it. Her enthusiasm and positive attitude was obvious in the training, so much so that the company decided to have her trained as a trainer. Charlotte was unstoppable in her championing of strengths. A natural optimist, she got alongside people to bring them with her. Her enthusiasm was so contagious that she even persuaded the cynics. Along with a few of her colleagues who also became champions she played a huge part in making the change to SBR work. Here's what she said:

> SBR has changed my life. I am convinced I wouldn't have got this promotion if I hadn't found [SBR]. Also my son, who is 16, wouldn't be studying engineering now. I changed the way I guided him after the training. I asked him questions like 'What do you love doing? What gives you a real buzz?' People can see my enthusiasm and I love the results SBR brings as well as the effect it has on people.

What makes a great strengths champion?

The main thing is that champions *really* believe in SBR, have been inspired by how much you get to know the real person at the interview and they want to be part of something that is very positive. Like Charlotte they often comment that SBR has an impact on their lives outside work too – whether it's noticing in shops or restaurants whether a person really seems to love their job, or helping children decide what subject choices to make at school. We heard from Hilary Chapman earlier in this chapter why she chose the SBR leads that she chose. She talked about them having influence and being the sort of people who really care about quality. I would agree with that. Below are some of the other qualities that I have observed in really effective SBR champions, whether they are leading the implementation or not.

They start with the end in mind

Successful champions are driven by a vision of the kind of organization they want to work in – one where people love what they do, and deliver great performance as a result. To convince others, they share the vision and provide practical examples that clearly show how focusing on strengths helps build a better organization. Whether it's about improving patient care, transforming customer service or increasing engagement levels and productivity, the champions are always clear about what improvements they want to see.

They influence others

Champions are great communicators who recognize the importance of talking to people and answering their questions. They get alongside people and seize every opportunity to tell their colleagues about strengths. They share personal anecdotes and success stories that help others to understand the power of the strengths approach.

They recognize that people are more likely to support change if it builds on what's already working. This is why the starting point for SBR is profiling great performers who are achieving outstanding results within the organization.

Champions tend also to be good listeners. Understanding and talking through others' reservations and concerns means they get and keep people on side. They know that if people don't feel able to challenge they will feel 'done to'. They appreciate that the more involved people are in the change process, the more committed they will be to it.

They care about quality and getting things right

Embedding SBR doesn't happen overnight. It takes time and everything about the change needs to be done thoroughly and to a high standard. Champions are patient but they are also sticklers for standards. They pay attention to quality and make sure things are done right.

They build a network

The best champions know who the key influencers in their organization are. They make sure they give them feedback and keep them informed and involved. They create a coalition of senior people who understand the potential of strengths, and are committed to helping in different ways. They invite key stakeholders to attend, or interact with, delegates on training sessions. They find ways for them to *feel* the difference that strengths can make.

They integrate the strengths interview effectively with the overall selection process

It is necessary to incorporate the strengths interview into the overall selection process. This means reviewing the person specification and deciding which elements are still necessary and how each will be assessed. It also means deciding at which stage the strengths interview is best conducted. Usually assessment centre activities and behavioural competency interviews are no longer necessary because knowing whether a person has the necessary strengths means you know they will have the behaviours needed. So these two elements are normally replaced in their entirety by the strengths interview. Table 4.1 is an example of a person specification for a carer. It shows the essential criteria, the desirable criteria

TABLE 4.1 Person specification for a carer

Essential criteria	Desirable criteria	Assessment method
Qualifications GCSE English and Maths at Grade D or above (or equivalent, which would include Key Skills Level 1 at English and Maths)	NVQ Level 2 or above in Care	Application form
Experience No essential experience needed	Experience as a carer useful (in professional or personal setting)	Application form and pre-screening telephone interview
Further training Willingness to undertake and complete NVQ Level 2 in Care		
Aptitudes (Verbal, numerical)		Numeracy and literacy aptitude tests
Strengths/values/motivators Possess all the strengths in the organization's Carer Strengths Profile		Strengths-based interview

and how each is assessed. The order in which this company carries out its assessment is as follows:

- Application form
- Telephone screening
- Numeracy and literacy test
- Strengths-based interview

When they are going through the process of reviewing their person specifications to integrate SBI, many organizations find that some of the criteria they were previously using are too vague and therefore not very useful – for example, 'must be a good team worker'. So the review is useful in itself.

Organizations that recruit people in large numbers sometimes worry that introducing SBR will add too much time to the recruitment process. In fact it normally reduces the time taken to hire, for a number of reasons. First, the strengths-based job advert attracts more of the right people so less time is wasted sifting through applications of the wrong types. And second, the SBI normally eliminates the need for assessment centres and behavioural competency interviewing. Even in cases where the existing selection process takes less time than the new strengths selection process, time is saved overall because it greatly reduces the time wasted in managing the performance of those who are not right for the job.

They pay close attention to quality

As with any big change, it's important to do it well if it is to produce the lasting results you want. SBR is a new way of doing things as well as a mindset shift to a focus on what works well. In order to make sure it works, it has to be done right with no corners cut.

The kinds of things that organizations do to ensure quality are as follows:

- Appoint an SBR lead who they know is a stickler for quality.

- Carry out in-depth strengths-based interviewing training to give interviewers specific knowledge and skills to conduct a good strengths interview. Ideally they should attend a minimum 1.5-day training programme to develop the skills and confidence to master this very different style of interviewing. A regional manager in a financial services organization put it well: 'The quality of the training is key. It's not easy to observe body language accurately and to follow the discipline of the interview questions, but with the right level of training you can quickly grasp the technique.'

- Give newly trained interviewers plenty of early opportunity to practice their strengths-based interviewing skills. Ideally pair them with more experienced colleagues.

- Ensure that strengths interviewers are occasionally observed by someone who is experienced to coach them and ensure they are doing it right. With the best will in the world people can forget things or slip into bad habits. Partnering with people who are relatively new interviewers can help them refresh their knowledge of the process and conduct excellent interviews.

- Check the interview notes to make sure that evidence of the candidate's strengths (and non-strengths) is recorded.

- If someone hasn't interviewed for a while, give them a chance to refresh their knowledge in a conversation with another experienced interviewer or the SBR lead.

Successful implementation is always characterized by close attention to quality, particularly in the early days. This is really about making sure that people develop good habits so that correct interviewing becomes the norm.

Elisabeth Pullar from Guy's and St Thomas' set a lot of store by the strict monitoring of quality:

> I've ensured that high-quality standards have been maintained. I've had to do a lot of work on making sure that people have followed the process correctly. I want to be sure that the quality of interviewing is right. I have sat on nine out of ten interview panels and have been alongside newly trained interviewers. I will be following up with successful candidates to find out whether they are still feeling positive and fulfilled in their role. So up to now quality control has been a bit dictatorial, but necessarily so.

They measure its effectiveness well

The measures of effectiveness vary from one organization to another and depend upon the desired impact. So, for example, if your key goal is to reduce employee attrition rates it will be important to know what your current attrition level is before you start and then to measure it at regular intervals following the introduction of SBR. Table 4.2 lists some commonly used metrics in public and private organizations in financial services, healthcare, restaurant, retail sectors and travel sectors.

Quantitative evidence of SBR's effectiveness usually follows the qualitative measures such as feedback from recruiters, managers, interviewees and customers. This is because it takes time to gather and record numerical data, whereas qualitative feedback can be sought immediately.

TABLE 4.2 Commonly used metrics in public and private organizations

Measure used	Issues to be addressed
Attraction	Too few job applications or too many applications from the wrong type of person
Attrition	High attrition and difficulty retaining the right people
Attrition during crucial periods	Such as induction or initial training periods
Customer service/feedback	Low service ratings and poor or mediocre customer feedback
Engagement scores	Low or mediocre employee engagement levels
Net promoter score (a measure used by some businesses to gauge customer loyalty)	Low service ratings and poor or mediocre customer feedback
Performance	Low or mediocre performance or a need to improve performance vis-à-vis competitors
Progress in training	The speed, quality and enthusiasm with which new employees get to grips with the job
Sales	Number of sales, cross-sales and up-sales achieved
Sick absence	The amount of time that employees take off sick (which can be an indication of lack of engagement and/or wrong role fit)
Ratio of applications to interviews and interviews to appointment	Some organizations have too many of the wrong applicants, others have too few

The following box gives an actual example of an evaluation proposal that an SBR lead developed for their organization. It shows the range of measures that were appropriate to this organization and provides a good illustration of how to approach the evaluation of SBR.

Evaluation of strengths-based recruitment – an example proposal from one organization

The move to strengths-based recruitment will enable us not only to assess people's past performance but also to evaluate their future potential by focusing on what candidates are naturally good at, enjoy doing and are energized by. It is hoped that the addition of a strengths-based interview to the recruitment process will enable us to identify more confidently the right people who'll be motivated and energized in their work.

Whilst very positive, the move to strengths-based recruitment for these large staff groups has the potential to be a challenge and will initially involve an investment in time. It is therefore essential that its use is evaluated. The following simple metrics are proposed to monitor the impact:

- Selection ratio – number of people hired divided by the number of applicants.

- Proportion of staff passing the probationary period – a measure to help establish whether great people are being selected.

- Composite engagement score (using questions from our engagement survey) – it is well documented that staff engagement has significant associations with employee and customer experience, performance outcomes and productivity. The more engaged staff members are, the better the outcomes for our customers and the organization generally.

- Turnover rate – the percentage of people recruited via strengths-based recruitment that leave during a cumulative 12-month period.

- Reason for leaving – We need to know whether there is a reduction in people leaving because the job is wrong for them.

These metrics are all part of business as usual or are easily obtained, and therefore should not require additional work.

It is proposed that all metrics are benchmarked in April 2015 prior to the organization commencing the implementation of strengths-based recruitment. These metrics will then be re-evaluated in April 2016.

Pitfalls to avoid

One of the benefits of not being the first to do something new is that you get to learn from others. It's hard to know which and how many SBR projects have suffered from pitfalls as I clearly don't have inside knowledge of them all. However, here are some of the common mistakes that I have seen organizations make, or they would have made if they had not have been given good guidance and advice.

Lack of senior level buy-in

This is a rare occurrence, as senior executives' endorsement is normally necessary to introduce SBR. However, if the main sponsor leaves the organization and there is not enough support amongst the rest of the senior team, things can go wrong. I saw this happen once when a new chief executive came in just after the main sponsor left. It wasn't so much a case of a lack of support for SBR, but it was a relatively early stage in the journey, it had not yet become business as usual and so it was swept away as large technological changes took centre stage. This happened even though there were a good number of champions in the organization and the data was proving that SBR was saving money and improving customer service. The antidote to this is to involve the right senior people from the word go so that there is more than one senior advocate who is committed.

Appointing the wrong SBR lead

The SBR lead is a crucial piece in the jigsaw puzzle. As with any change you are trying to make, it makes all the difference if you have someone leading it who has vision, energy, influence and commitment. They have to want to make SBR work so much that their commitment is obvious and infectious. They don't have to be raving extroverts. I've seen fairly quiet people who are powerful and effective SBR leads. But they do need determination and a desire to successfully implement SBR. One organization appointed someone based on their project management skill alone. They weren't great at connecting, listening or getting alongside and influencing others. Their strength was getting tasks done and they tended to drain others rather than energize them. Not a good fit for an SBR lead role.

Losing momentum

Any new approaches or initiatives can lose momentum unless there is active senior level support and unless there are committed people pushing things forward operationally. For example I have seen projects slow down when the senior leader was off sick or a new HR director was appointed. Keeping up momentum, particularly in the early days, is crucial.

Starbucks UK didn't lose momentum, but Sandra Porter, when asked whether she would have done anything differently, talked of the benefits of implementing the approach across the whole business versus what they did, which was to start with a pilot: 'The challenge of starting with a pilot and then a gradual roll out is that we were limiting how much momentum it could initially gain versus a "big bang" approach.'

Lessons learned from organizations that have implemented SBR

The following lessons are taken from the 'Welcome to the strengths revolution' report (North, 2013) of a study of five organizations that have implemented SBR. Individuals who had led SBR projects in their organizations were asked what might be useful to pass on to others thinking of adopting or piloting SBR. Some of this overlaps somewhat with points made in the rest of this chapter but they are worth repeating as they are 'from the horse's mouth', so to speak:

- The leader articulates their vision for SBR and is personally committed to it. Sometimes they see it as part of their legacy. They are always influential people who want to see a big change and are very visible in their leadership of SBR.

- People really understand the potential of SBR when they see their first strengths profile. They said that some people were intrigued by the potential of SBR but wondered whether it was too good to be true. Confidence in SBR and excitement about its potential increased when they saw a strengths profile for the first time. An HR manager in a financial services company said, 'Previously we'd been aiming to recruit the perfect person, whom we now realize didn't exist... at last we saw a clear description of our own great performers... it was real, we knew we had recruited these people from the local market before and that there would be more like them out there.'

- Technical competence assessment plus strengths assessment add up to great hiring decisions. Technical competencies will always be essential for some professional or more complex roles. So it is still important to assess for role-specific skills and knowledge as part of your recruitment process, and to give proper weight to these factors in your selection decision. However, it's also worth bearing in mind that, while some skills and knowledge will be prerequisites for selection, others may be able to be taught. Strengths, on the other hand, can't be taught.

- A review and re-vamp of the whole attraction and selection process needs to take place to reflect a strengths-based approach. Every aspect of the recruitment process needs to be reviewed and updated to reflect this approach. An HR manager in a financial services company said, 'We've turned our adverts, and all of our recruitment documents, into something we're now really proud of, and that represents who we really are.'

- Embed a support network to assure quality and sustainability. Getting strengths interviews right is a responsibility that everyone trained in the new skills needs to take seriously. One recruitment manager talked of the importance of colleagues at remote locations knowing that they 'are not on their own'.

- Team leaders create an environment in which individuals' strengths can flourish. It is impossible to overstate the value of input from managers and team leaders in successfully integrating strengths recruits. A project manager in a healthcare company said, 'Retention is about more than getting quality people through the door. You have to treat them right, too... enabling them to play to their strengths.'

- HR's role and mindset is important. Sometimes SBR is led by HR, sometimes it is supported by them but led by another part of the business. The active involvement of HR is important as they usually lead, and are guardians of, resourcing. Lynda Greenshields was very clear about the mindset she needed from her HR team:

> It's all about HR taking responsibility for business growth – alongside your people who are on the phones, or the sales managers who are leading the people on the phones – rather than HR thinking that they sit to the side of the front-line business. They don't. They are part of the business, and if they're not part of it they shouldn't be there. They need to think about solutions and they need to be a part of those solutions and not just

the department that people get sent to if there's a problem or if they need to be 'processed' in some way. That's the old mindset. The new mindset is HR acting as an integrated part of the business and being accountable for business results. ... For us SBR was the vehicle for an incredible shift in the role and value to the business of HR. As Group HRD, I left an HR department that no longer sits alongside the sharp end of the business, but that loves and is excited by being a fully integrated part of it.

Figure 4.1 summarizes the essential success factors for implementing SBR, and is a handy aide-memoire.

Advice from senior leaders to other senior executives who are thinking of implementing SBR

When I interviewed senior leaders for this book I asked what advice they would give to other leaders who are thinking about implementing SBR or who haven't yet considered it. Here's a summary of what they said:

- Only implement SBR if you really want change.
- See it as a long-term transformation, not a short-term initiative.
- Appoint an SBR lead – someone who is committed to SBR and will be focused and determined enough to make it happen.
- Support the SBR leads and champions as much as you can because they are pivotal to success.
- Be clear about what results you want from SBR and agree which metrics you will use to measure effectiveness.

Here are some direct quotes from those I interviewed. Hilary Chapman's advice was to embark upon SBR only if you genuinely want change: 'I would say, be ready to change. If you're not ready to change, don't do it. If you're not going to alter things, don't bother. Commit to it and follow it through. It's not just another initiative. Not everyone likes change, and you can't play at this. Get the sign-up of your senior colleagues.'

Lynda Greenshields of Acromas Group posed a question about the extent to which your brand is being correctly delivered: 'To those who haven't yet considered it, I think they could ask themselves, "Is my brand being delivered

FIGURE 4.1 Checklist: successfully implementing SBR

Understand what benefits you wish to derive from implementing SBR

Decide how you will measure success

Articulate the vision and goals for SBR and keep reminding people of these

Gain the support of key stakeholders

Appoint one or two SBR leads

Decide which SBR methodology to use

Identify the great performers in the given role(s)

Decide where the strengths interview will fit into the overall process

Identify and support the champions early on

Pay attention to quality

Communicate early successes

consistently right through our organization into our customer experience, every single time?" If it is, then maybe they don't need SBR, but if not I'd say, "Consider it!"'

Katherine Fenton was thinking about the importance of quality: 'I'd say don't try to take short cuts, do it properly. Take the time to understand SBR because once you understand it, you "get it" and you can convey the concept to your people so that they "get it" too. I'd also say it's essential to train your own trainers thoroughly, again no short cuts.'

Helen Lamont reiterated the importance of getting support and good planning as well as demonstrating credibility through showing that other good and respected leaders are supportive of SBR:

> I'd say it's a big change and it's important to get buy-in early and plan the implementation well. You have to be confident and brave. We are spending public money on this, so we had to make sure at the outset that we were very confident in the approach. The fact that ten chief nurses from the Shelford Group collaborated to implement it gave our executive board confidence. The Shelford Group chief nurses are a very experienced group who have done a lot of national work. That gave it strength.

Janice Sigsworth also reiterated the importance of buy-in, including from HR, and ensuring you have a clear project plan: 'In the NHS I'd say select a strong and consistent lead who straddles nursing and HR. Make sure your project plan is clear and that all the key people are signed up.'

Sandra Porter of Starbucks UK spoke of having ambition to improve things and finding the right advocates:

> Firstly, I would say it's about setting an ambitious goal – above whatever might be on a strategy document. Getting the attention of an organization by spelling out what is not good enough anymore and what the future could be. You need ambition and you need to secure money and resources behind it.
>
> Secondly, I'd say find advocates who are going to support the project. We had a great steering group who had credibility, were well connected and were ambitious. One of the key people from operations was a real asset. His business area was working well already so he could help us lead strengths-based recruitment while keeping the wheels on his bus. He spoke from the heart about why the current situation wasn't good enough from his own personal experience. It was obvious he wanted to do something significant and make a difference. He was great at influencing his colleagues during 'water cooler moments'.

Tips for the practitioner

- Make sure your key stakeholders are at the meeting where the strengths profiles that have been developed are presented. This is where real buy-in is cemented.

- Embed SBR well by supporting your interviewers until they become really confident with strengths interviewing and monitoring the quality of the interviews and evidence gathered.

- Report back early results and success stories to maintain momentum and buy-in.

Two-minute chapter summary

This chapter describes what organizations that have successfully implemented SBR did to make it such a success. We hear from people who have commissioned and led successful implementation. Knowing the pitfalls to avoid is useful too. So the chapter covers that as well. Finally, it contains advice from senior leaders who have implemented SBR and whose organizations have been using it for a number of years.

The full transcripts of interviews carried out for this book can be found in Part Two.

References

Damasio, A (2000) *Feeling of What Happens*, Vintage, London

Fenton, K (2014) Transform nursing with strengths based recruitment, *Health Service Journal*, February. Available from: www.hsj.co.uk/topics/technology-and-innovation/transform-nursing-with-strengths-based-recruitment/5067109.fullarticle (accessed 1 September 2015)

Francis, R QC (Chair), The Mid Staffordshire NHS Foundation Trust Enquiry (2010) *Independent Inquiry into Care Provided by Mid Staffordshire NHS Foundation Trust January 2005–March 2009*. Available from: https://www.gov.uk/government/publications/independent-inquiry-into-care-provided-by-mid-staffordshire-nhs-foundation-trust-january-2001-to-march-2009 (accessed 10 December 2015)

North, D (2013) Welcome to the strengths revolution: An in-depth study into the benefits of strengths-based recruitment. Available from: www.engagingminds. co.uk (accessed 21 July 2015) [A study of the impact of SBR in five well-known organizations from the following sectors: financial services, restaurant, retail, social care and travel. Findings were based on interviews with 20 key stakeholders and a survey of 80 employees.]

Notes on organizations referenced in this chapter

The **AA** is a British company that provides car insurance, driving lessons, breakdown cover, loans and other related services. It is a FTSE 250 company and has more than 14 million customers in the UK.

Guy's and St Thomas' NHS Foundation Trust comprises two of London's best-known teaching hospitals: Guy's Hospital and St Thomas' Hospital. It also includes Evelina London Children's Hospital and both adult and children's community services in Lambeth and Southwark. It also provides specialist services for patients from further afield, including cancer, cardiothoracic, women's and children's services, kidney care and orthopaedics. It has approximately 13,650 employees.

Saga is a UK company that is focused on serving the needs of customers aged 50 and over. It is listed on the London Stock Exchange and is a FTSE 250 company. It has more than 2.5 million customers and provides a wide range of insurance products, personal finance and package holidays including cruises.

Sheffield Teaching Hospitals NHS Foundation Trust is one of the UK's busiest and most successful Trusts. It comprises five of Yorkshire's best-known teaching hospitals: the Royal Hallamshire, the Northern General, Charles Clifford Dental Hospital, Weston Park Cancer Hospital and Jessop Wing Maternity Hospital. It provides a full range of local hospital and community-based care. It has approximately 15,000 employees.

The **Shelford Group** comprises ten leading NHS multi-specialty academic healthcare organizations. The ten members collectively employ over 83,000 people with a turnover of over £7 billion.

The institutions that make up the Shelford Group are of strategic significance to NHS care, the life sciences industry and the UK economy. Shelford Group members are: University Hospitals Birmingham NHS Foundation Trust, University College London Hospitals NHS Foundation Trust (UCLH), Sheffield Teaching Hospitals NHS Foundation Trust, Oxford University Hospitals NHS Trust, Newcastle upon Tyne Hospitals NHS Foundation Trust, King's College Hospital NHS Foundation Trust, Imperial College Hospital Healthcare NHS Trust, Guy's and St Thomas' NHS Foundation Trust, Central Manchester University Hospitals NHS Foundation Trust and Cambridge University Hospitals NHS Foundation Trust.

University College London Hospitals NHS Foundation Trust (UCLH) is a Trust based in London. It comprises University College Hospital, the Hospital for Tropical Diseases, University College Hospital at Westmoreland Street, the Eastman Dental Hospital, the National Hospital for Neurology and Neurosurgery, the Royal London Hospital for Integrated Medicine, the Royal National Throat, Nose and Ear Hospital and the UCH Macmillan Cancer Centre. It is one of the UK's five comprehensive biomedical research centres and employs more than 8,000 people. It has more than 1,000 beds.

Strengths-based development and performance management

05

This chapter answers these questions:

- Why do human beings focus on the negative?
- What are the flaws in traditional performance management and development approaches?
- What is a strengths-based approach to performance and development, and what are its benefits?

Two of the key elements in any successful talent management strategy are development and performance management. One helps people to develop their true potential; the other effectively manages them. This chapter explains strengths-based performance management and development, how they are different from other more traditional approaches and how they work in practice. It contains a step-by-step guide to implementing strengths-based development and performance management, and shows the benefits that some organizations have experienced from adopting the strengths approach.

The problem mindset

We know from evolutionary biology and neuroscience that it is human nature to focus more on the negative, because we are programmed to be alert to risks in our environment. Organisms that were alert to risk in their environment were more likely to survive. Early man had to worry about wild animals and neighbouring tribes, so it was essential to focus on potential problems. In an article for *Psychology Today* (2015), psychologist Ryan Niemec talked about the neurological wiring that gives human beings a negativity bias. He argued that this negativity bias means that there are times and situations when we are 'strengths-based' but that we quickly shift back to a problem mindset.

In today's context that translates to focusing on what is not working, including ignoring the good pieces of feedback that we're given, and obsessing about the one negative thing someone says. Certainly in performance reviews people tend to remember, and be affected more by, the conversation about their weaknesses. In my experience, unless you ring-fence conversations about weaknesses and talk solely about strengths first, the giver and receiver of the performance review ends up focusing most on weaknesses. It's certainly uncomfortable in some cultures and for some individuals to give praise and compliments, and in management we can be biased towards seeing what is wrong and trying to fix it. Indeed there are some jobs whose successful execution is dependent on that. You would want an airline pilot, for example, to spot what is wrong and you'd expect a manufacturing company to see errors and problems and fix them. But the same approach to human development and growth can result in a focus on the negative to the detriment of the positive.

Jones and Wade noted in their book *Strengths-Based Clinical Supervision* (2014) that a strengths mindset recognizes weaknesses but from a position of using our strengths as resources to draw on when we are in situations that we find difficult. This is in contrast to the deficit mindset, which focuses on our weaknesses and can cause us to feel constrained. I agree that thinking about our strengths as resources to draw on is a productive thing to do. Indeed in my experience working with organizations the inbuilt need to notice and focus on potential problems means that when people are given a chance to look at what's working well and/or their strengths they usually find it so refreshing and motivating. It opens up a new mindset and different possibilities for them.

The strengths-based approach to developing and managing people

Given that there are very good evolutionary reasons to explain why humans focus more on the negative than the positive, and why a negative occurrence has more of an impact than a positive occurrence, let's look at the importance of shifting the balance in our performance management and development approaches.

There are a number of reasons why organizations are adopting strengths-based development, including wanting a more balanced approach to development that focuses as much, if not more, on strengths as on weaknesses. There is a recognition that focusing on strengths as well as areas that need development presents an opportunity to significantly lift the performance of individuals as well as the organization. There are other reasons too:

- They want a fresh and engaging approach to development.

- Their managers are disillusioned with competency-based approaches (which can result in having the same performance conversation with an employee year after year and nothing changing).

- They want the employee to feel responsible for their own development (much easier with a strengths approach because it is far more motivational).

- It intuitively feels right to 'go with the grain' of human strengths versus the more uphill approaches to development that emphasize what's wrong more than what is working well.

SABMiller is an organization that understands, and builds into its development approaches, an emphasis on strength. In an interview for this book Samantha Rockey, Head of Leadership Development at SABMiller, told me:

> SABMiller has, over the years, introduced a number of approaches and programmes that are underpinned by a strengths philosophy. Firstly we encourage our leaders to create opportunities for people to talk about where they get their energy and how their job might support this. For example, we know from neuroscience that as human beings we are hard-wired to focus on the negative – this is a survival mechanism so that we are able to perceive problems and threats. As a company, we know how important it is to actively encourage people to focus on the positive. This balances the natural instinct to focus on the negative. You are only able to see the true picture when one perceives both the negative and the positive.

The idea of strengths-based development and management is not new, though. Peter Drucker, the management writer and consultant, first advocated it more than forty years ago in his book *The Effective Executive* (1967). Drucker was ahead of his time in his thinking about what makes for high performance. He realized that it is more productive to focus on building strengths than fixing weaknesses: 'Unless an executive looks for strength and works at making strengths productive, he will only get the impact of what a man cannot do, of his lacks, his weaknesses, his impediments to performance and effectiveness. To start from what there is not and to focus on weakness is wasteful – a mis-use, if not abuse, of the human resource.'

In an article he wrote for the *Harvard Business Review* in 1999 entitled 'Managing oneself', Drucker argued that operating from a position of self-knowledge and understanding of one's strengths is the only way to achieve excellence. Since then, a body of evidence has grown in support of Drucker's ideas, and an increasing number of organizations have adopted strengths-based approaches to development and management and are benefiting from its efficacy.

The problem with traditional performance management and development approaches

There are two main ways that organizations think about development. Some think of it in terms of identifying potential and encouraging growth. This approach tends to strike a balance by addressing weaknesses and developing strengths. Others, though, are based on the (often unconscious) assumption that people become better performers by fixing what's wrong. This is evidenced by the language used, ie there is no sign of words like strengths and talents. Sure, they acknowledge successes, but undue weight is given to improvement and fixing weaknesses (sometimes euphemistically called 'development opportunities').

Where competency frameworks are used in development, people are expected to work on achieving an acceptable level of performance in the competencies at which they are weak. Taken to the extreme, performance management and development approaches that seek to enable people to meet a framework of competencies are unrealistic. At worst they try to make someone into something they are not.

Words like 'learning', 'growing' and 'flourishing' are too scarce in the context of managing others. This is revealing and demonstrates the extent to which organizations tend to focus on deficit rather than abundance. Language use, time spent discussing weaknesses and competency frameworks to which people are expected to aspire all subtly and unintentionally lead to a focus on what's not working. A strengths-based performance management and development approach does the opposite. It places a firm focus on what people can already do well, how they can augment those existing strengths and how they can prevent their weaknesses from tripping them up and undermining their overall performance.

In an interview for this book Lynne Stainer talked about her experience working for a large insurance company. She became disillusioned and felt that management ignored her strengths and things she was great at and enjoyed. She eventually left to seek out a career that has proved to be a great fit for her. Her advice to employers was as follows:

> If an organization looks for a broad range of competencies and insists everyone has them, they are in danger of heading towards mediocrity. I believe the best teams, those that really are capable of exceptional results, will be made up of people who excel at a narrower range of skills individually; but, with the right blend of individuals all playing to their individual strengths yet working together, there is little limit to what they could achieve. You wouldn't turn down Lionel Messi as a team member because he wasn't much good in goal! If you've got the chance to recruit a 'flair player' with a strength you really need for a particular job, don't ignore them because they don't match the 'norm' you have tradition-ally gone for. Have more of an open mind.

What is strengths-based performance management?

There are a number of principles and features that characterize strengths-based performance management systems:

1 The focus is not just on *what* the person has done to achieve their goals. Weight is also given to *how* a person has done that, what they have learnt and their potential for growth.

2 Performance reviews place emphasis on leveraging strengths. Time is spent discussing the person's strengths, the extent to which they are using them, how they could possibly be over-using them and what they could do to bring them to bear in their work even more.

3 The manager explores, using specific questions, people's realized strengths, unrealized strengths, overdone strengths and weaknesses. Their role is to support and engage people in an exploratory conversation as well as to challenge any blind spots the person may have.

4 The performance review is not just a one-off event once or twice a year. It's an ongoing conversation and that is more important than the form filling.

5 It's not about ignoring weaknesses; it is about knowing what can be trained or improved, and what can't.

6 People are rewarded for 'how' they do things as well as 'what' they do. So it's not just about getting to a particular outcome without regard for the means they use. It's about what the person is like and how they carry out their work, not just the results they achieve.

7 They are used to understand individuals as well as team strengths and thus enhance the performance of both.

What is involved in a strengths-based performance management process?

1 First, managers need to be trained in the strengths approach. For some this involves a significant shift in mindset.

2 Ideally, managers undertake an assessment of their own strengths. The benefits of this are twofold; first they get to understand what their specific leadership strengths are, where they might be weak (and thus need to compensate) and, importantly, it gives them an experience of the strengths-based performance management process. Done well, it is a very motivating and engaging experience. This experience illuminates the contrast between more traditional approaches because it is generally far more engaging. Having had the experience, it gives them a feel for the benefits and the confidence to do it with their own staff.

3 A workshop for managers that includes how to have the conversation (it's very different).

4 Decisions must be made about what to do about people who are genuinely in the wrong job.

5 Stretch those who are already great to leverage their strengths to improve their own and the team's performance.

It's worth pointing out that managers can be nervous of facilitating a strengths-based conversation with their people. This is because it is much more of a conversation than a 'Do you meet this competence, yes or no?' type exercise. So they don't know what to expect and can feel less able to control it. Sometimes they feel as though they need to have all the answers to questions like 'What are your main strengths?' In fact, the most powerful and useful kinds of conversations are those where the manager poses the questions and helps the employee think it through, providing some of their own feedback and reflections but not giving definitive pronouncements on a person's strengths and weaknesses.

Implementation of a strengths-based performance management system is straightforward and is made up of the following three steps.

Step 1: Engagement (and strengths assessment) of senior stakeholders

I have found that by far the best way of engaging key senior stakeholders in a switch to strengths-based performance management is to give them an experience of discovering their own strengths. Ideally this will take the form of a leadership strengths assessment as part of a discussion-based workshop where they first work through an understanding of their own strengths and then enter into a discussion of how the approach will benefit their people, the organization and its performance.

In my work I have found that once you do this at senior levels there follows a demand by those attending such strengths assessment exercises to roll out the approach to their teams. This is because they find it enlightening, engaging and common sense.

Step 2: Re-design of the process towards a strengths orientation

Most organizations have paperwork that includes guidance documents and performance management record forms that need to be completed. Newly designed forms are usually very simple and contain four boxes (or slight variations of them) (see Figure 5.1).

The key thing, though, is to make the conversation the focus rather than the paperwork. For this reason it pays to keep the paperwork light and make it a useful reference document that the employee enjoys and wants to return to. Some organizations do away with a form altogether and encourage managers and employees to make their own notes in a format that suits them.

The key question is, what feedback if any does the organization want in relation to individuals' performance reviews, and for what purpose? Answering this question will guide what is needed in terms of the paperwork.

FIGURE 5.1 Developing strengths

Unrealized/unused strengths	Realized/used strengths
• The person doesn't know they have them as they have never had occasion to use them. • Something in the context in which they are working prevents them from using a particular strength. Questions for the manager or coach to ask: • What do you love doing and what are you energized by? • Given a choice, which parts of your job would you do in preference to anything else? • What do you love doing but for some reason feel prevented from doing? • What do you love doing that is not required in your current role? • How can you bring those strengths into your current role? • How might the wider organization benefit from you further developing, and leveraging these strengths? • What support do you need to do so?	• The person uses their strengths regularly • Sometimes other people can see strengths in a person that they themselves don't (people tend to take their own strengths for granted) Questions for the manager or coach to ask: • Which of the strengths in the profile are your strongest ones? • Which of the strengths in the profile do you think others see in you? • How can you use your strengths even more/better to increase your performance and satisfaction in your job? • How might the wider organization benefit from you further developing, and leveraging these strengths?

Overdone strengths	Weaknesses/non-strengths
• A strength that someone over-uses such that it becomes a problem in a particular context. • An overdone strength can become a weakness.	• The things a person is not good at and that drain them. • Realistically, everyone is weak at some aspects of their job. The thing to remember is that you

(Continued)

FIGURE 5.1 Developing strengths *(Continued)*

Questions for the manager or coach to ask:

- What do you love so much that you probably do to the detriment of other things?
- What are the consequences of this?
- How can you prevent yourself 'over-playing' your strengths in this way?
- What support do you need from others to do this?

cannot transform weaknesses into great performance. At best you can make it 'good enough'.

- Something that is not natural/ the person doesn't love/isn't energized by but does because they are required to in their role/situation.

There are different ways of managing weaknesses, including: (1) devolving to others; (2) focusing on strengths so much that certain weaknesses are less problematic; (3) using your actual strengths to help you to do something you find hard, eg challenging doctors by calling on other strengths (high standards, doing the right thing and making a difference); (4) acquiring associated learned behaviours, eg a person who doesn't naturally connect with people can learn some of the behaviours that natural connectors have, such as smiling and asking questions.

Questions for the manager or coach to ask:

Are there elements of the job that must be done but feel like weaknesses/non-strengths?

What other ways might there be to get these tasks done well?

How could you use your strengths to compensate for your weaknesses/non-strengths?

Step 3: Train managers in strengths-based performance management

The concept is simple, so it shouldn't take more than a day. In my experience it works well to run a day's workshop which includes the attendees completing their own strengths assessment, facilitate a discussion on the role of the leader in performance management, highlight the fundamental differences between traditional competency-based approaches to performance management and a strengths-based approach and give them the opportunity to practise facilitating strengths-based performance conversations.

The following case study is an example of a strengths-based leadership workshop that a financial services company used to introduce strengths-based performance management to their leaders.

CASE STUDY Strengths-based leadership training

The organization felt that their current system was not motivating for staff or useful for management. They described it as having degenerated into an annual form-filling exercise that added no discernible value for anyone. Managers dreaded it and felt it was not a good use of their time, and employees were either neutral or negative about it. They had introduced strengths-based recruitment the previous year and there was a groundswell of desire to extend it to their performance management approach.

Because of the introduction of strengths-based recruitment, most managers understood the concept of strengths and had bought into it so there wasn't a need to sell the idea. In fact some of them reported a frustration with the fact that they were recruiting people based on their strengths but the formal performance management process was still geared around competences. That said, we observed that some of the best managers had changed the way they managed people. Specifically, they were talking new recruits through the strengths profile that they had been recruited against and discussing with them and managing them according to what they knew about their strengths, values and motivators.

Engaging Minds conducted a strengths-based leadership workshop and train-the-trainer so that the organization could roll it out themselves to all their managers. There were three key elements to the workshop: the Leadership Strengthsmatch tool; developing the skills to have an engaging strengths-based performance management conversation; and an action planning template to support the attendees to put into practice what they had learned in a meaningful way.

Feedback and impact

A month after they had attended the workshop, nine of the managers who partici-pated were interviewed about the impact and value of it. They were asked the following questions:

1 What value did you get from the Strengths-Based Leadership Workshop?

They talked about the process of self-discovery that it facilitated and how under-standing their own strengths was key to them becoming a better manager. One of them reported: 'It prompted self-discovery. Instead of trying to teach me how to be a better manager from the outside, which most courses do, this training helped me to build my own approach from the inside.'

All of them also reflected on how they hadn't realized the extent to which they and the organization focused on people's weaknesses, often to the exclusion of positive feedback.

> '*I realized how much I, and my colleagues, have been stuck in the habit of trying to fix others' weaknesses, often being highly directive in the process.*'

> '*The opportunity to practise using the Engaging Conversations toolkit, and to get constructive feedback from my colleagues was very helpful.*'

They also said that now they understood the approach it was obvious to them that they needed to understand their people so much better: 'It reinforced the need for me to really understand my people to get the best from them.'

An overall comment that they made time and time again was how simple, ob-vious and common sense the strengths approach is: 'It's common sense really... why wouldn't you want to play to the strengths of your team members?'

2 What's your opinion of the Leadership Strengthsmatch tool?

Some of the managers had completed various forms of self-assessment tools be-fore but nothing with such a strongly self-reflective element as the Leadership Strengthsmatch tool. Some found it a bit daunting at first because they were not used to reflecting on themselves. However, they found it enlightening as well as useful:

> '*I was uncomfortable at the outset, but that wasn't about the tool; it was mainly because I'm not used to "blowing my own trumpet".*'

> '*It was mind-opening; it's not often I sit down and analyse what I'm good at.*'

They found that thinking about their own strengths made them think about what drove their performance and success. None of them had thought about it that way before. Whilst fairly modest, it was obvious that they found it engaging to discover their own strengths.

> 'It was highly relevant for improving my performance.'

> 'It confirmed some strengths I knew about and teased out others that were hidden, which was a nice surprise.'

3 How has the approach helped you become a better leader?

The impact at the front line had been immediate. They had been keen to implement the approach with their people. Whilst some had expressed some concerns about perhaps not knowing how to handle the unexpected, none of them had had this experience when they put it into practice for real: 'In a strengths-based discussion the conversation flows and employees accept more responsibility for their performance and development.'

A couple of them made the astute observation that a strengths-based performance conversation focuses on the future and possibilities. Some of them contrasted it with their previous approach where they felt they had dwelt too much on what had not gone well in the past to the detriment of successes and opportunities to perform well in the future: 'A strengths conversation is forward, not backward looking.'

They also came to the realization that a strengths-based conversation with their people led to them discovering what it is that drives their own performance. Previously it was apparently not something they thought about: 'Strengths-based discussions invite people to consider what drives their good work, and to think about how their strengths can be applied elsewhere.'

Because it feels very positive they also found previously hard-to-reach employees opened up more and were more engaged:

> 'It helps open up performance and development discussions with more experienced staff who can be defensive about feedback.'

> 'Providing unqualified positive reinforcement feels so different from talking about a few positives before highlighting all the things people aren't good at... people aren't waiting for the "but" any more.'

Some of them talked about how clearly knowing their team's strengths and weaknesses helped them to resource their work and projects more effectively: 'It's enabled me to more efficiently allocate tasks across my team, and to select the right people for project work.'

At the time of introducing this new approach, the organization was going through a lot of major changes. They said that, rather than adding to their responsibilities, rolling out the strengths approach helped them to lead through the changes:

> 'I can't influence a lot of things in this time of uncertainty, but I can positively impact morale by using the strengths approach.'

> 'I believe the strengths approach brings out the best in me as a leader.'

4 How is the approach benefiting your people?

They reported that people, even the cynics, were energized and engaged by the process. It had built their confidence and people were more positive as a result of the new quality of conversations that they were having with their managers. Interestingly, and pleasingly, they also said that because people clearly understood themselves more they had noticed that they were taking more responsibility for their own performance and development and talked about why they had achieved the results they had been able to achieve. This organization had long been trying to get people to take responsibility for their own development. The managers who were interviewed reflected that they realized that people didn't know how to do that before but now they automatically felt responsible because they were so engaged with the approach:

'It's been confidence building.'

'They feel more responsible for their contribution.'

'They enjoy "thinking for themselves".'

'They're more energized.'

5 How is the approach benefiting the organization?

This review was conducted only a month after implementation of the approach but a difference had already been noticed in terms of engagement, teamwork and productivity. Sales had even increased in one area:

'Better use of resources across the team.'

'Better teamwork.'

'People are more engaged, taking more ownership of their performance.'

'People are more productive.'

'Sales have gone up.'

These managers recognized the importance of continuing to practise what they learned about how to conduct a good strengths-based performance conversation. They also made the link to team-building by getting the team to understand each other's strengths. Some had already started to undertake career coaching conversations, particularly with people who they felt were displaying strengths that would make them suitable for other roles. And they were able to manage the expectations of those who had unrealistic career aspirations by engaging them in a conversation about their strengths, what would make them happy and where they would be most likely to be a round peg in a round hole.

What is strengths-based development?

Hopefully it is clear from the narrative about strengths-based performance management that development becomes an inherent part of the conversation. That is as it should be. Trying to separate the two is an unhelpful and forced divide. When discussing how someone is performing, you will discuss with them about when they are performing at their best, how that performance can be enhanced as well as how they might address the things that damage their performance.

The strengths-based philosophy is essentially about understanding what contributes to high performance and doing more of that whilst working out how to mitigate that which gets in the way. Peter Drucker put it this way: 'It takes far more energy to improve from incompetence to mediocrity than it takes to improve from first-rate performance to excellence' (Drucker, 2007: 144).

Recognizing and actively developing strengths is where the opportunity for excellence and high engagement lies. In contrast, focusing development activity on fixing weaknesses can be hard work and demotivating, as it is soul destroying trying to change something that is impossible to change. Have you ever found yourself having the same discussion with an employee year after year in performance reviews where you are talking about the same things they could improve and nothing much seems to change? Have you ever wondered why that is? It's probably not laziness or lack of will. It's more likely to be because the thing that they are not very good at is not a natural strength or interest of theirs so they will always struggle with it. There is a marginal gain in plugging away at trying to get them to be better at it. But if they spent that energy and time deploying their strengths to best advantage that would be time better spent.

An over-focus on weaknesses and what is not working eventually erodes people's confidence and can chip away at their self-esteem. It doesn't help the organization either. Small improvements can be made but the big opportunity for excellent performance is to build on what people are already good at and naturally drawn to.

A leap to a strengths-based approach to development is a big leap for some. We are used to looking for problems and gaps and trying to plug them. Conscientious people who want to do a good job and get ahead in their career want to improve things. There is nothing wrong with that per se but an overwhelming orientation towards improving what's not working has created organizational cultures that spend little or no time understanding what works and augmenting that.

As Marcus Buckingham pointed out in his book *Now Discover Your Strengths* (Buckingham and Clifton, 2005): 'Unfortunately most of us have little sense of our talents and strengths. We become expert in our weaknesses and spend our lives trying to repair these flaws – while our strengths lie dormant and neglected.' So the first step in strengths-based development is for people to understand what their strengths are.

Peter Drucker observed in his work *The Effective Executive* (1967), 'Most Americans do not know what their strengths are. When you ask them, they look at you with a blank stare, or they respond in terms of subject knowledge, which is the wrong answer.' This could equally apply to people of other nationalities.

So, what does strengths-based development entail? There are two important elements: first, understanding the principle of strengths-based development – that excellent performance comes from leveraging strengths, not fixing weaknesses; second, knowing what to do. That is:

1 Gain a clear understanding of your strengths.

This is typically done through some form of strengths profiling. This insight is obviously essential to the development process.

2 Adding skills and knowledge to strengths to create strong capability.

For example, a person might have a natural strength in loving to be in charge, but that alone is not enough. It means that they have the raw ingredients to be a leader. In other words, they are the right kind of person. But it doesn't mean that they have the necessary skills and knowledge to, for example, coach their people. An example of this was a ward sister who was promoted when she was relatively young. She had all the strengths of a great ward sister but had never learnt anything about what skills effective leaders need to develop, for example how to run a team or how to handle a disciplinary meeting. All important things for a leader in her position to know. So the key was for her to add the skills and knowledge to her natural strengths in order to achieve the capability of a great leader.

3 Enhancing performance by using under-used strengths.

Sometimes people don't bring their strengths to bear at work for various reasons. Perhaps they had been discouraged as a child or maybe their manager was not supportive of them using a particular strength. Knowing that they have these strengths and consciously using them at work is an important part of development.

4 Understanding and avoiding the impact of overdone strengths.

Our overdone strengths can become our greatest weaknesses or de-railers. For example, a leader who loves to be in charge can overdo it and come across as pushy and arrogant. It is much more helpful to think of the things that derail us as overdone strengths because then we can scale them back so that they become helpful to us and others instead of hindering our performance and impact. Think of the contrast between someone being told 'you are pushy' versus 'one of your strengths is being in charge and you're overdoing it to the extent that others are experiencing you as pushy and dominant'. That is more likely to result in a positive reaction rather than a defensive one.

5 Knowing how to manage weaknesses.

We all have weaknesses. The problem comes when we are in a job that doesn't play to our strengths enough and we end up spending too much time trying to fix our weaknesses.

There are different ways of managing weaknesses, including: (1) devolving to others; (2) focusing on strengths so much that certain weaknesses are less problematic; (3) using your actual strengths to help you to do something you find hard, for example ward sisters challenging doctors by calling on other strengths (high standards, doing the right thing and making a difference); (4) acquiring associated learned behaviours, for example a person who doesn't naturally connect with people can learn some of the behaviours that natural connectors have, such as smiling and asking questions.

How does strengths-based development and performance management work in practice?

Most people don't have a clear idea of what their strengths are. Even when they do they can assume that everyone is, or can be, good at what they are good at, so to them their strengths are no big deal. If an individual is given the opportunity to understand and acknowledge their strengths, they will be able to capitalize on them in the workplace, develop them further and excel more easily. In addition, it's crucial that people understand their own strengths so that they can avoid taking them too far such that their strengths become weaknesses.

Strengths assessment tools

There are essentially two types of tools:

- Questionnaires such as Strengthscope, Strengthsfinder and R2, and the VIA Survey, produce a report of a person's significant or so-called 'character' strengths. The benefit of these questionnaires is that they are quick to complete. The disadvantage is that they are generic and don't require much reflection from the participant. This means the employee will be less engaged when completing it and the resultant report is more of a 'tell' approach than an 'involving' activity.

- Self-assessment strengths tools such as Strengthsmatch and Leadership Strengthsmatch. The benefits of these tools are that they cause reflection about a person's strengths. They also result in real ownership by the individual, who must genuinely engage with the tool. The downside is that they take longer to complete.

These tools can be used as stand-alone tools, as part of a development programme or in a coaching context.

Strengths-based development conversations

A strengths approach to development emphasizes the discovery and best use of a person's strengths, an exploration of the over-use of strengths (that may become a problem) and finally, how to work around weaknesses. It doesn't ignore weaknesses, but, unlike a traditional approach to development, the greater emphasis is put on leveraging strengths to create superb performance.

It's a different way of thinking, so managers need a framework and some associated skills in order to have effective strengths-based development conversations. This is sometimes achieved with a face- to-face workshop, other times with a briefing process, which can be an online or paper briefing pack.

Performance and development conversations are all about building on strengths, acquiring associated skills and knowledge and managing weaknesses. Figure 5.1 (page 102) provides a development framework and guide to questions for managers to ask.

An honest approach

Strengths-based development is a more honest approach. It acknowledges that none of us is perfect and that we all have weaknesses. It doesn't use words to wrap up the truth. It calls a spade a spade. We have 'weaknesses', not 'development points' or 'learning gaps'. It is also realistic. It seeks to see people for who and what they are. All these are reasons why people find it refreshing and common sense. In reality, most people who are in the wrong job know it. They feel stressed, out of their depth and unhappy. They find the strengths approach refreshing and positive because they are not effectively being told that they are deficient in some way. It's about them not being a good fit for the role. They are a square peg in a round hole and usually they know it.

What's the case for strengths-based development and performance management?

The benefits to the organization

There a number of organizational benefits in terms of effectiveness of interventions and ownership by the individual:

- There is improved performance for the organization as a whole as people are focused on their strengths.
- People take ownership of their own development and performance, because they can clearly see what they need to do and are motivated by the focus on strengths.
- Strengths make sense and feel motivational to people, so they buy in (in contrast to deficit approaches that can be demoralizing as they force people to try to develop areas they find impossible to improve).
- There is increased employee engagement.

'Fit for job' is crucial to engagement. It seems like common sense to say that engagement in itself is not enough – people have to be in the right job in the first place. Research done by ANN INC, the US women's fashion retailer, showed clearly that having the right people and engaging them are both crucial to high performance but that getting the right person in the job makes the greatest difference. Their study was reported in an article by Jake Herway and Nate Dvorak in *Gallup Business Journal* (2014). They looked at which factor was most important in their store performance, selecting managers with the right strengths for the role *or* employee engagement. They analysed store managers in ANN INC's largest division to see if strengths and/or engagement affected how managers performed on the company's store performance metrics. The study revealed something they did not expect to find. While they didn't anticipate that engaged managers with few of the right strengths would lead to exceptional performance, they did expect their engagement to lead to better performance. Instead, they found that store performance dropped by 5.9 per cent for managers with few strengths and high engagement compared with managers with few strengths and low engagement. In other words, without the innate strengths to be a great manager, engagement did not result in significantly better performance.

There is growing evidence of the effectiveness of strengths-based approaches to performance management and development. Peter Drucker largely based his conclusions on his personal experience of observing thousands of executives in action. Since then, a great deal of quantitative evidence has emerged of the efficacy of the approach through its practical application. Key pieces of evidence as to the effectiveness of strengths-based development are presented by the Corporate Leadership Council and Gallup. In 2002 the Corporate Leadership Council found that emphasizing employee strengths in performance reviews increased performance by 36.4 per cent whereas an emphasis on weaknesses can cause a 26.8 per cent decrease in performance. This was from a study of over 19,000 people in 34 organizations across seven industries and 29 countries. Gallup reported a 12.5 per cent increase in the productivity of teams whose managers had received a 'strengths intervention'.

Anecdotal evidence from organizations like the AA, SABMiller and the Scottish Government report the impact of strengths-based development to include increases in engagement, motivation, focus, performance and sales.

Samantha Rockey of SABMiller talked about the organizational benefits: 'Commercially it makes sense to release people's potential and energy. To be at their best, people need to feel valued for who they are and what they bring.'

Below is a case study from an organization that decided to implement a strengths-based leadership development programme in 2015 and early feedback from those who were involved.

CASE STUDY Building strengths-based leadership

This case study is from a leading provider of analysis and communication services. Its clients include plcs, private equity companies, trade associations, universities, healthcare providers and charities. The company has grown fast, and has ambitious plans to build upon this success.

It is a 'young' organization, with many of the workforce in their 20s. The owners realized that the business's future will depend on how well this talented group of junior professionals is managed and led. They decided to invest in a formal development process for their emerging leaders that would equip them with the confidence and skills to develop their people and grow the business. Their objectives were for the participants to be:

- empowered, and identifying as leaders;
- ready to take responsibility and make decisions;
- clear about their strengths and how they could apply them to increase their personal effectiveness;
- confident in themselves and their leadership style;
- equipped with a strengths mindset for use in developing their own teams.

The programme challenged the team leaders to think differently, but also supported them in very practical ways. As well as providing a new approach to their personal development, it showed how leveraging strengths would help to deliver the business's growth plans.

The development programme had three parts:

1 Pre-work

This included:

- an article that questioned the purpose of leadership, and what each of us brings to it;
- Completion of the Leadership Strengthsmatch tool, a self-discovery guide that helps people identify and plan to use their leadership strengths.

2 Face-to-face workshop

This empowering workshop gave delegates the opportunity to:

- understand the idea of strengths, and the principles underpinning strengths-based development;
- confirm their 'clear strengths', and uncover potential 'hidden strengths';
- explore ways they could play to their strengths in their current jobs, and when thinking about their career progression;
- look at the weaknesses that could potentially trip them up and how they could mitigate those;

- start to prepare a personal development plan (PDP);
- agree some short-term actions to test their insights from the session.

3 Individual coaching sessions.

Each team leader received two follow-up one-to-one coaching sessions that were arranged one and three months after the workshop. These discussions gave delegates the chance to:

- review the outcomes of the actions they had committed to;
- think through any obstacles they had encountered;
- finalize their PDP.

The participants said the workshop was 'enlightening',' challenging', and 'valuable'. They particularly appreciated:

'The time and space to reflect and focus on strengths, rather than weaknesses.'

'Learning what colleagues think my strengths are, and understanding what drives them too.'

'The opportunity to prepare an action plan to use my strengths to become a better team leader.'

During the coaching sessions team leaders commented on the short-term and longer-term benefits of the strengths approach:

'I've increasingly started to apply strengths to different people and situations. It's providing an unconventional and helpful perspective.'

'It offers a potentially new dimension to staff reviews, which have not previously focused on building upon people's strengths. I believe that all our teams will have more effective leadership in the future.'

The leadership team met with the participants two months after the second round of coaching sessions. At this session the team leaders shared what they'd got from the process, and the group identified way of improving the approach and created an action plan to build on these insights.

From an organizational perspective, this company now has a group of motivated leaders who feel empowered to contribute to the business's growth and know how they can contribute using their strengths. They are also realizing what kind of talent they will need to employ to support their growth. They had not thought about this in terms of people's strengths before, only their experience and qualifications.

Benefits to the employee

Based on feedback from organizations that have moved to strengths-based development, there are clearly benefits to employees:

- They understand what drives their performance and therefore what to 'dial up' in order to be even better.

- They find it a very motivational approach because it puts the prime focus on the positive. It is specific and helps pinpoint the potential to excel, and is consequently confidence boosting. Clearly understanding their strengths brings a clear focus to their development plan and it feels realistic, in contrast to a focus on developing weaknesses that sometimes feels impossible to achieve. In addition, as we saw in the case study on page 113, they love to feel in control of their own development.

Talking about the benefits to employees and what it's like working in a strengths-based development culture, Samantha Rockey commented:

> Having the ability to create and define one's own destiny is very attractive. Couple that with a high-performance, high-engagement culture and you end up creating an environment where focused and energetic people tend to thrive. As an example, we have recruited senior people from top fast-moving consumer goods companies and one of the main reasons they cite for wanting to work for SABMiller is the opportunity to be genuinely empowered. We've always recruited bright, performance-oriented people. Put people like this in a strengths-based culture of genuine empowerment and self-management and it leads to fantastic performance and business growth. This in turn means that people get growth opportunities that they wouldn't otherwise have.

Frequently asked questions

Can competency and strengths approaches to development work together?

Yes they can. Most competency frameworks include things that people can learn to do. Adding strengths (what a person is innately good at, loves doing and is energized by) to skills and technical know-how competencies is the way to create solid and practical performance and development approaches.

How does strengths-based development fit with high-potential (HIPO) programmes?

HIPO programmes are characterized by giving people 'stretch' assignments. Stretch assignments are developmentally most useful where people understand their strengths, how they can improve them even more, how they can become potential derailers if overdone, and how they can mitigate their weaknesses. However, if HIPO individuals are moved into areas that are a very bad fit to their strengths, they can fail. Furthermore, if they don't understand exactly *why* they have failed, then their confidence, and their appetite for stretch assignments or for moving out of their comfort zone, can be severely damaged.

Knowing their strengths (and how to leverage them) makes them more resilient to being out of their comfort zone and therefore better equipped to extract the maximum learning from the programme.

What about weaknesses – how do we address a situation where an otherwise effective performer lacks a key strength for a job or leadership role?

The strengths-based development approach does not ignore weaknesses. If a person is weak at something that is crucial for their job it's essential that they either find a viable work-around, acquire the skills and knowledge that will enable them to be 'good enough', or move to a job that does play to their strengths. While it's clearly possible to learn certain behaviours to fix a weakness, the individual will likely find the activity draining and will struggle to achieve excellence.

How much attention should be given to strengths when supporting an individual to prepare a development plan?

There is no set formula. A good rule of thumb, though, would be 80 per cent of the focus is on leveraging strengths, and 20 per cent on things that might trip a person up… which could be actions to avoid over-playing a strength.

Tips for the practitioner

- Engage senior managers and key stakeholders by inviting them to do their own strengths assessment. Or ask them questions about when they are at their best and most energized, what stays at the bottom of their to-do list and what they love doing. A dialogue like this helps people to see the contrast between the deficit-based thinking that characterizes many organizations' approaches and the strengths-based approach.

- Pilot strengths-based development and performance management in one area of your business and seek feedback as well as tracking engagement scores if you have them.

- Keep the focus on the performance/development conversation, not on the paperwork and form.

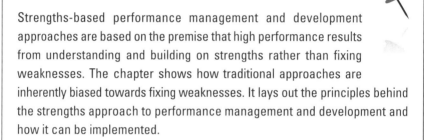

Two-minute chapter summary

Strengths-based performance management and development approaches are based on the premise that high performance results from understanding and building on strengths rather than fixing weaknesses. The chapter shows how traditional approaches are inherently biased towards fixing weaknesses. It lays out the principles behind the strengths approach to performance management and development and how it can be implemented.

The full transcripts of interviews carried out for this book can be found in Part Two.

References

Buckingham, M and Clifton, DO (2005) *Now Discover Your Strengths: How to develop your talents and those of the people you manage*, Pocket Books, New York

Corporate Leadership Council (2002) Performance management survey. Available from: www.teams-and-leadership.com/pdfs/better-performance-management.pdf (accessed 21 July 2015)

Drucker, P (1967) *The Effective Executive*, Harper and Row, New York

Drucker, P (1999) Managing oneself: Best of HBR, *Harvard Business Review*. Available from: https://www.cqu.edu.au/__data/assets/pdf_file/0004/26833/Managing-Oneself-Full-Article.pdf (accessed 10 December 2015)

Drucker, P (2007) *Management Challenges for the 21st Century*, Butterworth-Heinemann, Oxford

Herway, J and Dvorak N (2014) What's more important: Talent or engagement? *Gallup Business Journal*, April. Available from: http://www.gallup.com/businessjournal/167708/important-talent-engagement.aspx (accessed 10 December 2015)

Jones, JE and Wade, JC (2014) *Strengths-Based Clinical Supervision: A positive psychology to clinical training*, Springer Publishing Company, New York

Kaiser, RB and Kaplan, RE (2013) Don't let your strengths become your weaknesses, 2 April. *Harvard Business Review*. Available from: https://hbr.org/2009/10/dont-let-your-strength-become (accessed 10 December 2015)

Niemec, RM (2015) You are not strengths-based even when you think you are, *Psychology Today*, June. Available from: https://www.psychologytoday.com/blog/what-matters-most/201506/you-are-not-strengths-based-even-when-you-think-you-are (accessed 20 October 2015)

North, D (2013) Welcome to the strengths revolution: An in-depth study into the benefits of strengths-based recruitment. Available from: www.engagingminds.co.uk (accessed 21 July 2015) [A study of the impact of SBR in five well-known organizations from the following sectors: financial services, restaurant, retail, social care and travel. Findings were based on interviews with 20 key stakeholders and a survey of 80 employees.]

Strengths assessment tools referenced in this chapter

R2 Strengthsfinder – proprietary tool of CAPP.

StrengthsFinder 2.0 – proprietary tool of Gallup.

Strengthsmatch and Leadership Strengthsmatch – proprietary tools of Engaging Minds.

Strengthscope – proprietary tool of the Strengths Partnership.

The VIA survey – The VIA Institute.

Putting strengths at the heart of your talent management strategy

06

This chapter answers these questions:

- What is a strengths-based talent management strategy and what are its benefits?
- How can a strengths-based talent management strategy be implemented?
- What is a strengths-based organization?

This chapter looks at why a good talent management strategy is no longer a 'nice-to-have'. It explains how to take a holistic approach to strengths by creating a strengths-based talent management strategy. Each element of a talent management strategy is covered, and every aspect of the employee experience and lifecycle is included: employee brand, employee value proposition, recruitment and selection, development, performance management, leadership, engagement, diversity and inclusion, reward and recognition, career management and succession planning.

Once you have started on the strengths journey you will have already started to shift your organization's mindset. This is the most important thing. The rest of it becomes obvious. This chapter cuts through complexity and explains simply and clearly what you need to do to put strengths at the heart of your talent management strategy and become a strengths-based organization.

What is talent management?

The term 'talent management' was coined by McKinsey in the late 1990s when it published its work on the so-called 'war for talent' (Chambers et al, 2007). They had researched 77 US companies to discover the extent of the competition for talent. There was a growing concern about skills shortages all those years ago. McKinsey raised awareness of the seriousness of this issue amongst its senior readers and clients and asserted that talent management must be a 'burning corporate priority'. The article stated, 'Everyone knows organizations where key jobs go begging, business objectives languish, and compensation packages skyrocket.'

Talent management has been on the agenda of medium to large organizations since then. Most have talent managers and talent departments. The term itself is one of the latest jargon terms to beset HR. No matter its label, it is an important concept whose day has come. The world is becoming ever more complex, faster changing and global. And skills shortages and an ageing population are threatening the productivity of some countries and sectors. The expectations of key stakeholders, markets, investors, customers and employees are higher. If ever there was a time when talent acquisition and retention need be at the top of a CEO's agenda it is now.

There are numerous definitions of 'talent management', some more convoluted than others. I like the definition used by the consultancy firm DDI in their paper 'Nine best practices for effective talent management' in which they define talent management as 'A mission critical process that ensures organizations have the quantity and quality of people in place to meet their current and future business priorities' (Wellins et al, 2009).

There is no single formula for a good talent management strategy, because organizations' needs vary according to their strategy, goals, context and challenges. However, all talent management strategies must address three groups of questions: what does the organization want, what is the current situation, and how will the gap between those two be filled? The essential questions from which an effective talent management strategy will be derived are as follows:

What are we trying to achieve?
What is our current business strategy and objectives?

What are our short-, medium- and long-term goals?

What culture do we need and want?

Where are we now?

What are we currently doing well?

What is the gap between where we are, and where we need to be?

What is the gap between the talent we need, and the talent we have?

How will we get to where we want to be?

What capability do we need to deliver our business strategy and goals?

How will we find and nurture the talent we need now and in the future?

What do people need to do?

Answering these questions will elicit the organization's talent needs. The challenging part is answering the penultimate question, 'How will we find and nurture the talent we need now and in the future?' The answers to that question effectively become your talent management strategy.

There are plenty of books about how to create a good talent management strategy. My goal here is to show you how to put strengths at the heart of your strategy, irrespective of the exact details of the strategy.

What do we mean by talent?

Some organizations refer to their whole workforce when they talk about talent. Others define talent as a smaller group of employees who have high potential and are earmarked to become senior leaders. In some organizations 'key talent' might also refer to technical talent pools. Organizations that aspire to be strengths-based may have high-potential schemes but they also realize that: (a) all of their workforce are important in different ways and for different reasons; (b) everyone has strengths that, if nurtured properly, contribute to the organization's success; and (c) focusing solely on those with senior leadership potential is losing the opportunity to increase the value of all others.

For the purposes of this chapter I will define talent as all employees within an organization. For some organizations that, say, rely on seasonal staff that could also mean temporary or agency workers.

What's important about talent management?

'People are your greatest asset' is a worn-out phrase. However, its truth remains. Few, if any, organizations today have a rich supply of talent that they are happy with and know how to hold onto. Attracting great people to work for you and knowing how to manage, motivate and engage them is probably the most effective competitive advantage you have.

Organizations are increasingly competing globally for good people, and there are skills shortages in key professions, which means that global competition for talent is heightened. For an increasing number of sectors, including health and social care and engineering, it is now the norm to recruit from numerous different countries in a quest to addresses shortages. *The Economist*, in an article about skills shortages, reported in April 2015 how Dyson's expansion could be seriously stymied by a shortage of engineers – Dyson needs 3,000 but Britain only produces 25,000 a year. Dyson has been a technology and engineering success story, but its continuing success will depend on its ability to find and keep engineers. It is not alone. The article goes on to report that in a survey of British firms that employ engineers and information technology (IT) staff, carried out by the Institution of Engineering and Technology (IET), over half reported that they could not find the employees they were looking for and 59 per cent said that the shortage would be 'a threat to their business in the UK'.

Without the right talent, organizations will start to lag behind in their ability to innovate and create great new products and services. And even where they continue to produce what customers want to buy, it is relatively easy for competitors to innovate to get ahead.

In sectors where there is not much product or technology differentiation, brand and service become more important. And the quality of these is in large part dependent upon the quality of the people the organization employs. These organizations cannot keep doing what they have always done and expect to attract and keep the good people. A solid, practical and effective talent management strategy is a more important asset to any organization nowadays than it ever has been.

How a strengths approach to talent management can transform organizational culture

You don't need a complete strengths-based talent management strategy in order to have a positive impact on your organization's culture and to mitigate risk. Tackling one aspect alone can make an enormous difference. For example, in my experience with many organizations of all sizes in different sectors, introducing SBR has a hugely positive effect very fast. Once people experience and become fans of the strengths approach their mind wanders quickly into other areas of the organization. They start asking questions like how a strengths-based approach to reward and recognition would look, how the new employee induction process should change to be strengths-based. All because they are so excited by the concept and the difference they see it making. I have been working in the field of organizational change and development for many years. I have never witnessed anything shift an organization's culture as positively and rapidly as SBR does. In my work with clients I have repeatedly noticed that the introduction of SBR changes the atmosphere and enlivens the organization internally as well as having an effect externally with stakeholders, including customers. Managers and leaders have told me they notice it quickly, too, when they walk into one of their stores, contact centres, branches or wards. They will often say things like, 'What have you done? The atmosphere in here has totally changed.'

Why is such a culture change possible? I am not sure I have a complete answer to that question. It's obvious, though, that if you start selecting people who love what they do, are energized by their work and great at it you will transform the atmosphere, performance and service. Then you start to get a virtuous circle. The more that people do great work, the more those around them (including customers) will notice and react positively, and so it goes on.

So, if the strengths approach has such a positive impact, it makes sense to systematically weave it into all aspects of your organization and people practices.

Implementing a strengths-based talent management strategy

Questions that may be central to any talent management strategy, but are certainly key to strengths-based ones, are as follows:

1 Which of our employee groups are the most important to delivering our mission?

2 Do we know what makes the great performers in those groups great?

3 Who else supports them to do their job well?

4 How are we supporting them?

5 Where can we find these people?

6 Will we mainly grow our own talent or bring people in from outside, or a mix of both?

7 How do we select to these roles?

8 How do we engage, manage, reward and treat them once we have appointed them?

These questions help guide the organization to take the necessary actions to implement a strengths-based talent management strategy that will deliver their organizational goals.

CASE STUDY: A strengths-based talent management strategy

To illustrate how this works in practice, here is a case study of a group of ten organizations, The Shelford Group, who began the journey towards a strengths-based talent management strategy for their Nursing Directorates in 2013. At the time of writing they are a good way down the road of addressing questions 1 to 6 for their key roles.

The Shelford Group Chief Nurses knew the answer to question 1. That is that ward sisters were amongst the most important group of staff in terms of delivering good patient care. Katherine Fenton, former Chair of the Shelford Group Chief Nurses, said, 'One of the key roles with great potential to influence the quality of patient care in UK nursing is the ward sister. If you have a great ward sister in place, you get a happy ward, low staff turnover and, most importantly, great outcomes for patients.' She also said that she knew a great one when she saw one but she said 'we couldn't articulate their strengths, qualities and attributes to be sure we were recruiting the best people for the role.' So question 2 needed to be addressed. And, using a strengths approach, it was tackled by profiling the strengths, values and motivators of the great performers in the job.

The NHS chose to profile the ward sisters first as they have a big influence both amongst the ward-based team of nurses and nursing assistants but also higher up the hierarchy with the doctors and managers. In answer to question number 4 there is a whole range of people who support the ward sisters in doing a good job, including nurses, nursing assistants, porters, consultants and ward clerks to name just some. A holistic strengths-based talent management strategy would include profiling all of those roles too over time so that there is a real clarity about what it takes to perform well in each of these roles. Indeed, that is what is gradually happening with the nurses and nursing assistants having been profiled too now. Then comes the question of how to find these people. There are two issues in relation to this: one is finding qualified people and the other is to use the staff nurse strengths and motivator profiles to select student nurses so that they ensure that the right kind of people enter the profession in the first place.

Attraction is an important part of any talent management strategy. That includes ensuring that you have an employee value proposition that people find appealing. In other words, is what you offer as a company – your culture, ways of working, type of work, reputation, types of customers, management style and so on, appealing to the types of people you want to attract? The Shelford Group had no problem with this – they are known to be the top ten NHS academic teaching hospital Trusts in the UK. Their reputation, quality and standards of research and innovation mean that people want to work for them. The other part of attraction is of course about ensuring that the right people see and are attracted to the roles on offer. As with many organizations, the job adverts were fairly flat, unappealing and didn't do a good job of describing the sort of person that they were looking for. So the job adverts were rewritten using the strengths and motivator profiles. Now people could read the adverts and get a good idea of the sort of person that was being sought. Indeed, job agencies and managers were able to talk to people with great clarity about what kinds of individuals would be a good fit for the roles. The end result was that more of the right people were applying. For roles in the NHS applicants tend to look at NHS Jobs online so there was no need to find new places to advertise.

In terms of selection for these roles, strengths-based interviewing has been implemented and forms part of the overall selection process, which includes assessing for the necessary clinical experience and competence too.

Where to start?

You have to start somewhere, and most organizations start by introducing either strengths-based recruitment or strengths-based performance management/development. These are the logical places to start, as well as a way of gaining enthusiasm and buy-in early. SBR is a good starting point because having the right people in the first place is fundamental to a high-performing organization. Other organizations decide to start with strengths-based development or performance management and use the enthusiasm generated as a launch pad to introduce strengths approaches into other aspects of talent management.

Elements of a talent management strategy and what makes them strengths-based

Underpinning a strengths-based talent management strategy is the principle that we have explored in detail in this book – that the greatest success at an organizational and individual level is achieved by understanding and leveraging strengths, not by fixing weaknesses.

Perhaps the easiest way to approach the question of how to put strengths at the heart of your talent management strategy is to look at each element in turn and explain what can and does give them a strengths orientation.

Employer brand and employee value proposition

An employee value proposition (EVP) is the jargon commonly used to describe the benefits of working for an organization, such as its culture, rewards, leadership style and ways of working. The employer brand is simply how the EVP is expressed and communicated.

By their very nature the EVP and employer brand emphasize the positive parts of an organization and the benefits of working there. If the organization understands the strengths, values and motivators of its high performers it understands a lot about what is important to them, so can communicate those things in the EVP. Sometimes, though, the problem with employer brands is they don't reflect the reality of the organization. In other words, the promise doesn't match the actual experience of working there. That can be a big problem for good people who accept a job and then feel let down when they experience the reality of life with that employer.

Being a strengths-based organization and one that uses SBR and strengths-based performance management and development immediately sets you apart, as relatively few can genuinely make that claim. So it is a major asset to any EVP. The process of being selected using SBR is very motivational and positive. As Keith Jones, Recruitment Manager for a major financial services company, said, 'Candidates love and feel energized by the strengths interview. We've never had any negative feedback.'

Recruitment and selection

Most of this book has been about SBR so I won't repeat here what makes a selection process strengths-based. It's worth underlining here, though, that understanding what makes your great performers great is a fundamental underpinning to a talent management strategy. Unless strengths profiling is done for your key roles, you can never be sure what makes for great performance. Therefore you can't be certain that you are investing in people who will enable you to achieve your organizational goals and vision.

Performance management and development

As with SBR, we have discussed at length strengths-based performance management and how to embed it. Managing and developing key talent is crucial to guaranteeing that you have great performers and successors. If you know about your workforce's strengths you remove a lot of the risk that you will find yourself with not enough of the right people. Most businesses spend a great deal of time and money gaining insight into their customers – what they love, what's important to them, what motivates them, how they like to be communicated with, etc. Until the strengths movement came along, most organizations knew way more about their customers than they did about their own employees. Some might claim that employee engagement surveys give them insight. They do, but they are based on a standard set of questions, the subjects of which may or may not be important to a particular group of employees. I always remember answering an engagement survey that asked, 'Have you got a best friend at work?' I didn't, and it wasn't important to me to have a best friend at work. Luckily I had a good manager who made it his business to find out what made all of his people tick. I doubt whether the company's engagement survey gave him any more insight into us than he already had.

Genuine insight into employees and prospective employees gives any talent management strategy a richness and depth that it otherwise wouldn't have. This is a major area that a strengths approach can add via strengths profiling.

Leadership

Leadership is another huge topic. But when it comes to what leaders do in a strengths-based organization, it's simple. They understand their own strengths and those of their people. They use that knowledge on an ongoing basis to develop, support and stretch themselves and their teams. Most of all, though, their orientation is to build on what is right and what is working well about the organization and their people and to augment that. They don't ignore problems that need to be fixed but they realize that most gain is to be had from having people play to their strengths and stretching them as much as possible to do so. An example of this was a leader in the publishing industry during the dotcom boom of 1998/99. Everyone was a novice when it came to digital publishing strategy. No one really knew what to do because digital publishing and commerce was in its early stages. This leader had a woman on his team who he knew to be a great researcher and networker. He tasked her with figuring out as best she could what questions needed to be asked about this digital revolution and who could help the company work out their strategy. This challenge was very motivating because it played to her strengths as well as her motivations and values, which included learning and making a difference. Her boss knew her well enough to know that she was the one for this assignment, which, at the time, was mission critical for the entire organization.

Engagement

Employee engagement is an output, not an input. In other words, it is the result of a lot of other things happening, such as being in the right job, doing work that you love and having good support from your manager. So the strengths approach increases employee engagement simply because it has the right people in the right roles for them, managers know what motivates them so can manage them better, they are valued for who they are and managed accordingly. We saw in Chapter 2 the qualitative and quantitative proof that engagement increases with SBR. Engagement is an important thing to measure. The value that the strengths approach can add to that aspect of an organization's talent management strategy is to ensure that what is being measured is actually what is *known* to engage your employees rather than generic questions that may be inquiring into factors that are not actually all that important to people, ie that don't engage them.

Reward and recognition

Knowing what is important to people and what motivates them means that you can reward and recognize them in a way that matters to them. Strengths and motivator profiles give you that insight. I worked with an organization that, at considerable expense, introduced a scheme whereby employees could get a discount from certain brands and stores. In fact, what was more important to these people was that they got to speak to their manager every day about what they had achieved that day. They were motivated by that kind of recognition. It's not that they were unhappy about the discount scheme, but they said they would much rather have had something much easier and cheaper – time with their boss!

I have worked with a number of organizations that pay low wages, and in the UK that pay the government statutory minimum wage. Their bosses have sometimes commented that they believe that they cannot attract the right people for the jobs because they don't pay enough. In all cases we have found that pay is not the most important issue for those who are in the right job and love it. I have spoken to care workers who say that they cannot believe that they get paid to do the job they do – and care workers are notoriously low paid. I am not advocating low pay, I am making the point that getting to know what matters to people means you will find out what kind of reward and recognition they want.

Career management

The strengths approach makes a really important contribution to career management. Managers have consistently told me that once they understand their people's strengths and the strengths needed for the jobs they aspire to they can have a really meaningful conversation about whether the latter is likely to be a good fit. One of the most common frustrations in organizations in relation to careers is that of people feeling like they have not had enough guidance or opportunity. An example would be a staff nurse who had always assumed that her next career move would be a step up the ladder to become a ward manager. Seeing a strengths and motivator profile of a ward manager led the nurse to realize that it would not be a good fit for her and she would not be happy in the job. She realized that she would be much more suited to being a specialist nurse. All those years of aspiring to be something that was just not a good fit. Without the strengths and motivator profile she may well have been promoted to ward manager and been unhappy, as well as not doing a great job. As it is, the NHS has a very high-performing specialist nurse in this person. This is effective career management in practice.

The other benefit that strengths brings to career management, as we have already seen, is that people feel much more ownership of their own career as well as feeling empowered to make the right decisions for them. This is because they know themselves and what will make them happy, and so feel confident in choosing the right path for them.

Succession planning

Succession planning requires careful attention if organizations are to avoid risky gaps in talent and continuity. Effective succession planning means really knowing your people and developing them such that they obtain the experience and knowledge they need to fulfil the roles of the future. A question that is sometimes asked is, what does 'stretch' mean in the context of strengths-based succession management? The first thing to say about this question is that strengths approach is not the antithesis of stretch. In order to develop their potential, people can be stretched to use their strengths more and to greater effect, they can be stretched to increase their knowledge, skills and connections, and they can also be stretched to find ways to mitigate their weaknesses. So a stretch assignment for someone in a succession pool could be a project that helps them work on addressing important weaknesses relevant to the requirements of the role. However, if someone is fundamentally unsuited to a particular type of activity (eg leading others), then it becomes counter-productive to expect them to perform well in it and become a viable successor. So the real question to look at is 'why' is someone out of their comfort zone and is that 'stretch' a positive developmental activity or a counter-productive one?

Mobilization

Mobilization of your workforce so that each person and team is doing the best work they can is much easier if you know their relative strengths. Leaders who understand each of their team member's strengths can allocate work and projects accordingly. In practice this means that people are doing what energizes them so that projects don't stall due to lack of interest. One leader, when he learnt about the strengths of his team, switched responsibilities for a couple of projects that were late. He allocated them to people whose natural strengths were a good fit. Lo and behold, the projects got done and those with responsibility for them did a good job.

Diversity and inclusion

Clients often comment that strengths-based recruitment leads to a greater diversity of appointees.

SBR leads managers to be more open-minded and curious about the types of people who could do the job. Previously their safest default might have been to hire people like them and/or the types of people that they have always hired; this leads to a distinct lack of diversity as well as 'group think' (the psychological phenomenon of a group in which conformity or desire for harmony results in poor decision making).

SBR can improve the number of successful candidates from different gender, age and ethnic groups. There are a number of reasons for this. First, for some jobs previous experience is not necessary. This means that people who could have the right strengths for the job but who have had limited or no previous experience in the particular job or sector can still pass the interview. Also SBR levels the playing field in that it's about what kind of person someone is, irrespective of their age, background, nationality or gender.

SBR can also improve social mobility because people aren't debarred due to lack of connections with people or experiences that are wrongly assumed to be necessary for the job. For example, an underprivileged young person is just as likely to have the strengths to become a lawyer as an Oxbridge graduate. Provided they can also demonstrate the intellectual ability needed there is no reason that they couldn't be appointed. SBR levels the playing field. People are people and SBR challenges some of the reasons why people are wrongly turned down for jobs.

The strengths-based organization

Reorienting your talent management strategy towards strengths ultimately leads to a strengths-based organization in which people would be more engaged, driving excellent performance and growth, managing people would be easier, greater employee diversity would mean that the organization becomes more innovative and reflects a diverse customer base. The organization's reputation as a great place to work would also grow.

The model of a strengths-based organization in Figure 6.1 shows the key elements of a talent strategy from attraction to mobilizing strengths to meet customers' needs. It starts with attracting the right people and the end result is outstanding results for stakeholders. The culture is characterized by being relational, appreciative, inclusive and positive. Leaders are role models of authenticity and there is clarity of purpose and goals. The underpinning approach to people is to maximize strengths and minimize weaknesses.

Diagnostic: To what extent is your organization strengths-based?

Listed below are the principles, processes and individual actions that characterize each element of the strengths-based organization model. Take a look at the descriptors for each element and consider:

How does your organization match up?
Which are the elements where your current practice comes close to
    reflecting a strengths-based approach?

FIGURE 6.1 Model of a strengths-based organization

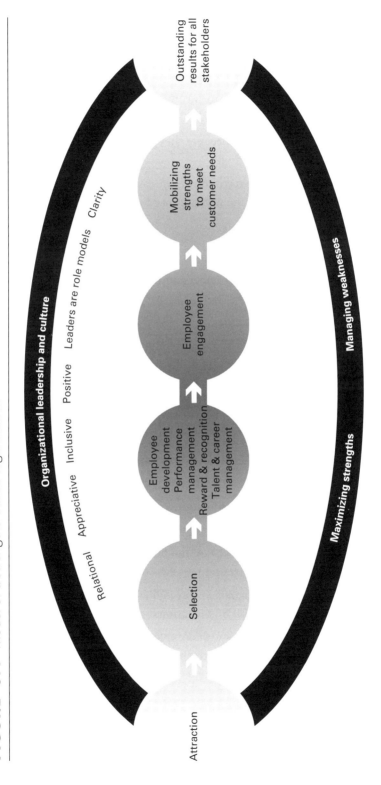

Which are the elements where you have the furthest to go? These could be a good place to start, especially if they are causing your organization pain.

1 Attraction and selection

- Strengths and motivator profiles describe what it takes to be great in key jobs.
- People are selected because they are exactly right for the job – they can and want to do it.
- All aspects of the recruitment process, from adverts to induction, are aligned to reflect the strengths needed to succeed in the role.

2 Employee development

- You assume everyone has strengths.
- People are helped to understand their own strengths, values and motivators.
- You have moved away from the gap analysis, remedial approach to one that emphasizes strengths.
- Development focuses on building strengths, managing weaknesses and realizing the potential of under-used strengths.
- Teams are created and developed to be coalitions of strengths.

3 Performance management

- You strive to understand each individual and their strengths.
- You've given up on trying to make everyone an all-rounder.
- Learning is prioritized and rewarded.
- Employees are encouraged to contribute across the organization.
- There is a strong focus on the future and what might be possible, not just on the past and present.
- Performance is managed through everyday conversation, not process, forms and organizational cycles.
- Performance conversations explore strengths and how these can be deployed to achieve the best outcomes.

4 Reward and recognition

- One size fits one, not all.
- There is recognition of individuals' differing values and motivators.
- Reward goes beyond the material.

- The value of developing potential is recognized by all.
- How, as well as what, determines reward.
- Reward structures value specialists as well as generalists.

5 Talent and career management

- Strengths and motivator profiles indicate what's required for success in different roles across the organization.
- Individual career paths and succession plans are mapped using known strengths and motivators.
- People understand their strengths, their options and how to achieve a win/win career for themselves and the organization.
- People are supported to do their best and become fulfilled.

6 Leadership

- Leaders know themselves and manage with authenticity.
- Team members are appreciated for their strengths and who they are.
- Leaders set clear expectations and provide regular feedback.
- Leaders adapt their style to meet individuals' needs.
- Every day, leaders inspire their people to perform.
- The leader's primary responsibility is to coach and enable.
- Leaders aim to be role models for others.

A final point about strengths-based organizations is that it doesn't happen without the senior leader believing in the approach and actively championing it. It is also essential to have a senior person leading the operational changes, otherwise momentum can be lost.

Advice for senior leaders

- View talent management as a crucial strategy for competitive advantage and risk reduction.
- Have your team complete the strengths-based organization diagnostic and assess the most fruitful places to introduce or augment strengths approaches.
- Ask whether you have enough 'bench strength' to enable your organization to grow and flourish, ie do you have people who are capable and ready to move in to key roles in the organization?

Tips for the practitioner

- Facilitate the creation of a talent management strategy that addresses the businesses' needs and growth plans.
- Outline clear and simple steps to achieve each priority.
- Align your talent management strategy with the most important metrics, eg attracting more engineers, reducing attrition in call centres.
- Share the talent management strategy with employees so they can clearly see the strengths approach embedded in organizational priorities.

Two-minute chapter summary

This chapter explains what a talent management strategy is and why it is important. It breaks down the elements of a strengths-based talent management strategy and clearly explains how to implement it. It also provides a model of the strengths-based organization and a diagnostic for senior leaders and practitioners to assess the extent to which their organization is strengths-based and to help decide where interventions are needed.

References

Chambers, EG, Foulon, M, Handfield-Jones H, Hankin, SM and Michaels, EG, III (2007) The war for talent, *The McKinsey Quarterly: The Online Journal of McKinsey & Co*. Available from: http://www.executivesondemand.net/managementsourcing/images/stories/artigos_pdf/gestao/The_war_for_talent.pdf (accessed 27 September 2015)

Economist, The (2015) Mind the gap, *The Economist*, 11 April. Available from: http://www.economist.com/news/britain/21648003-lack-skilled-workers-and-managers-drags-country-down-mind-gap (accessed 10 December 2015)

Wellins, RS, Smith, AB and Erker, S (2009) Nine best practices for effective talent management, Development Dimensions International (DDI). Available from: http://www.ddiworld.com/resources/library/white-papers-monographs/nine-best-practices-of-effective-talent-management (accessed 10 December 2015)

Notes on organizations referenced in this chapter

Dyson is a UK cutting-edge household appliance company. James Dyson founded the company in 1993. Today, Dyson employs nearly 5,000 people, a third of them engineers and scientists. Their machines are exported to more than 65 countries.

The **Shelford Group** comprises ten leading NHS multi-specialty academic healthcare organizations. The ten members collectively employ over 83,000 people with a turnover of over £7 billion. The institutions that make up the Shelford Group are of strategic significance to NHS care, the life sciences industry and the UK economy. Shelford Group members are: University Hospitals Birmingham NHS Foundation Trust, University College London Hospitals NHS Foundation Trust (UCLH), Sheffield Teaching Hospitals NHS Foundation Trust, Oxford University Hospitals NHS Trust, Newcastle upon Tyne Hospitals NHS Foundation Trust, King's College Hospital NHS Foundation Trust, Imperial College Hospital Healthcare NHS Trust, Guy's and St Thomas' NHS Foundation Trust, Central Manchester University Hospitals NHS Foundation Trust and Cambridge University Hospitals NHS Foundation Trust.

University College London Hospitals NHS Foundation Trust (UCLH) is a Trust based in London. It comprises University College Hospital, the Hospital for Tropical Diseases, University College Hospital at Westmoreland Street, the Eastman Dental Hospital, the National Hospital for Neurology and Neurosurgery, the Royal London Hospital for Integrated Medicine, the Royal National Throat, Nose and Ear Hospital and the UCH Macmillan Cancer Centre. It is one of the UK's five comprehensive biomedical research centres and employs more than 8,000 people. It has more than 1,000 beds.

Well-being and happiness

07

This chapter answers these questions:

- What research on well-being and happiness can help inform effective talent management strategies?
- How does being in the wrong job impact a person's well-being?
- What practical things can leaders and practitioners do to increase well-being at work?

Knowing what leads to well-being and happiness at work is important for leaders in organizations. Such knowledge will help inform positive leadership and effective talent management strategies in the future. That is why, in this chapter, I examine this topic in relation to its connection to the workplace.

Happiness and well-being are complex subjects and are still relatively new fields of academic study. For years psychologists focused on the negative experience of human lives. Positive psychology and the study of what brings well-being are still in their infancy as academic fields of research. Their increase in popularity since the 1980s has partly come about because people in the Western world have now achieved a reasonable level of economic prosperity. This means that their focus has inevitably turned to deeper, more meaningful aspects of what makes a good life and what will help them achieve well-being and happiness. In addition, there is a recognition that overcoming psychological problems and traumas doesn't necessarily lead to happiness or well-being but only sets the clock to 'zero'.

Understanding the factors that lead to well-being and happiness is a work in progress and the field is evolving fast. Some genetic research indicates that permanently changing a person's happiness levels is probably impossible. However, research amongst academics in the positive psychology world is producing more and more findings that suggest there are ways to improve subjective well-being. Indeed, as I have shown in this book, there are strengths-based approaches that are being implemented in organizations that contribute to people's feeling of subjective well-being in their life and work.

By design, Appreciative Inquiry, strengths-based recruitment and development all have the intention of focusing on and building upon what's working. Academic research, coupled with the results of practical strengths interventions in organizations, is giving more and more insight into what gives people a sense of well-being at work. To my mind, academics and practitioners have a lot to learn together. There appears to be more and more interest in this field, and the more those of us working in business can learn from the academics and vice versa the more of a chance we have to devise ways to boost people's well-being, satisfaction and success at work.

So in this chapter I outline some of the research into happiness and well-being that is relevant to the world of work and can contribute to executives' thinking about how to create and maintain powerful talent management approaches.

Definitions: subjective well-being, life satisfaction and happiness

Subjective well-being (SWB) is an umbrella term meaning the experiencing of pleasant emotions, low levels of negative moods and high general life satisfaction.

Life satisfaction is the feeling of satisfaction with life as a whole rather than transitory emotions and feelings that fluctuate depending on different contexts and situations.

Happiness as a term is sometimes used interchangeably with subjective well-being by psychologists. But it is actually a related but distinctly different concept. People can have a sense of well-being but not be happy and vice versa.

Why is it important to understand happiness and well-being?

Happiness is an important idea because it's how people judge their satisfaction with their lives. Ed Diener et al's research (1995) showed that college students around the world rated happiness and life satisfaction as very important or extremely important in the 41 nations he and his colleagues studied. Most people can probably say whether they are generally happy or not but they may benefit from understanding what exactly leads to their happiness and what they can do to be more happy, more frequently. So I would argue that it's important to individual citizens to understand what contributes to happiness. It should also be important to government, policy makers in the areas of health and education and, of course, to employers.

In Western countries, where subjective well-being has been studied, it turns out that people who have high levels of SWB on average have stronger immune systems (and there is some evidence that they live longer), are more creative, are better employees because they help others and are more conscientious, are more successful, earn more, have better marriages, get job interviews more frequently, have better quality relationships with others, are more sociable, are better liked, make better leaders, are better able to cope with difficult situations, like themselves and other people more, are also more helpful and altruistic, on average. With this list of payoffs, it's definitely worth understanding more about.

The characteristics of happy people

Park et al (2004) investigated the relationship between a number of what they call 'character strengths' (defined as positive traits reflected in thoughts, feelings and behaviours) and life satisfaction among 5,299 adults. They found that the character strengths most strongly and consistently correlated with life satisfaction were those of hope (expecting the best in the future and working to achieve it; believing that a good future is something that can be brought about), zest (approaching life with excitement and energy; not doing things half-heartedly; living life as an adventure; feeling alive and activated), gratitude (being aware of and thankful for the good things that happen; taking time to express thanks), curiosity (taking an interest in all aspects of ongoing experience; finding all subjects and topics fascinating; exploring and discovering), and love (valuing close relations with others, in particular those in which sharing and caring are reciprocated; being close to people). This work supports some of the findings of some other academics, cited in the remainder of this chapter, who have studied happiness and well-being in people.

They have satisfying relationships

Ed Diener and Martin Seligman (2002) studied very happy people and compared them to people who were less happy. The only external factor that distinguished the two groups was the 'presence of rich and satisfying social relationships'. Having friends, family or romantic partners to share events, thoughts and feelings with is necessary because it gives us meaning, eases pain and means we can share good times with others. Having others that we are close to is therefore crucial (though not in itself sufficient) for people to feel happy.

They are positive

Happy people are generally positive and optimistic. They use positive language much more than negative language. They smile and people like being around them because of their positive energy. People who have a negative disposition can feel disempowered and like a victim. Viktor Frankl, in his book *Man's Search for Meaning* about his time in a concentration camp, said, 'Everything can be taken from a man or a woman but one thing: the last of human freedoms to choose one's attitude in any given set of circumstances, to choose one's own way' (Frankl, 2004: 74).

Barbara Fredrickson, in her research into positivity, as described in her book *Positivity: Ground-breaking research to release your inner optimist and thrive* (2009), found that people who have positive emotions in a ratio of 3:1 in relation to negative emotions are more likely to flourish. She posited that we need three positive emotions to lift us up, to every one negative emotion that drags us down. Her research showed that most people have positive to negative emotions at a rate of 2 to 1. 'By contrast, those who don't overcome their depression, couples who fail in their marriages, and business teams that are unpopular and unprofitable each have ratios in the gutter, below 1 to 1' (Fredrickson, 2009: 133).

Encouragingly, she says that it is possible for people to raise their levels of positive emotions. People should not put pressure on themselves to do so, which can make things worse and end up with people feeling insincere as though they are putting it on. Instead Fredrickson says that the way to cultivate positive emotion is to be appreciative, curious, kind and, above all, real.

They feel grateful

Happy people feel a sense of gratitude and sometimes use phrases like 'I count my blessings', 'I can't believe I get paid to do this job' (I have personally heard that phrase many times from care assistants who are low paid and love their work).

As for the research, Watkins et al (2003) asked research participants to do a number of different gratitude exercises, such as thinking about a living person for whom they were grateful, writing about someone for whom they were grateful, and writing a letter to deliver to someone for whom they were grateful. Participants in the control condition were asked to describe their living room. Participants who completed a gratitude exercise showed increases in their experiences of positive emotion immediately after the exercise, and this effect was strongest for participants who were asked to think about a person for whom they were grateful.

They are authentic

Happy people are true to themselves and feel they can be themselves. Carl Rogers, a key figure in humanistic psychology, emphasized the need for people to be genuine in his book *On Becoming A Person*. Rogers believed that all living things have a drive toward actualization. Many of his beliefs were formed from watching the processes in nature. As a scientist, he saw how organisms stretched to fulfil their potential. The organisms that succeeded, he believed, were those that channelled their natural strength and yet also embraced complexity. This enabled them to develop the resources to deal with challenges. Those that remained narrow did not have the variety to overcome adversity. He thought that people who can be themselves and follow their true nature are more likely to find fulfilment. He talked of being fully human and to do so people must be true to themselves yet also be willing to learn from experience. He suggested that psychological health arises more readily in people who pursue this drive successfully (Rogers, 2004).

They are kind

Being kind boosts people's mood and happiness levels. Individuals who reported a greater interest in helping people or who act courteously and altruistically were more likely to rate themselves as happy (Feingold, 1983; Rigby and Slee, 1993; Williams and Shiaw, 1999)

Kind people usually have a generosity of spirit and enjoy helping others, even in small ways. They love to give to others and help people to succeed.

Some have learnt generosity from their spiritual or religious traditions, some from their parents, friends, teachers, managers, leaders and others. Some learn it from growing up in a culture that encourages people to give.

Being kind can lead others to like us more which in turn can boost our sense of happiness and well-being. Lyubomirsky et al (2004) conducted an experiment where they asked students to perform five random acts of kindness every week for six weeks. They defined random acts of kindness as behaviour that benefited others at a cost to oneself, such as putting coins into a stranger's parking meter, donating blood or visiting a sick relative. They found that they experienced an increase in well-being.

The role of passion and meaning

Robert Vallerand looked at the role of passion in sustainable psychological well-being. He found that being passionate toward a given activity will lead the person to engage in the activity frequently, often over several years and sometimes a lifetime, and that generally leads to the experience of positive emotions which in turn leads to an increase in psychological well-being. He distinguishes *harmonious passion* from *obsessive passion*. The former, he says, originates from 'an autonomous internalization of the activity into one's identity', whereas obsessive passion 'emanates from a controlled internalization and comes to control the person' (Vallerand, 2012: 3).

Pursuing goals that are personally meaningful and match one's values also enhances well-being, according to research by Lyubomirsky (2001). Meaning and happiness are related, but people can feel that they have meaning in their lives but not happiness and vice versa. Happiness is an emotion that comes and goes but meaning is enduring. According to Baumeister et al (2013), finding meaning in life is to do with effort, giving and sometimes sacrifice, and it doesn't necessarily make people happier although does give them a great sense of well-being. Happiness is more to do with getting what we want; it is less about giving, and more about taking. Happiness is also more about the here and now, whereas meaningfulness involves integrating the past, present and future. And meaningfulness was also linked to higher levels of worry or stress and lower happiness. Baumeister et al comment, 'Happiness went with being a taker more than a giver, while meaningfulness was associated with being a giver more than a taker' (Baumeister et al, 2013: 14).

How important is our work to our well-being?

As we have seen, being engaged in a pursuit that you feel is worthwhile and you enjoy – having a passion – creates well-being and happiness. Feeling a sense of excitement and energy and being the real you are important factors that lead to well-being. So we can see that work and being in a job that we love and that we feel suits us is part of what gives people satisfaction and makes them thrive at work. However, people who do work that they find meaningful do and can feel anxiety, worry and stress as well as low levels of happiness. Meaningful work is about doing things that are important and allow us to express ourselves. A good example would be a nurse on a children's cancer ward. On a day-to-day basis her happiness levels may be fairly low, but the sense of meaning she has in her work is probably high and has been so in the past, the present and the future too.

Given that we spend a lot of time at work, our chosen career is a massive contributor to our sense of well-being. It therefore follows that a strong and effective talent management strategy has at its heart selecting and nurturing people into jobs that they love and bring them the sense of well-being that means that they will thrive.

Martin North, one of the interviewees for this book who talked about what it was like to be a square peg in a round hole in his sales role, demonstrates how a person's well-being can be seriously affected if they are in a job that is wrong for them. In his case it appears as though other factors that contribute to well-being, like positive social relationships, were also affected, which resulted in his well-being dropping even more:

> There was a sense of draining energy. I didn't ever want to do anything. There was an apathy and it was shared by a couple of my colleagues; we were a rather 'unhealthy' little trio. We liked the sport but weren't suited to sales roles. We were rebels… not overtly, but we were quietly not doing what we should have been doing, just passing the time commiserating. There was resentment about doing what we were being asked to do, even though it was our job! I was thinking, 'Why am I doing this? Why am I here?' I was probably putting about 60–70 per cent effort in, time-wasting, browsing the internet, putting off the parts of the job I didn't enjoy. I think the flare up of my medical condition was 100 per cent related to the frustrating situation, because there's real correlation: at times of stress my condition worsens. Then I'd feel ill and feel less like doing my work, then I'd feel more stressed… it was a vicious circle. I would count down the minutes to the end of the day. I'd look at the guys around me who were clearly 'sales guys'; they were always on the phone, going at it… it was their calling. I just didn't want to go into work at all. I didn't feel I was good at what I was doing, subconsciously I knew I was cheating the company, I didn't feel confident. I didn't even want to hang out socially with people from work, I just wanted to get out of there.

In this role Martin wasn't happy and it certainly had no meaning for him. Contrast this with what he says about the role that he later moved into, for which he is really well suited:

> I wake up in the morning and I *want* to go to work. I want to get in there. Because I love it, a lot of my social group is work people. I enjoy being with and working with my colleagues now, we're similar personalities. And because I enjoy my job, I'm a more pleasant person! I stay late, I keep working until 8, 9, 10 in the evening. It doesn't feel like work, or a job. It's my passion, something I'm genuinely interested in. It's about energy too. In the sales role, I never had any energy, I was lethargic, wanted to be anywhere else except at work. Now I have a very positive energy and attitude. I just want to get things done.

Mike Blake's story also shows how being in work that you're not suited for can have a very negative impact on your well-being and that of those close to you. He contrasts the experience of being in a role that he loves and is right for him, with one where he was 'acting':

> In the role I do now, having had a really, really busy day, I come home energized and wanting to do things. In roles where I didn't feel comfortable, I'd have nothing left, I was completely drained, so I probably tried to protect myself and limit what I did at work. I used to have to 'let off steam', and that caused me some problems in the past, people found it hard to cope with. When you're an actor, you can't act all the time, you have to have times when you can be yourself; the bigger the disconnect between who you are 'having to be' and who you really are when you are being natural, the more has to come out in other ways, not always nice ways, maybe it's swearing, drinking, shouting... not good... You're away from your natural happy equilibrium, your normal way of being. It's hard. I think I managed to hide my inner feelings quite well from my team, even though I was increasingly uncomfortable. It knocked me out of balance, I wasn't the rested, fulfilled person I would normally be. It amplified or made worse other aspects of life and even triggered some things... you should ask my ex-wife!

Mike's story vividly shows the impact on a person's life of not being happy at work and the difference is made clear to him when he changed jobs.

Another interviewee, Lynne Stainer, also talks about the difference it makes to be doing work you love and how it can change your life:

> I think it changes your life in ways that you can't even begin to possibly imagine. If you're in work that you love, you'll be surrounded by this positive

energy and that will have an effect on everyone you come into contact with and every experience that you will ever have. It will improve all your relationships, and even the way that you think. There's nothing that it won't touch.

Viktor Frankl, the neurologist, psychiatrist and holocaust survivor, said in his book *Man's Search for Meaning*, 'Everyone has his own specific vocation or mission in life, everyone must carry out a concrete assignment that demands fulfilment. People feel more at peace when they are pursuing their chosen purpose' (Frankl, 2004: 131).

There was definitely a sense of peace and purpose in all those we interviewed when they were talking about their work. It was a stark contrast to how they spoke about the roles they were in when they felt like square pegs in round holes.

Lessons for leaders and practitioners

- Show concern for your people's well-being by asking them what is currently making them feel good about work and what is not.
- Encourage positive relationships at work by paying attention to the individuals and team as well as the tasks and processes.
- Communicate your organizations' vision and the meaning of what you do – talk about why you do it, not just what you do. This will help to give people a greater sense of meaning in their jobs.
- Select people for jobs that they find meaningful, fit with their values and play to their strengths.
- Note that people may find their work very meaningful but, at times, may not be happy doing it – this is not necessarily a problem! If they are feeling unhappy talk to them about this and explain the difference between meaning and happiness. This will help them to understand that not being happy at work all the time is fine and that it is more helpful perhaps to think about the idea of well-being.
- Be authentic so as to encourage others to be the same.
- Try to appoint people to projects that they are interested in and will enjoy.
- Share research with your people about happiness and well-being and get them thinking about what they can do to increase theirs.

Two-minute chapter summary

This chapter examines the factors that make people happy and those that lead to well-being. It provides an important insight into the notion of meaning (versus happiness) at work. It is therefore an essential backdrop to the subject of strengths-based talent management for leaders and practitioners who are interested in developing a holistic understanding of how humans function at their best in life and work.

The full transcripts of interviews carried out for this book can be found in Part Two.

References

Baumeister, RF, Vohs, KD, Aaker, JL and Garbinsky, EN (2013) Some key differences between a happy life and a meaningful life, *Journal of Positive Psychology*. Available from: faculty-gsb.stanford.edu/aaker/pages/documents/somekeydifferenceshappylifemeaningfullife_2012.pdf (accessed 10 December 2015)

Diener, E and Seligman, EP (2002) Very happy people, *Psychological Science*, **13**, pp 80–83

Diener, E, Diener, M and Diener, C (1995) Factors predicting the subjective well-being of nations, *Journal of Personality and Social Psychology*, **69** (5), pp 851–64

Feingold, A (1983) Happiness, unselfishness, and popularity, *Journal of Psychology*, 115, pp 3–5

Frankl, VE (2004) *Man's Search for Meaning*, May, new edition, Rider, London

Fredrickson, B (2009) *Positivity: Ground-breaking research to release your inner optimist and thrive*, One World Publications, London

Lyubomirsky, S (2001) Why are some people happier than others? The role of cognitive and motivational processes in well-being, *American Psychologist*, **56** (3), pp 239–49

Lyubomirsky, S, Tkach, C and Yelverton, J (2004) Pursuing sustained happiness through random acts of kindness and counting one's blessings: Tests of two six-week interventions, unpublished data, University of California, Riverside, Department of Psychology

Park, N, Peterson, C and Seligman, ME (2004) Strengths of character and well-being, *Journal of Social and Clinical Psychology*, **23**, pp 603–19

Rigby, K and Slee, PT (1993) Dimensions of interpersonal relations among Australian children and implications for psychological well-being, *Journal of Social Psychology*, **133**, pp 33–42

Rogers, C (2004) *On Becoming a Person: A therapist's view of psychotherapy*, new edition, Constable & Robinson, London

Vallerand, RJ (2012) The role of passion in sustainable psychological well-being, *Psychology of Well-Being: Theory, Research and Practice*, **2** (1)

Watkins, PC, Woodward, K, Stone, T and Kolts, RL (2003) Gratitude and happiness: Development of a measure of gratitude, and relationships with subjective well-being, *Social Behavior and Personality*, **31** (5), pp 431–52

Williams, S and Shiaw, WT (1999) Mood and organizational citizenship behaviour intentions, *Journal of Psychology*, **133**, pp 656–68

The future of strengths

08

This chapter answers these questions:

- What are some of the big challenges for employers in the coming decades?
- How can a strengths approach help tackle the challenges employers and employees will face?
- What words of wisdom can three HR directors who have led transformational change offer about the contribution of strengths?

In the public and private sectors, the strengths movement is building momentum. Not just because more and more organizations are adopting strengths-based talent management strategies but because once people have a taste of what it's like to be selected and valued for their strengths there is no going back for them. They become advocates and, as some told me in the interviews for this book, they can't help but see the world through that lens now.

So far we've looked at what has happened and is happening in reality. Now I'd like to speculate about what *could* happen in the future – what contribution the strengths revolution could make in the coming decades. I'll look first at some aspects of the changing context that we live in, such as people living longer, the changing nature of employment, growth sectors in the economy and Generation Z entering the workplace. All are issues about which we are yet to grasp the full meaning and implications.

I will posit how a strengths approach could make a positive difference in all these areas and help us to navigate the changes that are happening now and will happen in the next few decades.

Finally I will leave you with some thoughts on what the strengths revolution could do for you.

The changing context

We all have the challenge of coping with the changing world. On a local level parents are trying to work out how their children can grow up physically and psychologically healthy when their lives are so dominated by social media. On a larger scale, how do big organizations ensure that they have the right people when there is such global competition for particular skills and experience? There are many opportunities in the world now, for example for different types of work and styles of working, for travel and for connecting globally like never before because of the ubiquity of the internet. But there are also threats on a micro and macro level, such as climate change, population growth, an ageing workforce and terrorism. Opportunities and challenges facing society always benefit from new and fresh ideas and thinking. Strengths approaches, with their focus on what causes people to thrive, must surely have a big contribution to make as well as balancing an over-emphasis on finding what is wrong and fixing problems.

Eva Sage-Gavin, former Executive Vice President of HR of Gap Inc, said when interviewed for this book:

> I am often invited to speak globally on the topic of how to unleash and engage people's strengths. The outpouring of interest is amazing. While we have all sorts of global challenges in our post-9/11 world including climate change, employment imbalance and terrorism, people want to make a difference and feel it's time to act. They feel liberated to bring their strengths and gifts to the challenges they care about.

You can read the full transcript of the interview with Eva Sage-Gavin on page 191.

Here I explore some of the realities and challenges that the early twenty-first century presents and speculate on how we might utilize strengths approaches to help us navigate them in a positive and productive way.

People living and working longer

Increased life expectancy was probably one of the greatest advances in human health science and technology in the twentieth century. Most babies born in 1900 did not live past the age of 50. Now, life expectancy at birth exceeds 81 years in several countries. Older people today spend many years in retirement. In Organisation for Economic Cooperation and Development (OECD) countries in 2007 the average man left the labour force before age 64 and could expect 18 years of retirement. The average woman stopped working at age 63 and could expect more than 22 years of retirement.

Despite the fact that life expectancy has been increasing, the retirement age of the workforce has dropped. Yet many countries where people enjoy high incomes want people to work for more years to slow the escalating costs of pensions. According to the American National Institute on Aging, cognitive and physical abilities do not deteriorate as quickly as is often assumed so there is the potential for people to work longer. Indeed, working longer may support people to live healthier, longer lives if it keeps them active, socially connected and gives them a sense of purpose and well-being.

There is a generally held attitude in many societies that ageing is bad and to be dreaded. In Western societies, we are so aware of all the people who end up unhappy as they grow old, we see media reports of care homes full of sad-looking elderly people and we read about the crisis in healthcare as people live longer and suffer complex multiple illness and disease. In many cultures youth and good looks are revered and millions is spent on trying to reverse the effects of ageing. There is no wonder that a negative and fearful view of old age prevails. Without doubt there are aspects of ageing that are difficult and many elderly people do have a negative experience of growing older. However, that is not necessarily the experience of all people as they grow older. Indeed, there is evidence that happiness actually increases with age. Blanchflower and Oswald (2007), in their paper 'Is well-being U-shaped over the life cycle?', describe how happiness increases as we age. The 'U-shaped curve' of happiness shows that well-being reaches its lowest in the mid to late forties and then climbs steadily thereafter. And Linley et al (2007) suggest that for some people the following strengths can actually grow with age: curiosity, love of learning, fairness, forgiveness and self-regulation.

Vaillant and Mukamal (2001), in their paper on positive ageing in men, say, 'Whether we live to a vigorous old age lies not so much in our stars or in our genes, as in ourselves.' They found seven factors that predicted positive ageing: not being a smoker or stopping smoking young, adaptive coping style (or use of 'involuntary mature defenses', for example the ability not to turn mole-hills into mountains), absence of alcohol abuse, healthy weight, stable marriage, exercise levels and years of education.

With the insight generated from research like this there is a lot more that can be done to support people to maintain, and even increase, their sense of well-being as they age. In a context where there are growing numbers of older people and fewer younger people to care for them there is and will be a strain on the social and healthcare systems that are needed to support them. Society and politicians need to be creative and find as many positive interventions as possible to promote positive ageing and alleviate the negative aspects that are difficult for individuals and their families and can be burdensome to the broader society.

A 2011 report *Global Health and Aging*, published by the World Health Organization (WHO), noted:

> Aging is taking place alongside other broad social trends that will affect the lives of older people. Economies are globalizing, people are more likely to live in cities, and technology is evolving rapidly. Demographic and family changes mean there will be fewer older people with families to care for them. People today have fewer children, are less likely to be married, and are less likely to live with older generations. With declining support from families, society will need better information and tools to ensure the well-being of the world's growing number of older citizens.

I agree that society will need better information and tools. New thinking and innovative approaches are also needed if ageing is not just to be seen as a problem and if elderly people are to be supported in different ways that emphasize overall well-being.

Potential contribution of a strengths approach

- raising awareness of what constitutes positive ageing and well-being generally as well as when a person starts to grow old;

- strengths-based careers advice for older people, not just young people;

- broadening the concept of careers and work to include unpaid and voluntary work so that older people can keep on finding meaning and purpose and younger ones can learn from their experience and wisdom;

- government policies that support older people to keep on working in jobs they find satisfying and fulfilling;

- encouraging older people to learn and pursue education, and support for organizations like University of the Third Age, which provides courses of education for retired and elderly people;

- thinking of a lifespan as one in which a number of different careers and types of work are possible at different life stages.

Insecurity in the global labour market

The International Labour Organization's (ILO) *World Employment and Social Outlook* report for 2015 found that, among countries with available data (covering 84 per cent of the global workforce), three-quarters of workers are employed on temporary or short-term contracts, in informal jobs often without any contract or in unpaid family jobs (International Labour Organization, 2015a). Another trend is the rise in part-time employment, especially among women. In the majority of countries with available information, the number of part-time jobs outpaced increases in full-time jobs between 2009 and 2013. Director General Guy Ryder commented that 'These new figures point to an increasingly diversified world of work. In some cases, non-standard forms of work can help people get a foothold into the job market. But these emerging trends are also a reflection of the widespread insecurity that's affecting many workers worldwide today' (International Labour Organization, 2015b).

Such insecurity potentially means that people accept jobs for which they are unsuited and so don't stay in those jobs, compounding the problem of an insecure job market. On the other hand, temporary job availability can be a very positive thing as it enables people who don't want to, or who are unable to, work full time to find work for which they are well suited and also that fits with their personal circumstances.

Potential contribution of a strengths approach

- schools and colleges help young people to think in terms of their strengths, rather than just their skills, and how they could be applied to a range of different careers. This will help with employability and at least help them to ensure that they choose roles that are a good fit and thus lessen the chances that they will end up in roles for which they are unsuited;

- helping people of all ages to make the connection between understanding their strengths and the confidence that that brings in themselves and their choices. Much could be done in this respect in schools and also, at the other end of the age spectrum, in elderly people's services;

- applying strengths-based recruitment to the temporary and part-time workforce would ensure the right people are selected and therefore reduce attrition amongst workers.

Job creation in growing sectors

Private sector services (such as business, administrative services and real estate) together with the accommodation and restaurant sector are expected to create jobs at the fastest rate of any sectors in the economy for the next five years according to the ILO's *World Employment and Social Outlook* report for 2015. According to the ILO predictions, these and related industries will employ more than a third of the global workforce over the five years to 2020. The ILO outlook also reports that public services in healthcare, education and administration will continue to be a major source of employment. While increasing at a slower pace, they will still represent 15 per cent of total employment.

The shift of employment to services-oriented work and the decline in manufacturing means a significant change in the skills demanded by the labour market. Individuals who once occupied jobs in manufacturing will continue to face a challenge if they are not able to transfer their capabilities to other sectors. It's not all good news for employers, either. Businesses in these growing sectors will be competing for enough of the best people. The majority of jobs in these sectors require a lot of face-to-face interaction and strengths in customer service. Employers would do well to gain a deep understanding of what it takes to be excellent at that type of work if they are to hire the best people. This is where excellent talent management makes the difference between an organization endlessly struggling to get and keep the right people or being a magnet for great people who are queuing up to work there. And for individuals there is an opportunity to look at their employability from a different angle. People who formerly worked in manufacturing could gain a new perspective on themselves by focusing not just on what skills and knowledge they could transfer but also on what their strengths and motivators are that might make them a great fit for an entirely different type of work.

This approach would benefit graduates too. A survey of *Guardian Careers* readers (White, 2012) looking at the biggest challenges facing graduate job seekers revealed that a quarter of those polled said that being rejected for jobs for not having enough experience was the toughest issue they faced as a graduate job seeker. The article described the graduate job market in 2012 as 'hostile' due to this and other issues such as unpaid internships.

As more and more employers adopt a strengths-based approach to recruitment it will become easier for them to see whether they are a good fit for the job and rely much less on making that judgement based on the candidates' experience. This means that they will have more people to choose from because they won't be unnecessarily cutting people out based on a lack of experience that isn't crucial to the job. The interviews in this book with people who have changed careers show that it is possible to move into work that might not have seemed like an obvious choice. For example, Joel Davies (page 224) started his career as a mechanic and is now a hairdresser. The key though is to understand who you are and not be trapped by pre-conditioned ideas about what you can and can't do, even if you have been in one particular line of work for most of your life.

Potential contribution of a strengths approach

- research by business into the strengths, motivators and values needed in the growing sectors of business services, restaurant and care;

- career guidance in schools and colleges that helps young people to work out their strengths early on so that they understand the spectrum of possibilities open to them and so that they can sell themselves to a range of employers;

- employers being clear about what strengths are needed in particular roles rather than always looking for people who have experience when it might not actually be necessary;

- career transition support to include a focus on what kind of person you are, ie your strengths, values and motivators, and not just the skills you have and previous experience you've acquired.

Generation Z

Every time period and each generation faces new challenges as the world changes. Each generation probably thinks their particular challenges are uniquely difficult. However, it is clear that Generation Z, those born approximately between 1997 and 2010 (there is no universal agreement on which years of birth define Generation Z) face a set of pressures that have never been experienced before. They are growing up in a time that is heavily influenced by the impact of the 2008 financial crisis both in terms of the resultant economic downturn and also the mistrust of large corporations, banks in particular. The environmental movement has never been as active, nor has the call for gay rights in different parts of the world. So they are a generation that has reason to feel empowered and has the wherewithal to make their voice and opinion heard via the internet.

Social media means that their lives are displayed and catalogued, not just by themselves but also by their parents from their babyhood. Those of us who grew up before the ubiquity of the internet benefited from not having our lives on display to a wide audience. Any mistakes we made were kept much more private, our appearance was not judged based on photographs posted on Instagram or Facebook. And the 'celebrity culture' didn't put pressure on us to look perfect. Today, social media means that wherever young people are they can post information about themselves and see the reactions in ways that can be devastating. Waiting for the 'likes' and 'you're pretty/beautiful/stunning' comments on social media sites can be an anxiety-inducing experience. On the positive side they can use the internet to create a personal brand and be seen by large numbers of potential employers or collaborators. Done well, this can result in productive connections and opportunities.

Against this backdrop of their early lives, it's hardly surprising that anxiety and desire to make a difference are real pressures for them. In an interview for this book Eva Sage-Gavin, former Executive Vice President of HR for Gap Inc, said:

> We know that globally, the Millennial and Gen Z generations are some of the most anxious. They face pressure in school, in sports, in social settings and experience a lot of anxiety just to be considered for a great education and good job. We've seen some tragic examples of what pressure can do to young men and women, including burn out and workplace illness that is all too common.
>
> At a global level they are also anxious about societal issues like climate change, poverty and terrorism. Today we have tools and resources to support individuals to understand what strengths they can bring to make a difference in their lives personally and to tackle bigger societal issues. That's why I focus on the power of positive energy and focus on strengths.

Potential contribution of a strengths approach

- raising awareness in the younger generation of the research on happiness and well-being and discussing with them what will make them happy, ie it's unlikely to be good looks, fame or fortune;

- help them to see their own value and worth through a deep understanding of their strengths from their mid teens;

- help them to make education and career decisions that are likely to lead them into work that they love and thrive in;

- expand the thinking of parents, careers advisors, and teachers to think in terms of multiple-career lives, different employment models and the notion of understanding your strengths, motivators and values in order to make good career choices.

Start with a question

In this chapter I've only briefly described some of the challenges employers will face in the coming years. Each is complex and far reaching. It can be overwhelming to think of how to even start tackling such issues. I find that questions can help to garner thoughts and elicit a few first steps. Here are three questions that I hope will help you do that:

- How can we make the most of the talents, experience, wisdom and strengths of older people?
- How can we prepare young people to thrive in the increasingly competitive and insecure global economy?
- How can businesses in the growing sectors truly understand what they need from employees to create great service and performance?

What if?

With these questions in mind, have a think about how a strengths-based approach could change the business landscape and workforce of the future. I invite you to imagine a reality where:

- young people are well prepared to thrive in the increasingly competitive global economy;
- careers support offers strengths-based careers guidance to people, of all ages and life-stages;
- businesses in growing sectors of the economy thoroughly understand what kind of employees will thrive in and be excellent at their jobs and know how to find them;
- the well-being and happiness of employees and customers are two of the criteria that stakeholders and society used to judge organizations;
- it's the norm for people to be selected for jobs that play to their strengths and that energize them;
- one of the ways an organization judges its own success is by how many of its employees are a great fit for their jobs – or round pegs in round holes.

This could be reality. As you can see from the interviews and case studies in this book, using a strengths approach can make a real difference to organizations and their people. By following the advice in this book you can implement strengths-based talent management for yourself and experience the difference for yourself. What difference could *you* make?

The strengths revolution is within your reach...

> When you are given the opportunity to put your foot forward and take ownership of a problem that no one else has been able to solve, and you see the potential to make something happen that you know will have unprecedented impact, it's a gift. It's irresistible.

That is what Lynda Greenshields, former HR Director of Acromas Group, said in an interview for this book, about why she placed strengths at the centre of her HR strategy:

> If your ambition is to make a difference to your organization's performance a strengths-based approach to recruitment or development will achieve that. If you are seeking something that wins hearts and minds there is nothing better than strengths. And if you want to leave a legacy of a culture that's inspiring and positive to employees and customers then a strengths approach will do that.

I hope I have convinced you of the power of strengths to improve businesses and public services as well as people's lives. Sandra Porter of Starbucks UK said, 'it's about setting an ambitious goal – above whatever might be on a strategy document.' Sandra, like the other senior leaders quoted in this book, of course had a strategy. And she was clear about what she wanted strengths-based recruitment to achieve. In her case it was about improving the customer experience and reducing staff turnover. For others it was about improving service or patient care, or saving money. Beyond their strategy, though, they all had an ambitious goal – I'd go so far as to call it a dream in some cases. They wanted big, transformational change. They wanted something that would excite and transform as well as being backed up by data. They put their faith in a strengths approach because it intuitively felt right to them.

Take the first step and, like the organizations and the individuals mentioned in this book who have experienced the power of strengths, you'll never look back. It changes organizations and it changes lives. It simultaneously achieves practical quantitative results whilst shifting mindset and thinking.

And the beauty of it is that dropping a tiny pebble in the pond can cause huge ripple effects. Small, simple steps, such as introducing strengths-based recruitment for one key role, can create disproportionately positive results.

It's the only organizational intervention I know of that has the power to create champions for whom the task becomes their mission. Organizations struggle and strive to get that kind of passion and commitment through all sorts of roundabout ways. It turns out that strengths-based talent management is a direct and fast route. There was no one more surprised than me when I first saw this happen. It's magic!

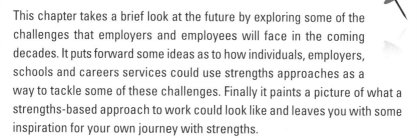

Two-minute chapter summary

This chapter takes a brief look at the future by exploring some of the challenges that employers and employees will face in the coming decades. It puts forward some ideas as to how individuals, employers, schools and careers services could use strengths approaches as a way to tackle some of these challenges. Finally it paints a picture of what a strengths-based approach to work could look like and leaves you with some inspiration for your own journey with strengths.

The full transcripts of interviews carried out for this book can be found in Part Two.

References

Blanchflower, D and Oswald, A (2007) Is well-being U-shaped over the life cycle? National Bureau of Economic Research working paper 12935

International Labour Organization (2015a) *World Employment and Social Outlook 2015*, ILO, Geneva. Available from: www.ilo.org/wcmsp5/groups/public/---dgreports/---dcomm/---publ/documents/publication/wcms_368626.pdf

International Labour Organization (2015b) ILO warns of widespread insecurity in the global labour market. Available from: www.ilo.org/global/about-the-ilo/newsroom/news/WCMS_368252/lang--en/index.htm (accessed 10 December 2015)

Linley, PA, Maltby, J, Wood, AM, Harrington, S, Peterson, C, Park, N and Seligman, MEP (2007) Character strengths in the United Kingdom: The VIA inventory of strengths, *Personality and Individual Differences*. Available from: personalpages.manchester.ac.uk/staff/alex.wood/VIA.pdf (accessed 10 December 2015)

National Institute on Aging and National Institutes of Health (2011) *Global Health and Aging*, World Health Organization, Geneva. Available from: https://www.nia.nih.gov/research/publication/global-health-and-aging/health-and-work (accessed 30 October 2015)

Vaillant, GE and Mukamal, K (2001) Positive ageing in two male cohorts, *American Journal of Psychiatry*, **158**, pp 839–47

White, Alison (2012) The biggest challenges facing graduate jobseekers today, *Guardian Careers*, 7 February. Available from www.theguardian.com/careers/challenges-graduate-jobseekers-face-today (accessed 16 October 2015)

PART TWO
Real-life insights and stories

Part Two answers these questions:

- What are the motivations of senior leaders who have introduced strengths-based approaches in their organizations, what strategic benefits has it given them and how do they explain its success?

- What do managers who have implemented SBR say have been the benefits and challenges, and what advice can they share?

- What does it really mean, in practice, for a person to move from work that is not a good fit for their natural strengths and values, into a role that suits them and where they know they are a 'round peg in a round hole'?

This section contains the transcripts of twenty interviews from three different groups of people, each of whom has a unique insight into the value of strengths-based approaches to talent management.

Chapter 9 contains the full transcripts of interviews with eight executive board level leaders who have made the decision to introduce strengths-based recruitment or development into their organizations. In Chapter 10 we hear from managers and recruiters who have been responsible for implementing strengths-based approaches, including day-to-day management. And in Chapter 11 we learn from individuals themselves what the experience of being in the wrong job or career is like and the contrast when they found work where they were a round peg in a round hole.

Interviews with senior leaders

09

It's rare to get this kind of insight into the strategic thinking of executive board level leaders. In these interviews they share their reasons for introducing strengths-based recruitment and development into their organizations, they talk about how they achieved support from executive colleagues and the broader organization and they discuss the success factors. We also get a glimpse into some of their personal motivations, lessons learnt and the legacy they hope that a strengths-based transformational change will leave in their organizations.

We hear from leaders in large UK- and US-based organizations in the public and private sectors including healthcare, fast-moving consumer goods (FMCG), retail and financial services. They are: Professor Hilary Chapman CBE, Chief Nurse at Sheffield Teaching Hospitals; Lynda Greenshields, former HR Director of Acromas Group; Professor Katherine Fenton OBE, former Chief Nurse at University College London Hospitals NHS Foundation Trust; Helen Lamont, Nursing and Patient Services Director, Newcastle upon Tyne Hospitals NHS Foundation Trust; Sandra Porter, former HR Director of Starbucks UK and Ireland; Samantha Rockey, Head of Leadership Development at SABMiller; Eva Sage-Gavin, former Executive Vice President of HR and Corporate Affairs at Gap Inc; and Professor Janice Sigsworth, Director of Nursing, Imperial College Healthcare NHS Trust.

Professor Hilary Chapman, CBE, Chief Nurse, Sheffield Teaching Hospitals

What is your role and how long have you been in it?

I am the Chief Nurse at Sheffield Teaching Hospitals. I have been in the role for over nine years. I have previously also been Chief Operating Officer alongside this. I am responsible for the nursing and midwifery services as well as hotel services and estates, which in total accounts for approximately half of our 8,000 people workforce.

What has been your role in implementing SBR?

As a member of the Shelford Group Chief Nurses I was one of the decision makers who evaluated the SBR proposal that was brought from outside the NHS. I listened carefully to the evidence and was one of the decision makers from the total group of ten Shelford Group Chief Nurses.

In terms of my own organization – Sheffield Teaching Hospitals NHS Foundation Trust – I was responsible for getting the right people and resources behind it. The first step was gaining the support of my executive colleagues, the most important of which in this context was the director of HR. He is responsible for recruitment overall and I needed to know that the strengths-based approach was going to become how Sheffield does things. He already understood the concept of SBR as he had implemented it outside the NHS. Equally I wanted my nine senior nurse directors across the organization to want to do it as much as I did. It was a case of presenting to them, answering their questions and a lot of ground work talking to people. I didn't have a lot of push-back to be honest.

Why did you want to do it as much as you did?

Because we were spending a lot of time trying to help people who were square pegs in round holes. And often the outcome wasn't good. I wanted to invest less time in the negative and more time making sure people are round pegs in round holes. I must admit at first I was wondering how you do this and knew we needed excellent leadership of SBR to make sure it was done well. We gave responsibility to two really good people who knew our existing processes, were well trained and were committed to the concept. They put a huge amount of investment into quality and controlled it tightly from the outset.

How did you choose the two SBR leads?

I trust them. They're professional. They understood SBR and could articulate the benefits. They had done the training and understood everything forensically, including the outcomes and benefits. I knew they would question things and that they would want to be absolutely happy with everything before implementation. They are strong enough to keep people within the golden rules too. Over time I have observed a huge energy and commitment in them. And when they came back to me to discuss things they would challenge me and hold me to how it needed to be done properly. That lovely thing as a senior leader to be challenged on things – they did that to me and pulled me back into line at times! They really believe in it.

Before they took the lead on SBR they didn't have a lot of influence, though they are both very good people. They are both gentle but forthright. Now they are flying. Somehow, leading SBR has given them the authority to influence. Through doing SBR they have been exposed to more people so their sphere of influence has grown and others' respect for them has increased.

What have been the benefits to the organization of implementing SBR?

We've made some very good appointments. Some of the people we appointed have been real surprises. They are showing huge strength in their very challenging ward leader roles. They are succeeding in their jobs and leading their clinical areas well. We wouldn't have made some of these appointments without SBR. Before, you would sometimes have a gut feeling about someone that you didn't think they were the right person, you had nagging doubts, yet they met all the criteria in the person specifications. Now we know whether they are definitely the right person. One of our wards had a very powerful, popular and good leader who had been there a long time. It was always going to be a hard act to follow but we have made a great appointment and the person is saying how much they enjoy the job. They really have been able to rise to the challenge.

I get feedback from line managers about what good appointments we are making with SBR.

Strategically it will make a difference when the university starts using SBR for student nurse recruitment. We need to recruit people with the right qualifications but we also need to make sure they are the right kind of people too so that we get the right people in as students from the start. There is a huge amount of time and cost involved in recruiting the wrong person; it's the cost of training the wrong person for however long they stay on the course, the lost place that could have been given to someone else, the loss of a registered nurse into our workforce and the time and effort we spend with people who are wrong for the job – that is huge. It will take time for SBR to flow into the whole process for nurses, ie from student nurse recruitment to more senior positions, but ultimately it will have a big impact on the quality of the workforce and of care.

We've just started to implement SBR for Band 2 Care Assistant recruitment and I expect it to reduce our staff turnover rate. We will be tracking that.

What, if anything, would you have done differently in implementing SBR?

I'm happy with how we have implemented it. We have taken our time to embed it properly so we haven't drifted off course at all. The only thing I may have done was got more people trained from the outset. But apart from that I don't think I would have done anything differently at Sheffield. And in terms of the Shelford Group, we have to keep the momentum going now that Katherine Fenton (former Chair of Shelford Group Chief Nurses) has retired. It is a challenging time for the NHS and my fear is that SBR gets lost. There is a shortage of nurses currently but does that mean you drop your standards? No it doesn't.

We would like to do more profiles, including those of matrons and senior leaders. Matrons are so important, and introducing SBR for that role would give us more confidence in those appointments. Having said that, even though we haven't yet got the profile I can see that my nurse leaders are thinking in a different way because of SBR. Previously we would always appoint someone with a background in that particular clinical area. Now we have realized that it's about the type of person and they don't necessarily need a background in the particular clinical area that they will be leading. For example, we have just appointed a matron with a renal background into older persons' care. SBR as a concept has shifted the mindset and created a different way of thinking about recruitment. My nine nurse directors have moved away from thinking people *have* to have worked in a particular speciality before.

I would also like us to develop a chief nurse profile. That is a tough job and the importance of appointing the right person is paramount.

There have been bumps in the road but not many, and we haven't had much kick-back in reality. It's working well.

What advice would you give to senior leaders who are thinking about implementing SBR or those who haven't yet considered it?

I would say be ready to change. If you're not ready to change don't do it. If you're not going to alter things don't bother. Commit to it and follow it through. It's not just another initiative. Not everyone likes change and you can't play at this. Get the sign-up of your senior colleagues. Also, choose your SBR project leads carefully because they need to believe it as they will be challenged. Do a lot of awareness raising and education to get people on the bus. And train people properly and carefully. Make sure they understand and stick to the golden rules. Once people see how well it works you will have created a desire – make sure you can meet the desire by having enough trained interviewers. Also, I would say ask for early feedback. Personally I haven't had to ask, people have come and told me.

In your experience, what kind of senior leaders can lead the kind of change that SBR brings about?

There are a number of things.

Bravery is crucial because if a candidate is everyone's favourite and the SBR process means that you appoint someone else you have to be brave.

A person who is open to challenge – it's comfortable carrying on doing things the same way. Even if those things are not working for you. So they have to like that disruptive change and challenge.

Any senior executive who is thinking about adopting SBR I would ask them: Do you *know* what you're doing now is working? If not then make the change. But you have to embed it properly and don't just allow it to be yet another initiative. Above all you have to want what is best for your clients – in our case it's our patients and patients' families.

I haven't got money to throw away on high attrition rates. I want us to be efficient. I would ask what they are wasting money on and do they want to be efficient.

I would also say encourage people to ask and say what they want when you are talking to them about SBR. If they don't feel able to challenge they will feel 'done to'. We presented to people and got all their questions out and we didn't get kick-back. If there was any cynicism at the beginning we drew it out and answered people's questions and concerns early. And as the Chief Nurse I fronted the sessions as I wanted to speak to people and listen to them myself. If people asked, 'Have we got time to do this?' I replied, 'Do you have time to manage the wrong people?'

The two SBR leads were instrumental in this education/awareness raising phase and the success we have experienced so far. They have not let standards drop. They keep the quality standard high and they are approachable too.

Thinking about the wider economy, what opportunity would you say SBR presents?

If people apply for roles that are right for them they flourish. If they are right and do well they can progress. In this way SBR will make a strategic difference to the quality of our workforce. Now that we have changed our adverts we are attracting people who wouldn't previously have thought of a career in caring services. SBR allows the NHS and social care to attract the right people, some of whom may not previously have considered such careers before. It will give us confidence in the future and in our ability to appoint well to new roles.

If I had a magic wand I would use SBR for every position in the organization because of the amount of time we spend with people in the wrong job. It would free up so much time. We can't do it all overnight. It's got to be done properly.

Lynda Greenshields, HR Director, Acromas Group, 2011–14

What was your role and how long were you in it?

I was HR Director at Acromas Group, parent company of the AA, Saga and Allied Healthcare from 2011 to 2014, during the period immediately prior to the floats of Saga and the AA on the London Stock Exchange. I had HR responsibility for around 30,000 employees, the majority working in customer-facing roles. I believe that HR, as much as any other part of the business, should be concerned about customer experience, customer satisfaction and brand reputation; and at Acromas I proved that the way employees are recruited and treated can influence all of these. I made SBR the nucleus of my HR strategy.

Why did you place SBR at the core of your HR strategy at Acromas?

When you are given the opportunity to put your foot forward and take ownership of a problem that no one else has been able to solve, and you see the potential to make something happen that you know will have unprecedented impact, it's a gift. It's irresistible. At the time, we were facing a huge challenge with call centre staff turnover rates, and it was felt to be a problem with no answer. Both sales and HR managers felt that they had 'tried everything' and were at the point of resigning to the view that 'it's like this across the whole industry'. And on the other side of that, with respect to our customers, our AA and Saga brands were all about customer service. But, we realized, how can you hope to deliver amazing customer service when you have such high levels of turnover in your customer-facing people? I had introduced the concept of SBR and seen its potential to impact customer service at Morrisons. I knew it could be the nucleus of transformation at Acromas. With it we could get the right and best people into our roles, people for whom giving great customer service would come naturally as a result of their strengths. But I also knew that we would have to treat these people differently – like valued customers – if we wanted to keep them. Everything would have to be addressed, how we attracted them with our ads and websites, how we asked them to apply for our jobs, how we offered them jobs, how we trained them, how we managed them, how we celebrated their strengths and successes. I'd already seen that the 'great employee' profiles that would come out of the SBR process could help inform all these things. Place SBR at the centre and layer everything else around it, infused by what you've learned about your people from it – I knew this was a powerful combination that could deliver lasting transformation for our customer sales and service organizations.

What were your strategic aims in introducing SBR?

As I've explained, it all began with the challenge to reduce our employee turnover rates, and that was the immediate on-the-ground problem being faced by the business. But really, I think what I was trying to get to was this. Whenever a customer called us or we called them or visited them, I wanted to make sure that our employee on the phone or in the customer's home would be living our brand and that our customers would experience that as great customer service, every single time. Saga and the AA look after their customers. It's what they are known for. It's what they do. Allied Healthcare employees are literally doing it in domiciliary care roles. Recruiting people on their innate strengths with SBR makes sure that your customer is always dealing with someone who loves their work, who gives great service because they can't help it, because it's who they naturally are. Customers know when it's great service or when they're being treated fairly. They feel it through the person they are speaking with or being cared for by. Then they talk about it, they tell people about it. In the end, it may be about business growth, but your customer advocates and the great brand reputation they help to create are how your business grows. You can't separate out any part of it. Your employees, your brand, your employer brand, your employee brand, your customer experience of your brand – words that people so often use to describe what they see as separate things – I believe they're all one and the same, your brand... your business. I placed SBR at the heart of our HR strategy because I knew it could impact our brand reputation and business results.

How did you sell the idea of SBR to your senior colleagues?

The SBR component was part of the overall package of changes I was proposing, and I had hard numbers to show that, amongst other things, we were not holding on to our best people and what that was costing us. The fantastic thing about Saga and the AA is that they are honest, and my colleagues wanted to know the truth of the situation. People already knew there was a problem, but the numbers clarified the severity of the situation. Now they wanted to understand what had happened and try to put things right. They were up for it. And that was great, because to effect a massive change like this you need leaders who are ready and willing to move from a point of feeling that nothing can ever make a difference. In this case, though, there wasn't the need for a hard sell... the logic was there in the numbers. Something needed to change and we all wanted to make it happen.

There's something else, too.

HR can often fall into the trap of focusing on proving their own worth (and I understand why, because of traditional and at times negative attitudes towards HR), along the lines of 'What can I do to make a difference so people can see how marvellous I am?' But, when HR step up and propose an idea that will actually make the business better, and people see that's the motivation behind what you're proposing, then why would they argue with you?

What difference has SBR made to the organization?

It's been huge. The great thing about SBR is that its starting point is the good people you've already got. You're picking them out, shadowing them, observing them, questioning them and profiling them, and saying, 'We want more people like you.' At last we were giving our best people the right kind of attention. They were the subjects – it wasn't just HR coming in with some new process for them to follow – and they were excited by it. They loved it! We were celebrating our great people, and organizations don't always take enough time to do that. It transformed their attitudes. Then what we did was to take the profiles we'd created and used them like 'customer plans' for our employees. So, we said, 'If this is our employee customer and this is how they think, then how must we treat them?' For example, in healthcare, great carers naturally operate from a place of deep respect and integrity, so you need to infuse all communications – your written materials, your website, your conversations – with those qualities so that you attract more of those people and give them the respect and integrity that they themselves need, so they feel valued, want to do great work for you and want to stay with you! One year after we began the project, one of the businesses reported that the turnover rate in the first three months of employment had fallen from 22 per cent to 10.8 per cent. An incredible result.

We've talked about the strategic benefits; what were the operational changes and benefits that were brought about by introducing SBR?

Let me give you some examples to illustrate this.

Starting with the recruitment process itself. Prior to SBR I'd say that all too often people came to work for us in our call centres because they needed a job and we were the only option locally. We were almost saying to people 'Come and get a job', because we constantly needed to re-fill positions. With SBR, our new job ads and descriptions attracted a wider range of people (from different walks of life), but they were 'self-selecting' because, increasingly, only people who could actually spot themselves in the carefully phrased descriptions applied to join us. It became less about 'Come and get a job' and more about 'Do you recognize yourself as the exact type of person we are looking for?' Our conversion rates (ratio of invitation to attendance at interview and ratio from verbal offer to day one induction) went up accordingly, saving us time, money and energy. SBR effectively does a lot of the work for you.

Next, the wider impact of SBR... I was visiting a site fairly recently on an unrelated matter and a manager came to me and said, 'You haven't come to take SBR away have you?' She went on to say that her own work had been transformed by its introduction. Pre-SBR she was spending the majority of her time reacting to problems arising from employees who were unhappy and underperforming at work. You know, we used to actually have to drop the targets for people when they came out of training so that they could have a chance of achieving them. We don't have to do that post-SBR, some now come out of training and beat the targets! For this manager, a whole raft of employee 'problems' had completely fallen away and she was able to fill her working hours with positively focused activities and proactive projects. She was less stressed, enjoying her own job and achieving far more. This is another example of SBR being the nucleus. You might start by recruiting the right people for your frontline roles based on their strengths, but the effects are wide reaching and impact the whole operation for the better.

And for the longer term, I think SBR has a great side effect that perhaps I'm only now fully appreciating. When you do a strengths-based interview you are potentially going to reveal, and name for the interviewee, strengths that they didn't realize they had. Of course the initial idea is that they will be using these in the role you are recruiting for, but what I've witnessed is that they can then transfer those strengths to amazing effect into other roles like training, coaching or mentoring. You give people the awareness and ability to know what other roles will suit their strengths and they will gain more opportunities to flourish within your organization into the future. Great for both them and you.

Why do you think SBR works so well, and are there any downsides?

To be honest, I might struggle to think of any downsides!

Why does it work so well? An Engaging Minds Strengths Profile presents as a very simple set of words, and that makes it brilliant, compelling and easy for your people to understand, connect with and buy into. It's not caught up in organizational rhetoric. It describes your greatest individuals exactly as they are and it immediately makes sense to everyone who sees it. That's because the Engaging Minds strengths profiling process reveals such carefully observed insight into your greatest people. Then discipline and rigour is applied to that insight to create the profile, in words that are clear and easy to understand. Because it's so clear and accurate, when you first present a strengths profile to people they might say, 'It seems a bit too simple, I could have written that.' I did see that happen, and it could be a potential 'downside', or at least a challenge for some people. The profile is so accurate that it feels absolutely like common sense, and it is, but the thing is, you see and recognize the profile only when it's been pointed out to you via a tried-and-tested process that has been incredibly thorough and that you know you can trust. The profiling process creates the profile, gets it in the open for everyone to see. Then you can have your 'aha moment', but you wouldn't have had it without that insightful, disciplined and rigorous methodology.

The reason it succeeded in our business was that we took it seriously. With such a huge change, everyone has to be behind it. And we all were. Everyone was involved. You have to be really rigorous and that involved procedural changes for us. For example, you must select the right people to be trained as strengths interviewers, and to become your in-house trainers of the next set of strengths interviewers. Any culture of just putting names in a hat or 'your turn next' won't work, and you have to realize it and get everyone on board with that. We succeeded because we all had an unshakeable belief in what we were doing and the impact it could have, and we knew the results could be measured and that was exciting. It wasn't about just crossing something off a list or getting a tick in a box. We all became guardians of the SBR process, and we challenged ourselves every single day to make sure we were doing the right thing for what we believed in for our employees and our customers. And SBR works. We went from less than 70 per cent of invited people attending a first interview to over 80 per cent in two years. And by then 95 per cent of people offered a job with us were actually starting work, a rise of 8 per cent. Those numbers, combined with the huge falls in turnover, meant significant improvements in bottom line business results. People can't argue with such an amazing outcome.

What advice would you give to other senior leaders who are thinking of implementing SBR or perhaps to those who haven't yet considered it?

To those who haven't yet considered it, I think they could ask themselves, 'Is my brand being delivered consistently right through our organization into our customer experience, every single time?' If it is then maybe they don't need SBR, but if not I'd say, 'Consider it!'

Once you've decided to go for SBR, you need to see it as the nucleus, in that it will get the great people you want in your organization. But, to deliver the wide-ranging benefits I've described, you need to make sure that once you have those people, you show you value them and always treat them with the respect they deserve. That doesn't necessarily mean financial reward, either. Procedurally, you might have to front up to the 'awfulness' of what you were doing before, and perhaps, in the face of your failings, if you can view things with a touch of humour it can be a saviour in the quest for lasting change... One day I was entering one of our buildings and I saw a big group of people hanging around outside the security gates. It turned out they were a new intake of trainees and they were being made to wait out there until every single one of them had shown up. I mean, if you'd invited people to dinner, would you make them all wait outside the door until all the guests had arrived? It may seem a small thing, but it's basically signalling, 'We don't respect you enough.' And you then expect those people to respect your customers? No. You have to step up to the mark and live your brand in everything you do for your employees as well as for your customers. SBR will help you know how to do that, because it shows you what your great employees value, but you have to follow through if you want success on the levels we achieved. You have to consistently do the right thing for your individuals.

Some might think, 'But how can you do that for 30,000 people?' Well, you can. You just have to keep breaking it down. You start with the SBR profile at the centre, that gives you a great employee with specific needs, you adjust your procedures to value and respect them, they perform brilliantly, you adjust your management procedures to celebrate that and introduce new possibilities, your managers enjoy their work and can achieve more, you adjust your expectations of them and the way you treat them... it keeps going on and on, until it permeates the whole organization. You just keep checking back with yourselves, 'Are we doing the right thing for our employees, our customers, our brand?' And the legacy is that it won't stop, because the whole mindset shifts; your people are doing it and they will keep doing it and training new people to do it. It's like you switch on the light and no one will want to switch it off again.

What do you think HR's role and mindset needs to be in order to successfully implement a positive change such as this one?

It's all about HR taking responsibility for business growth – alongside your people who are on the phones, or the sales managers who are leading the people on the phones – rather than HR thinking that they sit to the side of the frontline business. They don't. They are part of the business, and if they're not part of it they shouldn't be there. They need to think about solutions and they need to be a part of those solutions and not just the department that people get sent to if there's a problem or if they need to be 'processed' in some way. That's the old mindset. The new mindset is HR acting as an integrated part of the business and being accountable for business results.

I think that HR leaders have a responsibility to re-create what HR really means, because, in general terms, what is actually out there now in HR in many organizations is not good enough. It's not that HR is full of bad people or the wrong people, it's that they might be people whose light has not been switched on... yet. Some HR leaders may not even have realized that they can measure what is actually happening and take action. I urge people to be unafraid to look at the facts, because once you have them it's actually not that difficult to do something about them, if you have a tool like SBR.

For us SBR was the vehicle for an incredible shift in the role and value to the business of HR. As group HR Director, I left an HR department that no longer sits alongside the sharp end of the business, but that loves and is excited by being a fully integrated part of it. This is probably the most impactful job I've ever done, but I have been practising for a while! And I'll do it again, because I get such a buzz from watching people get their wings. In the end, it's the people themselves that transform things, not just the HR leader. At Acromas, every single HR employee was given a piece of the jigsaw and had to report on it. They made the changes and got the results. I loved seeing them realize what they were actually capable of doing. It was 'normal HR people' doing incredible stuff. It was wonderful to witness.

Thinking about the wider economy, what opportunity would you say SBR presents for leaders in large organizations?

SBR is about delivering your brand, it's about delivering what your organization stands for. It doesn't matter what your business is. It might be product, service or care in commercial business or in non-commercial organizations as with the NHS. SBR can work for anyone. And I don't see why the senior leaders in any organization wouldn't want to think seriously about that.

Professor Katherine Fenton, OBE, Chief Nurse, University College London Hospitals NHS Foundation Trust, 2010–15

What was your role and how long were you in it?

I was Chief Nurse at University College London Hospitals NHS Foundation Trust until April 2015. I was responsible for the leadership of 3,500 nurses. Aside from my other responsibilities as an Executive Director on the UCLH Board, it was my role as Chief Nurse to ensure that enough nurses with the right skills were developed properly and delivered high quality-care and patient outcomes. UCLH is a member of the Shelford Group, which comprises 10 leading NHS multi-specialty academic healthcare organizations.

How did you first hear about strengths-based recruitment and what inspired you to take the idea to the 10 Chief Nurses of the Shelford Group for their consideration?

In 2013 nursing in the NHS was under huge external criticism concerning poor quality of patient care – this was in the light of the public enquiry into the Mid Staffordshire NHS Foundation Trust.

One of the key roles with great potential to influence the quality of patient care in UK nursing is the ward sister. If you have a great ward sister in place, you get a happy ward, low staff turnover and, most importantly, great outcomes for patients. We intuitively knew who our best ward sisters were and we knew their qualifications and competencies, but we couldn't articulate their strengths, qualities and attributes to be sure we were recruiting the best people for the role. Sally Bibb [the founder of Engaging Minds] told me about the successes of strengths profiling great baristas in Starbucks and domiciliary care workers in the social care sector, and how it was possible to select the right people for the job *every time* by identifying their strengths and recruiting based on those strengths. I began to wonder if we could apply the same principles to our own recruitment process. It was a time when circumstance had handed us the freedom to do something new and radical. We were able to try something quite different, to see if we could really make a difference to the quality of patient care.

How easy was it for you to sell the idea of SBR to the other nine Chief Nurses in the Shelford Group, and beyond?

My Shelford colleagues are bright, they were facing the same challenges as me. SBR is such common sense that actually it was quite easy. Plus, I've got a reasonable track record of coming up with ideas that may take a different approach but work in practice, so it wasn't as hard as I thought it might be. If people like doing something then they are more likely to do it well, and if they don't like doing something it stresses them out and they can't be as effective. It's obvious. So, if we could identify what it is that all 'great ward sisters' love doing and do naturally, there's enormous potential to take stress out and put excellence in. That's inevitably going to impact patient care for the better. We all sensed the possibility. Then, when we started working with the relevant matrons and line managers of the ward sisters we found them saying again and again 'this has got the potential to transform the NHS!' and we really knew we were on to something. With each person we spoke to about it, the prospect of making a real difference to patient care with SBR grew.

What impact is SBR having at the front line?

To be honest it is too early for quantifiable results, but I can say that we have always had some wards that we might describe as 'worry wards' – the ones we know we may need to give extra support to – and of the 12 wards where we have recruited the ward sister using SBR, none of them are 'worry wards'. That, to me, is a great early result.

In terms of reaction from the front line, the ward sisters who have been recruited through the SBR process feel thoroughly investigated, that we really know them by the end of the process. They feel we are certain and they are certain they are the right people for the job, which inspires confidence. There was a bit of push-back from the recruiters at first because it does take more time to recruit a person using SBR, but my view is that it takes far more time and energy to remove someone later who has turned out not to be a good fit. It is essential to train the recruiters properly so that they truly buy into the whole process and believe in it. You can't just 'have a go' at recruiting on strengths, you need to be trained to do it by experts. Then your people will 'get it' and the process will work.

What are your hopes for the strengths profiling of staff nurses and nursing assistants?

Ultimately I hope it's going to mean better outcomes and experience for patients. In terms of nursing assistants, I think it will reduce the number of applications we get – because the new wording of the job description will enable people to easily recognize themselves as potentially good candidates or not – but the people who we do recruit will absolutely know what they are coming into, so we will get lower drop-out rates. We won't waste resources training people who aren't right and eventually leave us. I think we'll end up with happier people on the wards, and though that might be challenging to hear, it's what we need to ensure the best possible experiences for patients, and it is what inevitably comes from having people working on the wards who innately love the job. With respect to staff nurses, I think it will mean that we get the right candidates into the staff nurse training programme and into the profession. Overall, it's the potential to get the right people in place at every level of nursing that's the starting point for delivering the highest quality patient care. That's the goal. In the NHS, the end point of the SBR process is going to be improvement of the patient's experience and outcome – that's why we considered SBR in the first place and that will be the ultimate improvement we want from it.

Why do you think SBR works so well?

I think the Engaging Minds SBR method works because to create the strengths profile for a role, it forensically looks at the people we have already identified as being outstanding. The resulting profile is not a composite of the strengths displayed by the group of outstanding people overall, but it is derived uniquely from the innate qualities/attributes and strengths that all our outstanding people possess. And my view is that for SBR to work, once you have the strengths profile and you are recruiting against it, there can be no compromise, because the strengths cannot be taught or learned, you either have them or you don't. In conversations about the fact that someone possesses 12 out of 13 of the strengths, I would have to say, 'Well, do you want a great ward sister or just an OK one?'

Are there any downsides to SBR as far as you're concerned?

One concern follows on from what I've just said, as you can perhaps imagine. For example, if we've got 50 ward sisters in post and we've got 13 strengths that we know they must have if they are to be great ward sisters, what do we do about the people currently in post who don't exhibit all 13 of the strengths? It's different with the recruitment of nursing assistants or students because we're starting at the beginning there, getting the right people in post from the outset. But where existing staff are concerned, there's a potential challenge to face in moving people into jobs that they are better suited for. That requires strong leadership and honest conversations. On the upside, we've seen that where a ward sister has been performing poorly in post, it has really helped them to see the list of the 13 strengths and realize that they are not inadequate people, they are just not suited to the job; it has made them feel better about themselves and it has been easier for them to move on into a position where they can be 'a round peg in a round hole', which will inevitably be less stressful and more successful for them.

Secondly, for some leaders, there might be an initial concern that you may not find enough people, with the right strengths profile, to fill the available positions; in our case, as we face challenges in recruiting junior nurses, it could feel risky in that context to adopt a new uncompromising approach.

What advice would you give to other senior leaders who are thinking of implementing SBR?

I'd say don't try to take short cuts, do it properly. Take the time to understand SBR because once you understand it, you 'get it' and you can convey the concept to your people so that they 'get it' too. I'd also say it's essential to train your own trainers thoroughly, again no short cuts.

What opportunity would you say SBR presents for the NHS?

I think SBR could transform how we run the NHS, because it really has got the potential to make sure that every single patient gets a great experience. But, for the NHS to benefit fully from it, future NHS leaders who follow me will need to buy into it, have enthusiasm for it and be willing to drive it through fully. Over the months before I retire I'd like to see it gain supporters and momentum so it has a real chance to embed and last. When I've retired and can only influence from the sidelines, I hope that others will carry the flag for SBR and see it through.

What legacy did you want to leave when you retired and how might your pioneering work with SBR play a part in that?

The thing I am most proud of in my career is that all of my deputies – I think there are 22 of them out there now – have become chief nurses themselves. I'm proud of the part I've played in their development and that they are now all working as credible and effective nurse leaders within the UK NHS. I guess where my introducing SBR to the NHS fits in with that is that it would be wonderful if it could help us recruit the right people for all nursing roles *from the start*. If we knew we were choosing the best people to be student nurses every single time it would be amazing. The overall resulting impact on patient care, experience and outcomes would be a tremendous legacy to leave.

Helen Lamont, Nursing and Patient Services Director, Newcastle upon Tyne Hospitals NHS Foundation Trust

What is your role and how long have you been in it?

I'm the Nursing and Patient Services Director and I've been in this role for 6.5 years. I'm responsible for approximately 4,500 of the Trust's total 14,000 strong workforce. My role is extremely diverse, providing professional leadership to approximately 6,000 nursing, midwifery, and support staff, operational management of approximately 20 functions, and over 2,000 staff. I have responsibility for executive leadership in relation to infection prevention and control, safeguarding, and the quality of the patient experience, underpinned by safe patient care. The role of Nursing and Patient Services Director extends beyond that of nursing, requiring a board level contribution across the whole spectrum of the Trust's operations.

What has been your role in implementing SBR?

Along with my peers in the Shelford Group, I was responsible for bringing the issue to the table in Newcastle, and supporting the decision to implement SBR across the Shelford Group and I have overseen its implementation in Newcastle.

Why did you want to implement SBR?

Over the years I've worked with fabulous nurses who didn't do well when they were promoted to a ward sister role. They were ok but not great, their wards didn't have a buzz like the wards that were led by great ward sisters did. So I hoped that introducing SBR would mean we would appoint the right people every time and avoid the situation of having people who weren't right for the job and so weren't performing well.

When you walk onto a ward that is run by a good leader you just know. It's similar to the '15 step challenge', which came from a mother who often had to take her daughter to hospital saying, 'I can tell what kind of care my daughter is going to get within 15 steps of walking onto a ward.' You get a sense of whether a ward is well run – is it tidy, is the patient information up to date, are the staff smart, do the nurses look calm, are they chatting to patients, do they greet you? All of this starts to paint a picture of whether the ward is run by a good leader. Leadership is key.

When I first read the ward sister profile, which was clear and written in plain English, and resonated with me, I immediately wanted to share it with my senior team and engage people in the implementation of SBR.

What have been the benefits?

People are very positive about it. This is a big place and I am not close to day-to-day recruitment but my team tell me that we are making good appointments. We are yet to do a systematic evaluation but feedback from matrons and those involved in recruitment is good. There is a buzz about SBR.

What, if anything, would you have done differently?

I wish I had got more directly involved and perhaps got other disciplines involved early on rather than restrict it just to nursing. This is a big organization and I have an excellent team leading the project but I would have liked to have spent more time on it myself, so that I could see for myself the impact and the difference in recruitment methods.

I think it would also have been worthwhile for the Shelford Group to have agreed some detailed ground rules about roll-out at the start for a common approach to implementation. Having said that, the network of SBR leads across the Shelford Group share their experience and learning formally on a monthly call. They also jointly make recommendations to the Chief Nurse group, which is very useful. This network has become a very positive 'unintended consequence' of the SBR project as they are senior people who are collectively driving SBR forward very well, and developing a good network of peers.

What went particularly well?

The team leading the SBR project in the Trust are excellent. They understand and have an interest in people and what makes them tick. They also have the credibility of having been in clinical roles themselves. One of them had recently turned a ward around, in terms of performance, and she is a person who really gets things done. They are all very hard working and committed. People know them and they know a lot of people in the organization.

The team have done really well at promoting it widely including training people early on in strengths-based interviewing. We also secured funding from Health Education North East for a ward sister to be seconded to lead the project – as a result of that commitment we got good buy-in and support.

We established a steering group that meets regularly and which I am also a part of. It does make a big difference for people to see that there is senior level buy-in for this and that I am personally interested in it. It also helps that the Shelford Group is behind it. Everyone is so busy it would be easy for them to say we're doing recruitment now so let's carry on as we are. The commitment from myself and the others has meant people realize this is important and we're going to keep on doing it.

The ward sister profile was the right place to start. Ward sisters are pivotal and we also needed to get them involved early so that they understood it when we rolled the approach out to staff nurses and healthcare assistants.

What advice would you give to other senior leaders who are thinking of implementing SBR?

I'd say it's a big change and it's important to get buy-in early and plan the implementation well. You have to be confident and brave. We are spending public money on this, so we have to make sure at the outset that we were very confident in the approach. The fact that ten Chief Nurses from the Shelford Group collaborated to implement it gave our Executive Board confidence. The Shelford Group Chief Nurses are a very experienced group who have done a lot of national work. That gave it strength.

What are your hopes for SBR as you roll it out for staff nurses and healthcare assistants?

We all have some wards that don't perform as well as others. Knowing for sure that we are appointing the right people will, hopefully, sort that out. I would also hope for even better patient feedback and an improvement in staff attitude. It's impossible to isolate SBR as the sole cause of such improvements but if it means we can recruit people that we know are right for the job, and those people who are going to deliver great care, that's a great step forward. Our recruiters' feedback on SBR is positive because they can see people for who they really are at the interview. My hope is that we continue as we are with SBR and that in the next few years we will have some good evaluation of its impact, and that it will be well embedded in the Shelford Group organization, and beyond.

Sandra Porter, HR Director, Starbucks UK and Ireland, 2007–11

What was your role when you led the implementation of strengths-based recruitment?

I was the HR Director of Starbucks UK and Ireland.

Why did you want to adopt strengths-based recruitment?

I'm from a psychology background and am really interested in what makes people tick and how that affects their performance. When spending time in stores, it was clear that some baristas weren't comfortable connecting with customers. This is a crucial part of the baristas' role and has a huge impact on the customer experience and how the team work together. I felt that there was a huge opportunity to improve the effectiveness of our recruitment if we could tap into what someone is genuinely good at and has a passion for. Our existing tools asked *could* they do something, but we needed to ask did they *want* to do something? It's so apparent when you see someone who loves what they do. We needed to find a way of finding the right people and we needed a clever approach that would deliver that in a tight time constraint.

We knew from our customer data and from what store managers were telling us that we needed to change the recruitment mindset. I knew I had to respond with something bold that would make a difference, tinkering with what we had was not going to be good enough. And I knew I had to do it fast.

How did you sell the idea of SBR to others?

I had a good relationship with the recruitment team in the USA who agreed that recruitment was a huge key to unlocking improved customer experiences in store. They were interested in the principles of strengths-based recruitment, which aligned closely with our approach to development once on board. They were keen to observe the pilot and review the outcome. I communicated with them closely as we progressed with the pilot and roll out.

I have always pushed at things if I felt they weren't good enough and was probably seen as a bit of a rebel in that way. But I always came back to the customer data. No one could argue with that – the customer experience was paramount in the Starbucks vision.

The senior leadership team trusted me because I talked about what this project could deliver. As first adopters of the strengths-based approach, while it felt like a 'leap of faith', they seemed to buy into it rationally and emotionally. There was genuine buy-in because people could go into the stores and see for themselves first-hand what it was like when we had the right people and what it was like when we didn't. If keeping it the same wasn't the answer, then it needed to change! Talking passionately about the customer experience and setting a challenge created energy and ambition to enable us to progress with the project.

Many of the senior operational managers were really keen for the change and totally bought into the depth of insight that strengths-based recruitment could give them about people. Some were happy to go along with it, while a minority weren't truly engaged at the start as they felt strengths-based recruitment was just another change amongst so many that they had experienced.

Everything rested on the initial pilot. If the customer data had stayed the same but store managers said that strengths-based recruitment was a much better way of doing recruitment then it would have gained interest. But making customers happy *and* making store managers' lives easier meant we were onto a winner.

How did the store managers react to the idea of strengths-based recruitment?

With over 600 store managers we were always going to get those who were keen to try a different way and some who wanted to stick to what they had always done, even if it didn't seem to be working that well for them. When we piloted it they enjoyed the process and realized what they were missing – many were recruiting to fit a slot on their schedule but were forgetting to read the candidates' responses to see and hear what they really enjoyed doing. Some of them had forgotten how to interview candidates properly and had developed some bad habits.

The outcome of the first few training workshops was that they began to think differently. They realized that some of the challenges they were trying to cope with were the result of not having recruited the right people. The challenges their team brought them were their responsibility. They needed to pay more attention to the strengths of candidates to see if they were going to enjoy the environment and feel happy and confident delivering an experience to customers. There was a realization that the barista role doesn't suit everyone and it was their job to find out.

What difference did SBR make?

The difference began to show in the data. You can't attribute all the changes to one thing but the shift was significant and we started to see changes come through in store manager, barista and customer feedback. The 90-day attrition rate began to improve, which was a crucial measure for the pilot. Ninety-day attrition caused store managers significant operational difficulties and wasted a lot of their time.

For many store managers they felt very differently about recruitment. They got it. It was now obvious to them if someone was not right for the job.

What feedback did you get from baristas about strengths-based recruitment?

In the joiner interviews we did (after 30, 60 and 90 days) they told us they appreciated the recruitment process and felt that the store managers were genuinely interested in them. It was the start of a relationship with their store manager, which is *so* important because, as the old saying goes, 'People leave managers, not organizations.' Some people said that they hadn't thought about what they liked doing before their interview with Starbucks and they actually started to give that some thought. The interview helped them think about when they were at their happiest, what made them feel satisfied and which environments they would love... and hate. Before their experience with Starbucks some of them were just looking for any job rather than something that they knew they would be really suited to. After all, an early shift at Starbucks might start at 6am, so it really helps if you like it when you get there.

What was important to you personally about this project?

A driving factor for me was a desire to help the operations team with the problems they were facing and improve our customer experience. It may sound clichéd but it was really important to me personally and the HR team that our work made a real difference to the company and brand. I have never been someone that is keen to roll out a plan of off-the-shelf initiatives, as often the challenges and environments are so different that one size does not fit all.

What, if anything, would you have done differently?

The challenge of starting with a pilot and then a gradual roll-out is that we were limiting how much momentum it could initially gain versus a 'big bang' approach. I would have loved to have got all the store managers in a room together to think about how much better life could be if we cracked the challenge of recruiting people we knew would be great. This may have given the chance to learn from their peers' positive experiences. Peer influence was always so much more impactful than anything I could ever have achieved.

We were also rolling out this project alongside other operational changes. This is always the case within an ambitious company but if I could have had 100 per cent of their time and attention, to learn the approach and practise it, it would have been fantastic.

What advice would you give to other senior leaders who are thinking about implementing SBR?

Firstly, I would say it's about setting an ambitious goal – above whatever might be on a strategy document. Getting the attention of an organization by spelling out what is not good enough anymore and what the future could be. You need ambition and you need to secure money and resources behind it.

Secondly, I'd say find advocates who are going to support the project. We had a great steering group who had credibility, were well connected and were ambitious. One of the key people from operations was a real asset. His business area was working well already so he could help us lead strengths-based recruitment while keeping the wheels on his bus. He spoke from the heart about why the current situation wasn't good enough from his own personal experience. It was obvious he wanted to do something significant and make a difference. He was great at influencing his colleagues during 'water cooler moments'.

Have you any thoughts on why more organizations have not yet adopted strengths-based recruitment?

You have to have courage to make a big change. In some organizations competencies are tied into performance and reward so they might feel a change to strengths-based recruitment is too big a challenge. It's easier in some ways to stick with what you're familiar with even if you know it's not working. I guess the types of organizations that switch to strengths-based recruitment are ones where it's so apparent that there is the opportunity for so much more that they are compelled to change. If there hasn't been a moment of realization of a need for change, then make one!

Samantha Rockey, Head of Leadership Development, SABMiller

What is your role and how long have you been in it?

I'm the Head of Leadership Development for SABMiller and I've been in the role for about three years. I've been at SABMiller, in a range of HR roles, in South Africa and Europe for 16 years.

What is your experience of strengths-based approaches to development?

SABMiller has always had a conscious and deliberate strategy of encouraging and supporting people in the achievement of their full potential. This has played itself out in my own experience where fortunately I have always been in jobs that leverage my strengths. It's indicative of the organizational culture that I have been able to design and shape my roles in ways that mean I can really play to my strengths. It's a special culture and style of leadership that sees the value in maximizing strengths and actively encourages this.

Why do you think the culture has developed into one that empowers people in that way?

It stems back to the early part of the company's global growth. In the 1990s, our Managing Director, Graham Mackay (he later became CEO of SABMiller), introduced a performance management system that focused on people being able to achieve their full potential through meaningful roles, good conversation and a strong development culture. SABMiller has long believed that having stretch in people's jobs creates a high-performance culture. Mackay was a visionary in that he truly believed that if people could be encouraged to bring their whole selves to work, they would achieve great things. Philosophically this approach to development and performance has been part of the company 'DNA' for many years. This is borne out by the shareholder return, which has been over 1,400 per cent in this time, which overshadows the performance of all other companies, except one, on the FTSE.

Our South African heritage might also have made a difference to our remarkable growth, as South Africans are frequently seen as pioneering, resourceful, innovative and entrepreneurial.

What is it like working in such a culture?

Having the ability to create and define one's own destiny is very attractive. Couple that with a high-performance, high-engagement culture and you end up creating an environment where focused and energetic people tend to thrive. As an example, we have recruited senior people from top FMCGs and one of the main reasons they cite for wanting to work for SABMiller is the opportunity to be genuinely empowered. We've always recruited bright, performance-oriented people. Put people like this in a strengths-based culture of genuine empowerment and self-management and it leads to fantastic performance and business growth. This in turn means that people get growth opportunities that they wouldn't otherwise have.

What specifically has SABMiller done to develop a leadership approach and style that focuses on strengths?

SABMiller has over the years introduced a number of approaches and programmes that are underpinned by a strengths philosophy. Firstly we encourage our leaders to create opportunities for people to talk about where they get their energy and how their job might support this. For example, we know from neuroscience that as human beings we are hard-wired to focus on the negative – this is a survival mechanism so that we are able to perceive problems and threats. As a company, we know how important it is to actively encourage people to focus on the positive. This balances the natural instinct to focus on the negative. You are only able to see the true picture when one perceives both the negative and the positive.

We do look at where development needs to happen – that's important and cannot be ignored. However, we strike the balance by putting a great deal of emphasis on leveraging strengths. It's been very liberating for people. It's energizing and motivating for them to channel their energy into their strengths and passion.

Along with other leadership philosophies, our global leadership development programmes are underpinned by a strengths approach. For example, we have seen how the focus on strengths-based development has had an impact on graduate trainees, who have typically been used to a mindset of desperately trying to close gaps in order to get ahead. People now have a robust way of development that takes serious and proper account of their strengths. It's incredibly motivating for them as well as an effective way to engage your people.

Our flagship managing directors (MDs) programme sets a tone of exploring opportunities and entrepreneurial thinking. We also encourage our MDs to experiment with new behaviours and ways of working. This exploratory and experimental development approach seeks to help people direct their energy in a way that is enabling.

Ten years ago we introduced Appreciative Inquiry (AI) into our South African business. More recently, in our Latin American business, we introduced AI as part of a programme that focuses on the conversations that people have with each other in the business. The programme in Latin America specifically teaches people to have meaningful, positive conversations. This way of relationship building is yielding huge benefits to the business as well as to individuals.

The underpinning goal of our people management approach is for each person to become their best self at work. This means that individuals need to have self-awareness (understanding both strengths and weaknesses), a strong performance ethos and line managers who facilitate their individual growth. Inherent is a relationship orientation that we believe is core to successful business performance. It is important to point out that self-awareness is the cornerstone of development and as such people will have a balanced view of both their strengths and development areas. It is only by understanding both equally that true development can take place.

SABMiller have uniquely designed a performance management process that includes a structured one-on-one conversation every four to six weeks. We believe that if you get this coaching conversation right, everything else will follow. These conversations build trust and empathy and release a desire to perform well.

What benefits do you think your approach to development brings to the organization?

We don't have a huge number of square pegs in round holes in SABMiller because we recruit well and then encourage people to shape their jobs.

The company has always been encouraging of diversity of character. We have a lot of amazing people who are characterful and can be who they are. This is very powerful and it makes for an interesting and enlivening place to work. I think that one of the greatest strengths of the business is that there is a tolerance for different approaches and styles where people can and do hold different views but equally an understanding that we are a strongly performance-oriented business.

We don't have a singular approach to what is a good leadership style – a consistent set of leadership behaviours, yes – but a specific leadership style, no. This is important as organizations can often get hoodwinked into believing that emulating the MD's style will lead to success. Research into diversity of styles shows just how rich a culture can be built where people are able to 'be yourself more… with more skill', to quote Goffee and Jones.

What would your advice be to senior leaders who are considering adopting a strengths-based approach?

Commercially it makes sense to release people's potential and energy. To be at their best, people need to feel valued for who they are and what they bring.

As I've said, it's about the power of the conversation too. When the conversation is more oriented toward the positive, people can share their thoughts and ideas freely and this releases productive energy and is motivating. I believe strongly that our culture of regular one-on-ones has contributed enormously to high-quality conversations and clarity of direction. If the interaction between line manager and employee is robust and positive, the rest will follow.

What are you most proud of in terms of your individual contribution to developing the strengths-based culture?

Initially, the work that I did in the development space felt a bit counter-cultural. As a company we have great strength in logical, quantitative-based thinking. However, introducing new ways of approaching development seems to have taken hold and all of our leadership development has a strong strengths approach at its core. Strengths approaches don't initially seem to sit well in cultures where there is an initial instinct to identify gaps through logic and reasoning. But there is enough evidence to suggest that both approaches can co-habitat well together and that focusing on strengths is a critical counterbalance.

Which of your own strengths has contributed to this success?

I believe very strongly in the philosophy of individuals reaching their full potential and I haven't veered from that. It's taken courage sometimes as I've had to swim against the tide. I am people oriented and spend a lot of time building relationships and in conversation with people from across the business. This has enabled me to understand various perspectives, which in turn has helped me craft meaningful interventions. I've also had fantastic managers who have 'got me' and given me the space to do what I do well. It's probably been a combination of my willingness to take the counter-cultural view and having the support with that from some wonderful bosses.

What are you known for?

I think probably two things – one, having deep leadership development design expertise that focuses on facilitating the critical conversations the organization and individual needs to progress; and two, an insatiable curiosity for discovering/exploring new ideas/thinkers.

What legacy would you like to leave?

I would like the leaders I have worked with to be equipped to deal with the increasingly complex environment that we work in and to have a positive impact on the people around them. I would like the leadership development work we have done here to have contributed significantly to making our business a place where people thrive.

Eva Sage-Gavin, Executive Vice President of Human Resources and Corporate Affairs, Gap Inc, 2003–14

What is your background?

Over a 30-plus corporate business year career, I have been fortunate enough to have worked with some of the most admired companies in the world. Most recently, I was Executive Vice President of Human Resources and Corporate Affairs for Gap Inc for 11 years. Prior to that I held senior HR roles at Sun Microsystems, the Walt Disney Company, PepsiCo and Xerox.

I'm now serving on boards and as a senior advisor, including Vice Chair of the Skills for America's Future Advisory Board, a Director on the TalentSky Board and as a Senior Advisor to the Boston Consulting Group and the G100 Talent Consortium.

What is your own personal experience of applying strengths to career choices?

My strengths journey began when I was about 16 years old. I was blessed to have incredible mentors, including my mother and multiple high-school teachers. I'm not sure that the concept of 'strengths-based development' as we know it today existed back then, but my mentors intuitively knew how to help me tap into what I loved and was passionate about. I remember taking a career interest test and one of the potential matches the assessment highlighted was the field of 'personnel', as it was called back then (today it is known as human resources). My mother encouraged me to apply for university and study this new field in preparation for a career in business. As a child from a single-parent family of very modest means, I was astonished and delighted when Cornell University accepted me and offered financial aid to help me complete my degree in industrial and labour relations. I see now that my mother, who was a first grade teacher, was very advanced in her thinking and I benefited immensely from her optimism. Her focus on strengths and positivity built my confidence to take risks. I often reflect that it was her encouragement to follow my passions that led me to where I am today.

When did you first implement a strengths approach in business?

When I was at Gap Inc I read Marcus Buckingham and Donald O Clifton's book *Now Discover Your Strengths*. I was impressed and believed that focusing on a strengths-based culture was something that would be right for our business. In addition to Buckingham's work, we also worked with other organizations and partners who were expert in strengths-based assessments. We were focused on the power of leveraging strengths for talent development and selection. My team had also been doing a study on Millennial expectations and motivation and we were very proud to have a workforce that was more than 70 per cent female and diverse. We felt that having such a unique workforce was a great asset and we wanted to understand what it would take to better engage and motivate them. We found that the things that mattered to Millennials included having a clear purpose, receiving ongoing feedback and making contributions with a positive impact. Our vision was that people could bring their 'whole selves' to work, including what they cared about personally and professionally. This focus on strengths went from being a personal passion of mine to a global and robust set of HR strategic initiatives.

I knew that the positivity engendered by leveraging your strengths gets one further than just working on your development areas. One summer we tried a reverse learning experiment with our summer interns. We tapped into their passions and strengths by getting them actively involved in testing the relevancy of our people strategies to Millennials. We showed them our HR strategic plan and asked, 'You're our interns and target customers, what should we do differently?'

The interns suggested a whole range of ideas that we implemented, including contemporizing our social media approach. The idea of leveraging strengths to do great things was natural to our Millennials and an obvious concept to them. We leveraged their energy and ideas to change our strategy and take a different and much more impactful direction.

The strengths-based approach worked so well at Gap Inc because it was a natural fit with the culture. Employees welcomed it and we were ready and willing to re-invent our strategies. We succeeded by using a 'head, heart and hands' approach to roll it out globally. Using our 'heads' was about providing thought leadership, our 'hearts' was about believing in and living our values and our 'hands' was committing time, money and focus to implement our strengths-based goals.

After such an encouraging experience at Gap Inc, I am now leveraging the strengths approach in a much broader sense in my involvement with initiatives such as Skills for America's Future at the Aspen Institute. When you bring the concept of strengths into workplace development, you can activate a force field of positive change and performance. It's powerful and I am pleased to see that having implemented innovative approaches in business, many of the same concepts applied to government, policy and non-profit partnerships are equally effective.

In what ways do you think a strengths approach and tapping into people's passions is important in today's world?

I am often invited to speak globally on the topic of how to unleash and engage people's strengths. The outpouring of interest is amazing. While we have all sorts of global challenges in our post-9/11 world including climate change, employment imbalance and terrorism, people want to make a difference and feel it's time to act. They feel liberated to bring their strengths and gifts to the challenges they care about.

What do you think it takes for business leaders to introduce big change in their organizations, such as implementing a strengths-based approach?

Courage! Growing up I was encouraged to take risks and push for the things that I believed in. As a child of 12 years old in the 1970s, I challenged an education system that didn't allow girls to take woodwork and metalwork classes. Supported by my mother, I persuaded the school to allow me into those classes and that wasn't easy! After I successfully completed both classes, the school system subsequently opened up metalwork, woodwork and home economics classes to both genders.

I realized early on that I wanted to be a pioneer for positive change. Stemming from those early years, I tried to create new pathways and bring others with me. From my early years challenging school curriculum, to working as a woman in technology in the 1980s, I tried to show that there were new and different ways to get things done successfully. Ultimately, focusing on who a person is and what they bring, rather than on stereotypes, is a cornerstone of a true strengths-based approach.

What potential do you think strengths-based approaches have in the future to support the younger generation?

We know that, globally, the Millennial and Generation Z generations are some of the most anxious. They face pressure in school, in sports, in social settings and experience a lot of anxiety just to be considered for a great education and good job. We've seen some tragic examples of what pressure can do to young men and women, including burn out and workplace illness, which is all too common.

At a global level they are also anxious about societal issues like climate change, poverty and terrorism. Today we have tools and resources to support individuals to understand what strengths they can bring to make a difference in their lives personally and to tackle bigger societal issues. That's why I focus on the power of positive energy and strengths.

The movie *The Intern*, which was recently released, is a great example of how much someone in their seventies (Ben, played by Robert De Niro) can offer someone much younger (Jules, played by Anne Hathaway) new ways to be successful by nurturing their strengths. In the movie, Jules's life is crazy at work and at home and it's clear that she gains so much from Ben's wisdom and support. Young people like Jules are our future leaders in business and society. The baby boomer generation can offer so much by understanding and leveraging our own gifts and strengths. This is meaningful to me personally and a call to action for my 2.0 career. At this stage in my life, it is very affirming to be welcomed as a thought-leader for very different communities, from students in their 20s, to boards of directors, to non-profit and government partners. By leveraging complementary strengths and innovative problem solving, we have discovered wonderful synergies together that drive positive change.

Professor Janice Sigsworth, Director of Nursing, Imperial College Healthcare NHS Trust

What is your role and how long have you been in it?

I'm the Director of Nursing at Imperial College Healthcare Trust and have been in this role for seven years.

What has been your role in implementing SBR?

I am one of the Shelford Group Chief Nurses and was extremely supportive of the Shelford Group adopting SBR. For Imperial, I have taken the lead on SBR for the nursing, midwifery and healthcare workforce.

I have promoted the approach, got the CEO and executive to sign up by explaining to them the reason we're adopting it and the value it will add. I have championed it and stuck to my guns all the way through. And I have hung on in there when some people didn't want to use it.

Why did you want to adopt SBR at Imperial?

I could see the potential in recruiting people who had innate strengths in caring and compassion. I hoped that everyone we employed would be the sort of people who would go the extra mile for their patients and patients' families. I felt that we had been employing people who were competent but I was not confident that every single one was dealing with our patients in a personal and individualized way that was right for them (the patients).

When I first heard about SBR it struck a chord. In my own clinical practice I always tried to recruit people who shared my approach of giving good care even if you had to go outside the box to do it. I thought SBR would deliver that.

SBR was received enthusiastically at Imperial. I had four divisional nurses who felt the same as I did about it and understood it. It felt completely the right thing to do.

What have been the strategic and organizational benefits of implementing SBR?

I feel we have a strong set of ward sisters in place now. We have seen the patients' experience of care improve, as measured by the National Patient Survey. For five to six years we were behind our peer teaching hospital Trusts, now we're not. It's because we've now got ward leaders who are able to lead in a way that means the patient experience is good. Some of our consultants have also commented on what tremendous senior nurses we have.

When we roll SBR out for Band 5 Staff Nurses and Band 2 Nursing Assistants I hope that we will be able to recruit and retain more people who are aligned to the organization's philosophy and ethos, who are more compassionate and efficient. If we can get recruitment right first time it will improve the quality of care and save time in the long run.

The two divisional nurse directors of the two largest divisions in the Trust took to SBR very quickly. One took it global very early on. They have all the strengths you'd want from someone leading a change. They were positive and desperate to use SBR. They made a success of it and from there it took on a momentum of its own. It felt quite liberating as it's helped us to clearly describe the kind of nurses we're looking for. It's been a talking point around the subject of what makes a great nurse. People feel valued as a result.

Have there been any downsides of SBR as far as you're concerned?

There was some anxiety at first as some staff were worried about what would happen if they didn't match up to the profiles. There has also been some worry because SBR is a longer process than the one we had. But I'm not worried about that – if we get great people it's worth it. You have to stand firm on the approach if you want to see the difference it makes.

What, if anything, would you have done differently?

We've had quite a lot of changes in senior HR leaders since we introduced SBR and the transitions have slowed us down a bit. So it's taken longer than I wanted but there's not much we could have done about this.

What advice would you give to other senior leaders who are thinking about implementing SBR?

In the NHS I'd say select a strong and consistent lead who straddles nursing and HR. Make sure your project plan is clear and that all the key people are signed up.

What legacy do you hope SBR will leave?

When I first heard about the approach I felt it would go a long way to address criticisms nationally around lack of compassion in nurses. Nursing is more than just a job. Not everyone is suited to it. It's the innate strengths that make a brilliant nurse. This approach could go a long way to address shortcomings in nursing and make sure we get the right people in the NHS.

References

Buckingham, M and Clifton, DO (2011) *Now Discover Your Strengths*, The Free Press, New York

Goffee, R and Jones, G (2006) *Why Should Anyone Be Led By You? What it takes to be an authentic leader*, Harvard Business School Press, Cambridge, MA

Interviews with managers and recruiters

10

The interviews with recruiters and managers who have been involved in the day-to-day implementation of strengths-based recruitment bring an understanding of what it's like to be working on the ground to make it happen as well as the benefits, challenges and results they have seen. They also share their practical advice and tips. These six people are in roles where they have led and championed the introduction of strengths into their organizations.

Karen Coles, Nurse Staffing Review Project Lead, Newcastle upon Tyne Hospitals NHS Foundation Trust

What is your role and how long have you been in it?

I'm on a secondment as the Nurse Staffing Review Project Lead, which is in its third year. This role was set up in advance of the Francis Report's publication to review staffing levels, and skill mix across the Trust.

What has been your role in implementing SBR?

I attended the first strengths-based interviewing training and 'train the trainer' with my colleague in October 2013. We then became part of the Trust SBR Steering Group, which consisted of us, the nursing and patient services director, director of human resources, and the deputy director of nursing and patient services Royal Victoria Infirmary (RVI) who is the Trust lead for SBR. This group has since expanded in membership to include directorate managers and matrons.

As trainers, my colleague and I initially arranged four training sessions to include all staff who are involved with Band 7 interviews. This included ward sisters, human resources officers, the senior HR manager, the deputy directors of nursing and head of midwifery. We wanted to train as many people as possible in anticipation of the roll out of SBR for staff nurses and healthcare assistants. The early training of so many people was great as it spread the word and helped get buy-in. My role was also to provide information, advice and guidance to those interviewing.

The steering group also made a business case for funding for a project manager role to support the roll out and evaluation. This was successful and we appointed the project manager on a year's secondment and she has created a project plan for the roll out. She has also started working on evaluation including getting feedback from interviewers and interviewees.

What worked well in implementing SBR?

Training over 80 people initially in strengths-based interviewing worked well to spread the word quickly and get buy-in, therefore hopefully making roll out of SBR for larger numbers of staff nurses and healthcare assistants easier.

It was really useful to have senior people like heads of nursing and the senior HR manager as delegates in the training. It helped that they got first-hand experience of the strengths interviewing and demonstrated the Trust's commitment to SBR.

What have been the benefits to the organization?

It's a bit too early to quantify the benefits as it takes a while for a ward sister to settle into their role and get the ward as they want it. But we now have better insight at interview whether a person is going to be right for the job. You really get to know the person. Matrons love the process because they feel that they really get to know people at the interview. It helps them make the right decision.

For interviewees who are no good at doing PowerPoint presentations or don't interview well, it's a much better process because the real person comes through in a strengths interview. People who are definitely right for the role flourish in a strengths interview, whereas some of them just didn't come across well in the previous style of interviewing. For people who don't fit the profile I have found that they recognize themselves during the strengths interview that they don't have the strengths. In the past sometimes the only feedback that was possible to offer them was that there was a better candidate on the day. Now we can give them feedback about their strengths. Selection panels now have much more powerful information about candidates.

We've appointed about 34 ward sisters using SBR, most of those quite recently, so it will take a while to really know what the operational benefits are. When we implement it fully for staff nurses and healthcare assistants we will get quicker feedback on the impact because there are greater numbers and it's easier to assess their success in their roles.

What, if anything, would you do differently?

It would have been nice if there had been Trusts that had implemented SBR before us, but we were the first so we didn't have any to learn from. So it took us time to work out how we were going to implement it in a way that worked well for us. I would advise others who are thinking of implementing SBR to go and talk to other Trusts that have implemented it and have experience in SBR.

I would perhaps have had a broader range of people to train in the early training sessions so that the trainees could see a mix of people with different experience and examples.

What advice would you give to others who are thinking of implementing SBR?

I would say talk to people about it, as many as you can from a broad range of areas before you start. Then communicate with key people in the Trust, as you need buy-in from the people who are going to use SBR. If you include key staff and keep them up to date and support them with the process, you take them with you. We presented at the Matrons and Clinical Leaders Forum to explain SBR, answer any questions and provide reassurance. Also, it's useful to get senior people to sit in on interviews if they haven't done the training so that they can see how it works. I think the technique is so different it helps to understand SBR by observing it in action.

What are your hopes and dreams for the Trust?

It's for a workforce who are using all of their strengths equally and are in the right job, providing patients with the best care and not getting burnt out.

It would be nice for universities to introduce it for the selection of student nurses. That will be a big change, but we've got good links with the local university and are sharing our experiences of SBR with them.

Nick Corbo, Director of Customer Experience and Agent Development, Saga

What is your role and how long have you been in it?

I am the Director of Customer Experience and Agent Development. I've been in the role three years.

What has been your role in implementing strengths-based recruitment?

To begin with my role was to help sell it internally, gain momentum and help persuade any doubters and people who were worried and saying, 'This sounds very different.' I helped get people mobilized, shape the project and supported with implementation. To some extent it was internal sales of the project. I was well placed to do this because of my knowledge of the business, my strong operational background and the relationships I had. It helped that I was not from HR because sometimes people wonder whether HR really understand the operational issues well enough, whereas I have 20 years' operational experience in the company. If I say something's a really good idea operations people generally listen.

I went out on a roadshow talking to people about what SBR is and how it would work for Saga, and asked them for their feedback. Once we had started using SBR, I gave senior management early feedback including performance management data when it started to come through.

What made you decide that SBR was the right thing for Saga?

It made sense when Engaging Minds talked about the principle of picking the right people. I did find it frustrating that I wanted to know exactly how it worked from the start. But when I went on the strengths-based interviewing training it all fell into place. The training brought it all home very quickly. It was like it all clicked. It was good that the concept appealed to our logic first, ie you model your best people to find out their 'DNA'. Then the actual experience of the training made me completely jump onboard and know it was the right thing for us. A lot of people have the same experience on the training when they see the interviewing in action. If there are any sceptics I say to them, 'go on the training and then come back and tell me it doesn't work!'

Why did the company want to introduce SBR?

Turnover was where it originated. Frankly, we were using competency-based recruitment and we had a problem getting people to stick. The data screamed out to us that we were not bringing in the right people. They weren't enjoying it, they were saying it wasn't their kind of job and they weren't happy. We just were not selecting the right candidates.

So we knew something was wrong but we didn't know the answer. As soon as we did an interrogation of the data what stood out was the number of leavers with short service. Attrition and cost was the driver. We are a strongly performance-driven culture and improving performance was the strategic driver behind introducing SBR.

What have been the strategic benefits to the organization of implementing SBR?

I'll start with the operational benefits. Historically, new recruits were reluctant to go live and take calls. Strengths-based recruits were asking if they could take live calls and that was unheard of. The trainers were saying they are brilliant because they are the right people and have the innate ability to talk to customers. We got that feedback from the trainers early on. I spoke to one of our teams and told them they would be able to spot which were the SBR teams and which weren't. And they said they could and they saw the difference immediately. That early positive feedback helped build momentum.

Strategic benefits are about cost savings because of the reduction in attrition. Also, the service we are providing to the customers has improved because the SBR recruits connect well and are naturals with our customers.

What has implementation and embedding of SBR been like?

I was the custodian of it, the internal promoter and guardian of its integrity. Sometimes I had to fight my corner because if something started to go wrong with recruitment and training people sometimes said, 'Is SBR still working?' I'd tell them, 'You don't want to lose SBR.' A better question to ask is, 'Are we doing it right?'

One of the issues was that we had so much success with SBR that some people felt that SBR was the solution to all our problems. I had to say to people that they needed to be realistic. Some people will still leave during induction and the recruitment team will make mistakes sometimes. If you do it properly, though, the chances of making mistakes are less. With competency-based recruitment there was a 50/50 chance that someone would be right and it could take you a while to realize that they weren't. With SBR you see it very quickly, there aren't many shades of grey because we have the profiles, so we know. Because we had so much success so early it raised expectations so high. I had to spend time saying to people that there are still going to be people who don't stay. For a while the expectation was that everyone would be perfect.

You've done a number of things beyond SBR to build Saga as a strengths-based organization. Can you tell me about them?

In terms of going beyond SBR, we have now also looked at strengths-based development and our induction programme. We have the profiles so we know what people are like and I wanted to make sure their induction experience matched who they are. The one bit I would say we still need to do more on is their experience when they leave their induction training. We need to think more about how we manage, reward and incentivize them.

SBR is a complete mindset shift, it's not just a different way of recruiting. And these are different kinds of people with a different outlook and different motivators. We have to think differently and treat them right. We're recruiting people now who have engaging conversations with customers. We need to trust them and let them be who they are. It's important for people to be allowed to be authentic. We recruited them because we thought they were the right person so we should say to them, 'Go be you!' The right people don't want straitjackets. It's not just about SBR but also about how you manage large groups of people.

What, if anything do you wish you had done differently?

I would have invested the time to get more senior people trained quickly. Because once you go on the programme you become an advocate. It answers all the questions that senior operations people have. Once the senior person experienced the strengths-based interviewing training they bought into the concept immediately.

Thinking about the wider economy, what opportunity would you say SBR presents for leaders in large organizations?

In an area where there is high unemployment, low educational standards and an awful reputation we have managed to recruit some fantastic people. Some people never thought that was possible. But if you actually look at people's strengths it cuts across all walks of life. People who never thought they would be able to make a career for themselves realize that they can. Strengths is an opportunity because it unlocks people's potential.

It reminds me of when I was younger and I was going for an interview for a management training scheme. The guy gave me a big sheet of paper and asked me to write down all my significant achievements on the paper, for example winning a sack race and anything else that I considered significant. He then asked me, 'What does that tell you about you?' Focusing on your strengths gives you confidence. You can see the physical changes in people. It's amazing.

Charlotte Henderson, former Team Leader, financial services business

What was your role when you were involved in SBR?

I was a Team Manager.

What was your role in implementing SBR?

I was one of the first in the company to be trained as a trainer and I was an SBR recruiter. Initially I had to train all the managers in strengths-based interviewing because at the time we had to recruit 200 staff. When I did the training I remember thinking, 'Oh my god, I totally understand it.' It made so much sense to me. I could see the passion and drive in someone's face when they were talking about what they loved at work. I had seen that before in my family, my son and my friends but I just didn't understand what it meant. I could think back to conversations I'd had with people and understand, with hindsight, what it was I was seeing.

Why did the company implement SBR?

It was because of our high attrition rates. We were losing lots of people, including in the early stages of their induction training. We'd been aware of the problem for a while – a lot of people were leaving and some were staying but were unhappy. It had become the norm and it wasn't until we were introduced to SBR that we thought something could be done.

What was it like for you being involved in SBR?

I loved it! At the interviews you really get involved with the interviewees in that you see people come alive. You see the real person come through. They can't fake it. It doesn't feel like an interview, it feels like a conversation where someone is telling you about themselves and their lives. You really get to know the person in a way we never did with our competency interviewing.

We had very good feedback from joiners – they loved it and were very positive. A few times they said that they had gone home and told their partners about it and that it didn't feel like an interview and it felt like the interviewer really got to know them. They sometimes said they hadn't realized they were asked 16 questions as the interview just flowed so easily.

The people who we rejected were fine, too, because it's easy to explain to them why they weren't a good fit for the job. Because I knew all the different strengths profiles I started to be able to identify which type of other role might suit them. So we were helping people into careers that they had not previously even thought about for themselves.

What were the strategic benefits to the organization of implementing SBR?

Attrition improved greatly. We also didn't lose many people during induction training. They 'got' what customer service was and we didn't have to train them on how to listen to customers because it was natural to them. People enjoyed themselves in their jobs. They were better performers and they were doing better than people who had been there two or three years because they were thriving in what they were doing.

You could see the difference straight away. They were enjoying what they were doing. If you hired, say, seven new people in a team of 10, the others sometimes realized that the job wasn't right for them and left. Others upped their game and became energized because the SBR recruits' positive attitude was infectious. So others who maybe previously hadn't enjoyed their job started enjoying it.

The atmosphere changed for the better and customer service improved. Some of the SBR recruits had no previous contact centre experience but they picked it up really quickly. And they were really listening to the customers. Lots of customer commendations started coming through.

Senior management was really impressed because SBR delivered. There was less attrition and we were saving money because of that. And customer service and quality scores were so much better for the SBR recruits.

What were the benefits to you as a manager?

As a manager, walking away from my day-to-day work was so much better because I could see my people were energized. I didn't have to spend a lot of my time on performance management and disciplinaries. I was coaching and developing people instead. So it saved a lot of my time. I could have a much better quality of conversation with people because I knew them better and knew what motivated them.

I also changed the conversations I had with people who didn't seem to be right for their jobs. I asked them, 'Do you love what you do?', 'Is this the right job for you?' I helped them to understand themselves more.

I drew up a matrix of all my team and their different strengths. I tried to help them play to their strengths. I knew what motivated them now because of the profiles so was able to keep them very motivated. The profile gave us an understanding of the people. It was quite obvious once I had the profile. It was as if in your head you have a character and you understand them. You tune in with people because you 'get' them and can connect with them. And you become a great leader because you're leading and developing them in the right way.

What, if anything, would you have done differently?

I would have changed the induction training quicker as it was based on people having previous contact centre experience. So we needed to spend more time explaining why we did things like we did in a regulated environment because they wouldn't automatically know that.

What advice would you give senior leaders about implementing SBR?

Obviously to do it! To some companies it might feel like a risk as it is something new and they wonder whether the investment will pay off. But I would say to them, take that risk. If you are bothered about service, competency-based interviewing won't give you the right people to deliver great customer service but SBR will.

If they are not sure I'd say do the strengths-based interviewing training course and then decide. I had to train senior people including the head of the site I worked on. He was worried at first because he thought people would be able to fake the interview, but he realized when he did the training that they couldn't. People sometimes think of SBR in the same bucket as personality testing and they need to realize it's not the same thing. The training programme makes it click.

Ninety per cent of the people became advocates. I can't stress enough how transformational it is and I want to introduce it into my new company.

How has SBR affected you personally?

I believe that it's because I know my strengths that I have been promoted so quickly. It's because of what I know about strengths and how to tune into people and play to their strengths. Before I didn't know what my career looked like ahead. Now I know what to do, I know what I want my career to be like. I've got the drive. It changes you as a person because you learn so much about yourself and other people.

What has it been like being interviewed about your experience of SBR?

I'm so alive. I feel so energized. It's one of the only things in my entire career that I believe in 100 per cent. I have no doubts whatsoever. I see it in my day-to-day life and it makes so much sense. My son is 16 and if I hadn't known about SBR I would not have thought of guiding him to pick his options based on what he really loves doing and enjoys. He is doing engineering now and loves it and is flying. If I hadn't got involved in SBR he definitely wouldn't have gone down that road. I would have guided him to do what I thought he 'should' do.

Debbie Hutchinson, Assistant Director of Nursing, King's College Hospital NHS Foundation Trust

What is your role and how long have you been in it?

I am one of the four Assistant Directors of Nursing at King's College Hospital NHS Foundation Trust. I was appointed into this role two years ago and have been at King's for a long time.

What has been your role in implementing SBR?

Each of the assistant directors of nursing has a particular remit. Part of mine is responsibility for all matters relating to the nursing workforce. As with other NHS Trusts there is a huge challenge with recruitment and getting enough of the right people. Geraldine Walters, the Director of Nursing, asked me to lead on SBR because she knew I was very interested it in and we had talked a lot over the years about recruitment being about quality as well as quantity. It's a false economy if you recruit enough people but they are the wrong ones. I have seen a lot of good practice as well as complaints. Seeing examples of bad practice has always made me wonder why we get selection really right at times and why, at other times, we can get it wrong. And what is it about people (across all bands) who are really good and very happy in their work? And what makes others not?

When I started learning about strengths-based recruitment and saw the Band 7 Ward Sister profile I realized that the elements it described are what we had not been able to pinpoint before and they are the things that people can't be taught. It helped us to understand why some wards struggle and others don't.

Why did King's decide to implement SBR?

Geraldine Walters, our Director of Nursing, believed in it. We wanted the framework that SBR has now given us to pinpoint what made someone really good at their job so that we can be sure we are making the right appointments. It's about the quality of patient care.

Our overall commitment to maintaining patient safety, giving patients a high quality experience and good clinical outcomes is key. Geraldine won't budge on quality. She is consistent with that. Her belief that SBR can support our drive for quality was key to the decision to implement it.

Personally I believe in the tool. I think it's the right thing to do if we are to address quality issues. We need patients to trust us when they come into hospital, and on occasion we have lost that trust.

In terms of implementation, what do you think you have done well?

Geraldine chose two people to lead on it who were passionate about it and who she thought would roll it out well – myself and my colleague Matt Richards, who is a Senior Nurse with a background in recruitment. We both believe in it and we have complementary styles and experience. I was new in post so had the space that operational people don't get to think through how to implement this well.

We developed a good relationship with Engaging Minds, who were approachable, open and helped us to answer questions and concerns. Also, it has helped us to connect with the SBR Lead at Guy's and St Thomas' as they are a similar hospital and started implementing SBR at the same time. We have been able to share ideas and bounce things off one another.

A big part of what we have done is engaged others with SBR. Matt and I chose people initially for the training who we thought we could rely on to see the benefits of SBR and spread the word. It was valuable for me to hear about case studies from other organizations outside the NHS that had implemented SBR. It helped me to understand how it worked in practice so that we could learn from that. I talked to people outside the NHS who had used it and they said what a difference it had made. This background helped me talk to colleagues about it and answer their questions. I spent a lot of time doing that and getting people onboard.

You need perseverance because we are juggling so many things all the time. It's tough in healthcare and we have to think short term about results for the patients. But we also need to think long term and commit the time to the SBR training for it to bring us the benefits we need from it. Geraldine is supportive and behind us all the time with this as it's so important for the long term.

What have been the benefits of SBR?

Seeing the strengths in the profiles. Now we know exactly why the really good people are good.

We have not yet done the formal evaluation. Most people have been won over, though. When we started out with SBR for Band 7 Ward Sisters some people had doubts and wondered whether this was a trend that would come and go. But most have been won over because they can see the benefits.

What, if anything would you have done differently?

If money were no object I would have appointed a full-time coordinator for SBR. As we roll it out to staff nurses and nursing assistants that would be helpful.

We plan to do a formal evaluation as well as auditing for quality assurance. Our recruitment team are very organized so the gatekeeping and process side will become a routine part of how we do things.

What advice would you give to others who are thinking of implementing SBR?

It requires long-term commitment. People need to trust the leaders that they wouldn't be asking them to change unless there was a real benefit. Sometimes you need to use your powers of persuasion to get people onboard. Have a plan and persevere.

Initially it can feel slightly risky not to be asking questions that you are used to asking in the interview. It does take a bit of courage to not revert back to what you are used to.

Keith Jones, Recruitment and Management Information Manager, financial services company

What is your role and how long have you been in it?

I am a Recruitment and Management Information Manager in the financial services sector. I have been in the role for six years.

What has been your role in implementing SBR?

I was in the first group to undertake strengths-based interviewing and 'train the trainer' in 2012. I became the in-house expert and rolled out the SBI training for team managers. I developed into the natural leader for implementation of SBR and have been an informal advisor for the company's overall implementation of SBR. Being introduced to SBR was a lightbulb moment for me. I really saw the potential of the approach and found it exciting so took it on as my own. This involved explaining the approach to people, making sure that colleagues were being compliant in the way they did the strengths interviews, helping colleagues on other sites to implement it well and getting support and buy-in.

SBR has made me see things from a different perspective generally, not just related to recruitment. I tend to look at people differently now and I can help them more. For example, sometimes people have an idea of what job would be their natural progression but I can see that it would not be a good fit for them. Now I know about strengths I can have a really useful discussion with them and help them develop their career on a road that is right for them.

Why did the company implement SBR?

Our attrition rates were higher than we wanted them to be. The 0–3 months high turnover rate told us that something was fundamentally wrong with the process we were using. I asked myself why people were ticking the boxes in the interview but turned out not to be right for the job. Also, we'd been fishing in the same pool for recruits for so long and attracting the same kinds of people – some were 'can do' but didn't necessarily 'want to do'. We had to do something to attract more suitable people who would stay with us for the right reasons.

What have been the benefits to the organization?

Our 0–3 month attrition dropped dramatically. Reasons for leaving changed – people were leaving for what I would call good reasons, not because they were dissatisfied with the job.

We're also now fishing from different and bigger pools. We're attracting people of different ages, backgrounds and walks of life. It's brought us a good mix including a 50-year-old landscape gardener and ex-military personnel. It's been eye opening and has changed the culture in a positive way because they are self-driven people. They get on better and have really gelled together. Because they are all positive about their work they tend to keep an eye on each other and keep each other in line too. They have the right attitude. Heads of department notice it and say that they are great, they're not afraid to speak up and ask questions. They have much more energy. Sometimes it's challenging for longer serving people that they are sitting next to. It's raised everyone's game. I think it feels different in the contact centres now because of this. There's a much better buzz.

Team managers are very enthusiastic about people that they appoint – they want them on their teams. It's because they can really see what sort of person they are and what value they can add.

It was very positive too for the unsuccessful candidates. We ring them up and give them feedback about their strengths. They appreciate that. It gives them a positive feeling.

As an interviewer you get a real connection with the interviewees. You get to know them really well and it's great to follow the successful ones' progress.

Candidates love the strengths interview. We do workshops with them afterwards about their recruitment experience with us. They tell us they've loved it and feel energized by it. They don't realize how much they have talked and relayed to you in the interview. We've never had any negative feedback.

We're ahead of the game because we've got SBR. We're streets ahead of our competitors.

Were there any challenges?

These types of people have also created some different challenges for team managers because they're not used to managing people like this. They found it difficult initially because people were hungry, they were hitting their targets and weren't afraid to challenge. They were different from the contact centre norm.

We've moved from managing on competencies to managing on strengths and behaviours. We ran a course to help team managers to manage the new strengths-based recruits. It brought it all together because they realized that having the profiles meant they could understand what motivated people and what their strengths were. This makes it easier to manage people. It let them manage them as individuals playing to their strengths rather than managing everyone in the same way.

We did have a challenge with some of the agencies that were trying to train people to answer strengths interview questions. It worked against them because they came across as robotic.

What, if anything, would you do differently?

I don't think I would have done anything differently except having more time to dedicate to it. I'd like to do more refresher sessions for interviewers to make sure they are doing it as well as they can and keep engagement up.

What advice would you give to others about implementing strengths-based recruitment and development?

I'd say take that leap of faith and jump in with both feet. It's fundamentally different when you have been used to a competency-based world but you will quickly see the benefits and see the improvement in your numbers.

Let people experience a strengths interview. Once they have it makes what they might think of as a 'dark art' clear and obvious. I thought that it would be possible to lie until I experienced it for myself. When people experience it they see the benefit. I'd also say take the time to do the training course so that you can experience it for yourself.

It takes courage to introduce something like SBR because it's a different mindset. It's a new idea and feels very different. It changes your perception of people, it's not just about recruitment.

Elisabeth Pullar, Senior Nurse, Professional Practice Team, Guy's and St Thomas' NHS Foundation Trust

What is your role and how long have you been in it?

I am a Senior Nurse in the Professional Practice Team at Guy's and St Thomas' and I've been in the role nearly two years. The Chief Nurse asked me to lead on the implementation of SBR. I attended the strengths-based interviewing training in 2013 and went along with a healthy scepticism. I liked the sound of it but didn't really know much about it. I was hooked in the first five minutes when I heard the basic premise of the right people being in jobs they love with the natural attributes to do the job well. It struck me that people I've met over the years who are in the wrong job have got an underlying sadness because they have found themselves trapped in a role that they are ok at but not in love with. If we could just help people to get into the right job it would make such a difference.

Why were you chosen as an SBR lead?

I have a can-do attitude and my approach is always 'How can we make this happen?' rather than to see only the problems with something. I'm a doer. I consider it a necessity to role-model positive and proactive behaviour. I think the Chief Nurse asked me to lead on SBR because she sees me as a dynamic person with the ability to engage others and I'm not afraid of new things.

Why do you think Guy's and St Thomas' decided to implement SBR?

Our Chief Nurse, with colleagues in the Shelford Group, recognized that what makes a good ward is great leadership. They realized we would be in a stronger position if we could identify exactly what makes a great ward sister as that is what all outstanding wards have in common. Great ward sisters don't crumble when things get tough and, no matter how tough a decision they have to make, they always take the team with them. If people aren't right for the job it impacts on their team. At Guy's and St Thomas' we want to be pioneering, dynamic and forward thinking, but at the end of the day it's all about the experience of the patients and the staff. If you have the right people in place, everything else follows.

What have been the benefits of SBR so far?

We have not had a lot of ward sister vacancies yet but the people we have appointed using SBR have been outstanding. Several people have commented on what a good job they are doing and what a smooth transition it's been from one ward manager to the next. I feel comfortable that the appointees are good and have the right strengths. As we appoint more great people so the positive vibe about SBR grows across the Trust.

What do you think has gone well about SBR implementation?

We now have SBR-trained trainers in every directorate right across the Trust. So now it's not just me talking about it! People are very fired up and word is spreading. They're espousing the benefits of SBR and telling people how excited they are. People are now asking to join in rather than being forced to attend training. We've got real solidarity and engagement from the heads of nursing, matrons and ward managers. I'm determined to make it happen. We've planned it well and we've taken time to talk to people and explain it to them.

I've ensured that high-quality standards have been maintained. I've had to do a lot of work to ensure that people have followed the process correctly. I want to be sure that the quality of interviewing is right. I have sat on nine out of the 10 interview panels to date and have been alongside newly trained interviewers. I will be following up with successful candidates to find out whether they are still feeling positive and fulfilled in their role. So up to now quality control has been a bit dictatorial, but necessarily so.

What, if anything, would you have done differently?

I don't think I would have done anything differently. But we need to have a lot more discussions to work out how to roll out SBR for staff nurses as this is a much larger group than ward sisters. There are a lot of people involved in our recruitment process. I've been respectful and pragmatic when engaging people. I'm involving the right people and giving them a chance to talk and ask questions. I have set up a presentation and invited HR colleagues, the education team and universities that recruit student nurses for us. I will present alongside some of our newly trained SBR trainers. They are living and breathing SBR every day and are very passionate about it. We will answer any questions people have, we'll encourage the sceptics to challenge it, and we'll have a very honest discussion.

What would be your advice to other organizations that are thinking of implementing SBR?

Don't delay – do it! Engage people in a way that is right for them. Decide which roles to profile first and get it done.

Don't assume it's got to be a massive launch. We started SBR with one group of staff (ward sisters) and I found that gradually building people's interest has been valuable. There is now a sense of anticipation about implementing it for staff nurses and nursing assistants as they have heard how well SBR has gone with ward sisters. We know we can teach people how to do strengths-based interviewing, but we can't make them want it, so you have to spend time talking to them about it and answering their questions.

Why do people at Guy's and St Thomas' want SBR so much now?

Because they know that up until now career pathways have been built on a predestined idea of what a nursing career should be. And yet, despite having a lot of people in the profession who are great, they are not necessarily in the right job for them. People are beginning to get this and realize that you can't make people into something they are not – you can't make someone into a natural leader or into a naturally caring person. With SBR we have an opportunity to do things differently.

Reference

Francis Report (2013) *The Mid Staffordshire NHS Foundation Trust Public Inquiry. Chaired by Robert Francis QC, 2013*, The Stationery Office, London

Interviews with people who transitioned from the wrong job to the right job

11

Six individuals were interviewed, at a range of career stages in a variety of sectors and of various nationalities, countries of residence and ages. They all have something in common: they have each taken decisions to change the course of their working life in order to get closer to or to find 'a job' that is right for them; work that allows them to use their strengths and that fits with their values, work that energizes them and that gives them a sense of purpose, fulfilment and well-being. They each experienced varying degrees of misery and frustration working in roles that did not suit them. They all now do work they love. Their interviews offer fascinating insight into the difference it makes to a human being (and to everyone and everything around them including their organizations, colleagues and customers) when they realize who they really are and what they naturally do best, apply that knowledge to their work, and discover what it means, in practice, to be 'a round peg in a round hole'.

Mike Blake: from Technical Specialist to Sales Manager to Executive Briefing Consultant (IBM UK Ltd)

Mike is 53 and has worked for IBM since leaving Cambridge University where he studied economics. He's had at least 'five careers in one'. He moved from technical sales support and specialist roles into marketing, sales management and team leadership, eventually choosing to become an Executive Briefing Consultant at the high-profile IBM Client Centre (Hursley, UK) around 10 years ago. He organizes, runs and presents at product and development briefings that are requested by IBM sales people for their customer executives and their teams.

Mike is a baby-boomer who has so far fulfilled the promise of a 'job for life', remaining with one organization for his entire career, and he believes that he will stay in his current role, which he loves, until he retires. He's enjoyed aspects of much of his career, but felt least comfortable in management roles, when he struggled with the formal administrative processes involved and felt 'exposed', uncomfortable and drained. He sees the value of the experience he gained in these jobs, but the cost was a negative impact on his well-being and various other aspects of his life at the time.

Mike is a 'large character', a natural communicator and performer from an early age – 'I was never shy... always up for presenting at school assembly'. He loves building happy relationships with people. He likes to solve immediate problems, quickly. At work, he draws on his interests in business and economics, his technical knowledge and his extensive experience to do it 'on the fly'. Outside of work he fixes his motorbikes and never turns away from a practical DIY challenge, which illustrates his innate need to 'fix it'. He becomes energized when he says that, in the job he loves, he is like the 'United Nations' or a 'maître d', making sure everything runs smoothly and that everyone gets the best value out of the briefings he organizes and hosts. He loves the opportunity to speak (perform) at the briefings, to connect and build great relationships with everyone involved, and the way he can use his communication skills to ensure a successful outcome for his 'clients'. He likes to get positive feedback, and to feel valued for who he really is (which he now believes to be synonymous with the job he does, because he loves it and feels natural doing it); it's important to him that people come back and 'ask for' him.

What are you like as a person, and what are your interests outside of work?

I love motorcycles, history, castles, monasteries, mountains, supporting my football team (not on TV, I go to the matches), I'm a passionate consumer of real ale. I'm seen as 'large' and possibly loud. I'm very outgoing, keen to engage, always very happy to stand up front, funny, a good communicator, likely to have a lot of good ideas (though not always very politically correct about how I might express them). I tend to like to challenge authority... especially when it's stupid!

Tell me about your career, before you became a Briefing Consultant

I joined IBM straight from university. I liked the idea of working for a company that actually made something. My compatriots all went into finance, became global hedge fund managers (probably earning millions by now!), and I originally applied to IBM for a job in finance, even though I had no idea what that would mean. But they actually never considered me for finance and interviewed me for a completely different role – probably the best thing that ever happened to me. I started in tech sales/pre-sales. I was the technical half, like the technical accomplice, of a sales team. I'm so glad they did that. They might have seen something in me, but also they were expanding their sales organization, so that's what I got. I did that for around 12 years, moved into marketing for about six years and ended up working in the USA. When I came back to the UK I wanted to go back to being a techie, but when I tried to pursue that they made me a manager of a technical team for about five years (which I enjoyed) and then a Sales Manager (which I enjoyed a lot less). I took a sabbatical and returned as a Sales Team Leader. Then, eventually, a colleague (who I shall forever be grateful to) made me aware of this Briefing Consultant job in the Client Centre.

Have you ever felt like a square peg in a round hole, and what was that like?

Yes, when I was Sales Manager of a specialist sales team, and also when I was a Sales Team Leader. These weren't impossible jobs for me, but there were elements that I really had to force myself to do. I enjoyed working with the IBM teams and the customers we were trying to sell things to, the people side of the job. But, I didn't enjoy the processes that as a manager I was required to implement. I guess I wasn't happy carrying out the more formal side of the HR process. There was a lot of administrative stuff that has to be done as a manager, that other people seemed able to do with their eyes closed. But having to 'get things right to three decimal points' or 'get all these forms filled in by next Tuesday', very formal reporting and forecasting, it's just not me. I'm a bit process phobic. If there's so much process that it outweighs the positive elements of the job, then I'm in trouble. Words like 'compliance' and 'regulation' are not ones I leap towards!

I felt a bit exposed to be honest. I was doing an OK job, but I wasn't performing as well as I had in other roles, or as well as I knew I could. I felt a bit like a footballer being forced to play cricket. It's tiring, it's wearing. You can do it but it's not natural. Trying to be something and fit into a shape that you're not. Pretend. You're away from your natural happy equilibrium, your normal way of being. It's hard. I think I managed to hide my inner feelings quite well from my team, even though I was increasingly uncomfortable. It knocked me out of balance, I wasn't the rested, fulfilled person I would normally be. It amplified or made worse other aspects of life and even triggered some things… you should ask my ex-wife! In any case, I was front of the queue to take a sabbatical from IBM when the opportunity arose.

How did you make the transition into your current role at the Client Centre, and what is the job you do as an Executive Briefing Consultant?

It was the first time in my career that I'd made a conscious decision to choose a job. Normally I'd been directed by the company… made changes at their request… even when I wanted to go back to being a techie, they made me a Tech Sales Manager. This job came completely out of left field, it was a completely different situation. I just walked in and said, 'Look, this job is what I want to do, I don't want to do what I'm doing anymore.' I came here [to the IBM Client Centre at Hursley, UK] thinking I'd probably be here for a couple of years, but I've been here for a decade and I suspect I'll be in this role until I retire.

The purpose of the Executive Briefing Centre is to bring together our customers, potential customers and partners with the development staff in the labs who create the technologies and products which we sell. So, for example, take a customer like a global bank, they might have been using our products for many years, they might want to hear about new products we're coming up with, what's in the next version of software, tell us what they think should be in the next version of software, discuss any areas they might be struggling with. Part of my job is to work with the sales team to put together a programme for them… half a day or a couple of days or even longer. It could involve seeing new products, hands on sessions, executive level or technical discussions. The IBM sales team will have objectives (related to customer relationship and IBM sales targets), and the customer will have objectives that might include solving a technical issue, but that are more likely to be business driven… how they can achieve their business goals, and they want to know how we can help them do it.

The other part of my job is to facilitate the programme itself 'on the day', and I usually make an introductory presentation myself to kick the day off, engage everyone and set the tone for the day. Then I make sure the programme runs as planned, both sides get their objectives met, that we're flexible and adjust the content according to how things go, and that everyone leaves feeling they've had a worthwhile time and that they are looking forward to coming back again.

Being in a job that feels right for you, what's that like?

I'm in a role I'm naturally suited for. People say to me things like, 'You were born to do this' or 'Did IBM invent this job just for you? This is *you*.' I'm liberated. I've got far more of my energy and creative capability to apply myself to the challenges, because I'm not having to fit myself to a role and then deal with what's going on around me... I've got both hands free as it were to address the problems, because I'm in a role I'm naturally suited for.

What do you think you do that makes you really good at your job? What energizes you about it? What do you love the most?

I'm a big picture person. I'm interested in technology, but only up to a point, I'm not a geek. I operate at the 'systems level'. I can take a broad view and I'm good at understanding what's really important and what's not – what's just a detail and what's crucial. Combine that with the fact that I'm interested in people's businesses and how they work, the external pressures on them and what they're trying to do. I'm like the United Nations!

[At this moment in the interview Mike's phone rings and he answers. It's a salesman having to cancel a briefing that Mike has worked on shaping ('lovingly' is the word he uses to describe it) for the past two weeks. He remains completely calm, sounds happy, accommodating, totally positive, says 'Don't worry.' He adds zero stress to the situation for the salesman and appears to feel none himself. He explains afterwards that he takes such moments in his stride because he is happy in his work, he doesn't react like perhaps he may have when in a job he enjoyed less, when he felt more pressure.]

OK, United Nations... well, you could see the people involved in my briefings as two sides, people who are selling and people being sold to. My role is to try and bridge that gap. I position myself as a neutral. If the customers are being a bit shy, I put myself in their shoes and I ask the questions, try to create a dialogue (it shouldn't be a lecture) and then the meeting will warm up, I intervene to keep the dialogue going... I enjoy that. We've got it in our heads what the customer needs to know, but they're not going to get the full value if they just sit there and listen to what we want to tell them.

They'll get the best, most relevant information if they direct us with questions, but it doesn't always happen easily. Especially in some cultures, outside the UK, people are very unwilling to interrupt the flow or admit they don't understand. It could even be a linguistic issue. Sometimes I'm looking round the room, see glazed expressions, and I'll put myself on their side for a while, interject and say to the speaker something like, 'I'm not sure I'm getting that, can you explain it again?' or 'Can you tell us why that's important?' It could be a weakness in the speaker, they're giving information but not putting it in context. Whatever the reason, if the communication isn't happening, it's my job to fix it. I think I'm good at that because although I work for 'the company', because of my interests in business and economics, I can see things from the customer's side very easily. I try to get to know them even before the session starts, meet them on the doorstep and show them to the room, talking with them all the way there, finding out who they are, what their backgrounds are… I'm a bit like the 'maître d' in a restaurant, making sure everything runs perfectly and people get what they really want from the experience.

I like it when I feel I've made a difference, and often it's when I've had to react, intuit what the problem is and find a way to deal with it in the here and now. I'm a problem solver but in a unique kind of a way, I'm not a completer–finisher, but I want to get the fix and move on so we can make progress. I want to keep things moving forward. We ask for feedback from our visitors at the end of all our sessions and it matters to me that they've found the experience valuable and, dare I say it, enjoyable! I like to form relationships with the customers; sometimes they're with us for a few days, and I might take them for a historic tour of Winchester, or perhaps have dinner with them. I like it when customers go away with a real buzz and tell me that they want to come back and bring their colleagues and their bosses and their director. There are several of us doing the same job as me, and we're trained in the same programme with best practices, but we all do it slightly differently, we all have our unique ways, and it is nice when people do come back and ask for you because they like the way you do it.

The thing I love to do most in the whole world is stand up and present or perform in front of an audience, and I get the chance to do it in this job. At the beginning of every session I give a presentation, in the context of introduction to the day and background to 'the lab'; I show exciting examples, talk about things that are relevant to the customer that make a difference to people's lives. I try to get people emotionally engaged, focus them, spark their imagination, make them feel comfortable that they're in the right place, give them confidence they're going to have a great day and leave them wanting to know more. I put a lot of thought and effort into each customer, how they're different, what might be interesting to them. I think my contribution to the start of the day is very important in setting the tone of the day and I love doing it.

Looking back over your life, were there any early signs that seem to make sense now? Were there things you loved doing, or did people say things about you?

Well, I was never shy! I was always up for presenting at school assembly… performing, debating, acting, karaoke… I was always on stage, loved making people laugh, wanted to be a stand-up comedian, and I even did musicals. Little old ladies in Southampton would remember me 10 years later, come up to me when I working on the checkouts in the supermarket in my summer holidays, say, 'Ooh it's Mr Scrooge!'

I was popular, a 'large character'. I was noticed more than most, always had a lot of friends and big networks around me. I loved networking. I might have antagonized a few people, not afraid to say what I think, there is a mischievous side to me… I've had to work on that!

I've always loved fixing things – like DIY at home or my motorbikes, people call me 'Practical Man Grade 1'. I've always liked problem solving… short-term things though… I'd be no good at a three-year-long siege, I'm like a serial monogamist with problems! I like to solve one quickly and move on to the next.

What do you think is important for you and others about being in work you love?

In the role I do now, having had a really, really busy day, I come home energized and wanting to do things. In roles where I didn't feel comfortable, I'd have nothing left, I was completely drained, so I probably tried to protect myself and limit what I did at work. I used to have to 'let off steam', and that caused me some problems in the past, people found it hard to cope with. When you're an actor, you can't act all the time, you have to have times when you can be yourself; the bigger the disconnect between who you are 'having to be' and who you really are when you are being natural, the more has to come out in other ways, not always nice ways, maybe it's swearing, drinking, shouting… not good. Also I always felt, in roles I didn't fit with, that my managers didn't know who I was, they might even have been praising me, but I felt it wasn't me they were praising, just a false image they had of me. I've probably got the need to 'belong' more than most people, and it's a great feeling to know that when people are happy with what you do, they really are happy with you yourself, because what you are doing *is* you.

The people I work with now like working with me, because I never say no – I'm known as 'the man who never says no', I don't want to say no in this job, I don't want to have to disappoint anyone. I want to accommodate every salesman who wants to bring a customer and every customer who wants to come to visit us. Maybe I take on too much work occasionally, but it's because I enjoy the work, I can't get enough of it! The organization gets the most possible out of me, and I think the best of me. I think I'm a much nicer person to work with now too. Would I come to work if I wasn't paid for it? Well I think in this job, probably. There's a huge difference between doing a job because it's what you're paid to do, and doing something you'd love to do anyway because it is you – you feel you're getting a lot out of the job yourself, so it's win–win. I was in jobs where I wasn't the best person for the job, there were other people in the organization who could have done a better job than me. Organizations should be more aware of that, if they want to get the best out of their people.

How does your experience affect how you recruit/ treat/coach your employees? And what advice would you give to other employers about people being in a role that's right for them?

I've learned to try and understand people's real motivations. When I was a Sales Manager, I'd have a stream of technical people coming in wanting to be a salesman, usually because there was more money in it, but I'd want to get under that to try to find out whether the actual job was what they really wanted to do. Most of them I talked out of it. A couple I coached them through the transition and one of them I coached back out of it, because he didn't enjoy it – even though he was reasonably competent at it – and he realized that he'd rather do his old job for less money. Now, lots of people in the lab want customer experience because it helps them get promoted, but the environment of building relationships, 'selling yourself' to others, networking, is so different to working in a lab; most of them realize it's not for them once we've talked.

What advice would you give your younger self about your career?

I think I made a good choice of career and company because the company I joined can offer so many different roles, and has done to me. I've had about five careers in one! I don't know many other places I could have gone where that could have happened. I've developed and changed over time, and it's taken time for me to learn about myself, but I've been able to try different things in IBM, and eventually find something that was the perfect fit for me. IBM and I have worked it out together. I've never been forced to do a job, and I haven't taken every job that I've been offered, for example I turned away from becoming a manager of managers because by then I knew it wasn't for me. But, I learned a lot from my time as a Sales Manager, and because I've sat round tables with those people, it means I understand them and their motivations, and it helps me do the job I do now; I'm dealing with the people I used to be. I wouldn't have been ready for this job when I was 35 – I needed all that experience. So, I'd probably say, keep learning about yourself, stay open to opportunities that could benefit your experience and/ or be a good fit to who you really are.

What's it been like to talk about this with me?

I've enjoyed it. It's provoked a few thoughts about myself that I've never really considered before. All good.

Joel Davies: from Woodwork Tool Apprentice to Hairdresser/Hairdressing Salon Owner

Joel is 41. He began his working life in carpentry as an Apprentice Woodwork Tool Maker when he was 16. He quickly realized it was not for him and left when he was 17 to start an apprenticeship in hairdressing. In terms of the 'career nurturing' Joel received, his father taught him the importance of choosing a skilled trade with its own specialist tools, and hairdressing does fit that profile. However, from a strengths perspective, Joel 'comes alive' especially when talking about helping or serving others, and the energy in his voice as he talks about being a little boy delighted to learn to make a cup of tea, so he could make cups of tea for people, is a clue that he felt joy in service from a very young age. The other 'buzz point' for Joel is the process of co-creation with his clients, in order to serve them and help them become more than they thought they might be. It's not enough for him to create alone, for himself. When he made wooden spice racks when he was a kid, he gave them away; someone else had to be part of the process of creating, even if back then it was simply to receive his gifts. He needed the 'giving' to feel he'd done a great job. Hairdressing allows him to co-create with his clients to add something more to their lives than they had imagined possible. The fact he co-creates, mixing his own vision with theirs, to give them something that builds on what they had in their own minds, strengthens Joel's sense that he is serving each person; thus he feels that his work has real value and meaning every time.

What are you like as a person, and what are your interests outside of work?

All my activities outside of work tend to be quite solitary… because since my work is so very sociable, I need time on my own. Sometimes I feel too outward at work, and my other activities balance that. Maybe my work moulds the other interests. I love anything to do with motorcycles – vintage and modern. I ride alone. There's a big fitness aspect to my life – the gym, climbing, dancing, sport, yoga practice.

Tell me about your career before you got into hairdressing

It was always important to me to know what I was going to do for a living. My dad was a motorcycle mechanic and he told me, 'Don't waste your time doing unskilled work.' He was always appreciative of skilled tradesmen, he'd say to me, 'Look at all his specialist tools, he's a specialist.' We'd talk about different trades – carpenter, auto-electrician for vehicles, glazier, the old guy we knew who 'timed the magnetos on the racing Nortons' – and how great it was for someone to have their set of tools and do something many other people can't do. I could see the respect it demanded from people. I thought it was important to get to know what I wanted to do and I'd always liked working with wood. I bought lots of woodworking tools. I had a bit of a rose-tinted view of what it would be like, that I'd live in this utopian place and be able to make anything out of wood and I'd be in demand. First, while I was still at school when I was 14, in the evenings and on Saturdays, I worked in a woodworking yard making stairs and windows. I wasn't very good academically because I wasn't interested really. Then I found a better place, a place where they made dining tables for the Royal Yacht Britannia, a bit more 'high end', so when I left school [at 16] I started an apprenticeship there. But it was very much the old guys that were doing the cool, interesting stuff, it was like when you got to your early/mid thirties that was when you'd start doing the good things... and I was like, 'Wow, that's a long way off!' And the old boys (they were from Vosper Thornycroft) ran the show. The younger guys doing their apprenticeships there didn't command much respect, they weren't highly regarded. I spent days just sharpening chisels... I'd think, 'I'm sure there's a tool that could do this... do I really have to do this when I know there's a tool, just because the old guys used to do it that way?' I'd started the apprenticeship early in the holidays because I was so keen to get started on a trade, and it was that same summer that I realized, 'I really don't want to do this.' I'd always had an interest in hair, I guess it's about shape, proportion, lines and balance. I can visualize things. Even when I was at school I'd talk to girls about their hair and experiment with highlights and undercuts and stuff with my own hair. I'd always be disappointed with the barber I went to, I always felt he didn't pay much attention. I remember reading in a Sunday magazine about Princess Diana's hairdresser at the time, John Frieda, and thinking, 'These guys, they're not like the hairdressers round here... they're doing great work, they're meeting beautiful women, they've got a great life! There's this other world out there and I want in on that!'

What was it like being a square peg in a round hole?

It was mind-numbingly boring. It didn't challenge me. I felt lethargic. My motivation levels went down. It didn't bring out any of my higher qualities. I gradually resented being there. I could have stuck at it and made a go of it but I wouldn't have been that engaged in it. I wanted to find something I could engage in.

How did you make the transition into hairdressing?

In Hedge End and Botley where I grew up it wasn't that usual for guys to go into hairdressing... I did come across some nasty comments which hurt me at the time, comments like 'you must be gay', which kind of bothered me, until I met some gay people, and I thought, 'Well, they're alright!' So, I just threw myself into the hairdressing. I did my apprenticeship at Blinkers in Southampton, and there was a great guy there who'd worked at Vidal Sassoon and he used to say, 'Don't walk around with the chickens, fly with the eagles! There's load of chickens out there, don't be one of them.' I moved on to split my time three days a week working in London and the rest at Storm in Southampton. I started charging full price (being 'on the floor') when I was 19. I felt like I hit the ground running, but then there was a spell when I struggled, lost my confidence, used to cut my fingers to ribbons, some haircuts I could do really well and some I just couldn't. There was a lot of doubt and negativity in me for a time; I thought I wasn't good enough. I was into it but there were some aspects of it I find incredibly difficult, like 'hair up'. I wanted to do it all, but I realized I had to concentrate on my strengths, go for the cutting and colouring, restyles, the more technical aspects of hair-dressing… the shape, balance, proportion. That's what I'm good at. I started to specialize, and I was persistent and pushed through the doubts because I believed I could do it and I wanted to do it.

Being in a job that feels right for you, what's that like?

On the best days when I go into the salon, it's like, 'Yes, we're ready, today's going to be a great day!' Once I've agreed what I'm going to do for a client and I'm working on the hair, I'm totally present in the moment. I'm not thinking about anything else. I forget what day it is, I forget what time it is, I can't remember if it's morning or afternoon. Sometimes I'm drying or taking the towel off and I can't even remember which client I'm working on because I'm completely focused on what I'm doing, on my craft. I feel I've created something greater than was possible in the client's mind before they came in, there's been a connection, a mixing of energies and ideas in the process, and I've been of service to them and made them happier, and helped them feel more confident and empowered, good about themselves.

What do you think you do that makes you really good at your job? What energizes you about it? What do you love the most?

When the client comes in, I can see the haircut or colour there, but I like to find it with the client, or let it find us. I get an idea but I constantly check with the client to bring out their ideas and get confirmation that my idea is going to fit with them… 'Is it this?', or 'Do you like this part or that part?' I want to amplify and develop their ideas. I look at the hair and listen to the client to see where we are at, to know this is our starting point. I get very frustrated when hairdressers don't do that, they don't acknowledge the existing hairstyle, they don't check everything through and understand what we've already got, they go into it blind, like a stab in the dark, pushing their own idea onto the client. I'm not interested in just doing 'great hairdressing'. I want to serve the person. I want to take the result on beyond their expectations, beyond what they'd have been capable of imagining... that's the thing for me. I don't care about egotistical things like impressing other hairdressers, I'm not interested in competitions or photo-shoots – I've done some of that, but it's boring and like, 'So what?' – there's no 'juice' in that. I want to contribute to people's well-being and happiness, that's where the real 'juice' is. I get energized at the point when the answers are coming as part of my dialogue with the client, when I feel that together we've 'got something'... If a client says 'Just do what you want' it's no good. I need another energy to bounce off. And you've got to be open, because things can change at any moment. You've got to be aware and sensitive to the conditions that might crop up with the client or the hair itself. You can't be fixed in your idea, like you can't be mad if they change their mind, you need to adapt. I can do that. My part is to be a co-creator, maintaining my openness and going with the flow of it, not getting in the way of the natural process.

Looking back over your life, were there any early signs that seem to make sense now? Were there things you loved doing, or did people say things about you?

Well, I was always very slow to learn to do things for myself, things that would have been useful for me, like I was a lot older than I should have been when I learned to tie my shoelaces – I relied on other people to do things like that for me, but I loved learning to do things for other people. Like, it was a big thing when I learned to make a cup of tea, and I could make a cup of tea for someone! I loved to help my dad, he used to do 'autojumbles', selling old motorbike parts, I enjoyed doing all the manual work for him, helping get all the bits out. It was kind of an unusual thing for a kid to do on a Saturday, on their day off, to go off in a van with their dad to help him shift a load of bike bits! I loved running errands and making things like little spice racks and giving them away to people too. I was solitary, though, not sociable at all, so it's strange that my energizing moment in my job is in the process of co-creation with the client, that I need another's energy to bounce off for that, but maybe I've got more confident and I think it's the intention that's important, the wanting to do a good job, to do it right, to be available to help others – like I do for my clients. And I was always fascinated by hair and hairdressing, I loved to watch my mum's hairdresser, and I started experimenting with my own hair when I was still at school.

What do you think is important for you and others about being in work you love?

It's important to cultivate that feeling, when you get to work, of 'I really want to be here. I'm in the right place now. I'm ready.' You can only be of service to people (and to yourself) when you've cultivated those conditions. It's as if there's a moment-to-moment awareness and you are operating in the essence of what life is about, and then you can really be of service to others. You've found your thing. It's doesn't matter what the job is, if you're the right person for it, you're serving others, and yourself.

How does your experience affect how you recruit/ treat/coach your employees?

Well, I look for the ability to do what I do, but it depends on how much they are getting in the way of things, how fixed or not they are, how open they can be as opposed to how they might push their own ideas and not listen to the client. But to be honest, I'm not spoilt for talent in my geographical area so I have to try to develop the people I can get along the lines I want, to work in the way I do. I find if I focus on the higher aspects of myself, I tend to see elements of those in other people and then I can nourish that in them and bring them on. So if I'm energized and showing my people the best way to work, then it gives them permission to do the same. It's like being it rather than preaching it means that they mirror it. That's why it's so important to love what I do.

What advice would you give your younger self about your career?

I'd have encouraged myself to really do everything that I really want to do and to believe that there is nothing that I can't achieve. The journey of being a hairdresser has been great but perhaps there would have been other routes I could have taken. If I've discovered qualities in myself now, I wonder what I could have been like and achieved if I'd understood those qualities earlier. Now I've proved to myself I can push through to succeed as a hairdresser, I feel I might have been able to have been a great sportsman or musician, for example. The degree to which I've realized I can focus means I could have taken a tougher path and succeeded. But, it does come back to my need to be of service… would those things have nourished that? I'd have maybe become a coach, or teacher. I sometimes think I would have liked more money or fame or something, but I was on that route for a time and I turned away from that when I was 24, even though I was attracting famous clients. I enjoyed showing off and impressing others for a while, but it seemed that people were falling over themselves to serve the famous, I was a tiny part in it all. I know I can give more in the environment I am in, I can make more impact on my clients' well-being.

What advice would you give to other employers about people being in a role that's right for them?

The most important thing is to create the conditions that mean that people feel energized by what they do, because only then can they be of service to others.

What's it been like to talk about this with me?

It's been wonderful. There's a richness in talking about the energy that is generated in the moments and process I've spoken of. It's more than just an interview about hairdressing or about me, it's really been about that mysterious thing, the essence of life.

Martin North: from Salesman to Marketing Manager (US-based e-commerce football speciality retailer)

Martin is 32 and British, but has lived and worked in the United States since soon after leaving university with a degree in journalism. All his life he has been 'crazy about football', and has an in-depth knowledge of the professional game. He knew from the start of his career that he wanted work that would allow him to use his knowledge as well as his creative abilities and written communication skills. He sought out an organization that seemed perfect for him and was recruited by them. However, when he was offered two very different roles within the company, he chose the role that would give him a salaried position and the medical insurance he needed, rather than the role that would have matched his innate strengths, interests and talents. Within one year he was ill and under-performing; he was often late, 'counting the minutes', and he felt demotivated, frustrated and resentful that instead of sharing his knowledge of the game, he was in a role that was like 'selling polyester to people'. His performance was so poor that he was fired by the company. But, after a few months and a serious think, he managed to get re-hired by the same organization. This time, he was determined to prove his true value and took every opportunity to work on projects that would allow him to do the things he was good at and loved to do. Five years on, he is a Marketing Manager running the marketing for a business unit responsible for $20 million a year in sales. Sharing and using his knowledge of the game is integral to the role, the creative project elements of the job excite him, and he has been able to build in-depth working relationships that suit his nature of being a person who 'warms up gradually' to people. He says, 'It doesn't feel like work, or a job. It's my passion, something I'm genuinely interested in.' He wants to go to work. He works late. He has a 'positive energy and attitude'. He is succeeding in the company and derives enormous personal satisfaction from his work. Martin's story is a great example of an incredible career turnaround within the same organization.

What are you like as a person, and what are your interests outside of work?

I'm a creative person. I'm probably more subjective than objective, and quite emotional in the sense that I allow my emotions to drive my actions. I go with my gut rather than being too analytical when making decisions. I'm not that comfortable meeting new people. I am the sort of person who warms up gradually, rather than being immediately outgoing. I quite like to stay in my comfort zone and I don't take a lot of risks in my personal life. I'm passionate about football. I play it, but especially I love to follow it, and I have developed an extensive knowledge of the professional game.

Tell me about your career, before the transition to Marketing Manager

I graduated from Leeds University with a degree in journalism in 2005. My family had already spent a couple of years in the US for my dad's work, but I'd gone back to the UK for uni. I got a job working in Sainsbury's until I could find something more permanent, and after a few months I made the decision to come back to the States to the town where my brother was living. Fairly soon after arriving, I found out about a company nearby, an e-commerce retailer of sports equipment, specifically football, as well as lacrosse and rugby. So, having been crazy about football all my life, I thought yes, this is the company I want to try to work for. I knew of them because they publish a direct-mail catalogue and I'd seen it when I'd been at high school, so I knew they were one of the biggest football speciality businesses in the US, so it would be great to work for them. I was thinking something like communications marketing where I could use my creativity and my written and verbal skills. I met with the Head of Marketing and as they didn't have any marketing vacancies at the time, he encouraged me to start working in the call centre, with a view to moving if any other opportunities came up, because the organization liked to promote from within. I began working full time there in a position paid on an hourly rate.

The thing is, though, that in the USA there is no National Health Service as in the UK, so the average person must buy their own health insurance (which can be expensive) or obtain it via being in salaried employment – there have been some changes more recently, but at the time the situation was very black and white. I have a chronic (though not serious) medical condition that requires me to have regular medical checks and care. It's essential for me to have medical insurance, so I was really seeking a salaried position of employment in the company. Because of that, a few months in, I actually turned down the first offer of something that might have suited me well – one of my contacts in the company, a product trainer, offered me the chance to become his assistant (the job seemed to fit my skillset, I could have used my extensive knowledge of football and my passion for the product, and I knew I liked the work because I'd done some projects for him), but it wasn't a salaried position. At the same time, I was also offered a sales position in the 'team sales' part of the organization, selling kit and 'uniforms' for playing direct to clubs and schools. The main attraction for me was that it was a salaried role. So I went with the sales position because it most immediately fitted my personal need for health insurance. Initially it was OK; I was mostly working on the phone with existing clients, cold calling lists and placing orders. But over time, I didn't enjoy it. I'm not a very 'aggressive' person by nature, the cold calling didn't appeal, trying to win someone round without actually meeting them. I didn't really like the environment either, because although we were a team, each of us was focused on our own goals and efforts. I didn't like the sales 'dog eat dog' mentality. Eventually I lost interest in the work. My heart wasn't in it. My interest and knowledge in football is in the professional game, and in this role I felt like I was selling polyester to people. It was all about price. It wasn't what I'd thought a job at this company would be like. I'd imagined I'd be spending my days talking about players and the game.

A year down the line, my performance was poor, my numbers weren't good, I was late in to work a lot. I made promises that I'd work on it, but it didn't get better. I had a flair up of my medical condition. I probably gave the impression that I wasn't ever there. Eventually everything unravelled. They sat me down and said, this isn't working out, we're going to have to let you go. And I actually left that day. It was a real shock. Throughout my education everything had come fairly easily to me, I hadn't ever had this sort of challenge in my life.

To pay my medical insurance I took a short-term admin job in a travel agency and wrote some freelance articles, but I basically wasn't making enough money. I was 25. My parents were supporting me financially, and suggesting I should move back to the UK. Eventually, to try to cover my costs, I took a job on the deli counter of a supermarket. On the very first day, two or three people came in that I knew from my company. It was so embarrassing. I was there in my hair net, slicing cheese for people... it was not good. I quit after a couple of days. I thought, 'What am I doing? I've got a degree. I'm a reasonably smart guy. I have abilities.' I spent a week thinking hard about what I really wanted to do... and it all just came back to the same sports retailer that had let me go. I knew it was the sort of place I wanted to work. I'd just had a bad experience there. So, I contacted the owners of the company direct. I said, 'Look, I know I made a lot of mistakes last year, but I still think I have a lot to offer. I'd like the chance to come back to the call centre.' They accepted. So, I began again.

How did you make the transition into your current role?

I'd only been back in the call centre a few months when a project came up in the group that manages our websites. They needed someone with an extensive knowledge of football, and I was sent on secondment. I put a lot of effort in to the project because I was determined to prove everyone wrong about me, so I worked long hours, became friendly with the manager of the department and began helping him out using my knowledge, with writing content, managing our social media channels, that sort of thing. I felt enabled by him, trusted and very motivated. When the guy responsible for web content and social media moved on and his job came open, I was the natural person to take it over. It was a great fit for me. Writing for the web. Facebook. Twitter. Sharing my knowledge, online-chatting to people, interacting a little here and there. Maybe I'm a product of my generation... more comfortable with online communication than meeting new people in person! I excelled in that role, working nights, weekends, we did really well, and grew the business. I was the Social Media Manager for four years. Then, about a year ago, as a result of restructuring, I was approached to take on one of the new Marketing Manager roles, running the marketing for a business unit responsible for about $20 million a year in sales. A real vote of confidence in me, after all that had happened! It's more of an organizational role than the social media job where I was writing most of the content myself, but it's creative. I'm coming up with campaigns. It's still about telling stories. It's really good, I enjoy it.

What was it like being a square peg in a round hole, in your sales role?

It was frustrating. I felt so close to doing something that I thought was my dream job, working at a company that was all about football, but I wasn't really doing anything to do with football, just sales. There was a sense of draining energy. I didn't ever want to do anything. There was an apathy and it was shared by a couple of my colleagues, we were a rather 'unhealthy' little trio. We liked the sport but weren't suited to sales roles. We were rebels… not overtly, but we were quietly not doing what we should have been doing, just passing the time commiserating. There was resentment about doing what we were being asked to do, even though it was our job! I was thinking, 'Why am I doing this? Why am I here?' I was probably putting about 60–70 per cent effort in, time-wasting, browsing the internet, putting off the parts of the job I didn't enjoy. I think the flare-up of my medical condition was 100 per cent related to the frustrating situation, because there's real correlation: at times of stress my condition worsens. Then I'd feel ill and feel less like doing my work, then I'd feel more stressed… it was a vicious circle. I would count down the minutes to the end of the day. I'd look at the guys around me who were clearly 'sales guys'; they were always on the phone, going at it… it was their calling. I just didn't want to go into work at all. I didn't feel I was good at what I was doing, subconsciously I knew I was cheating the company. I didn't feel confident. I didn't even want to hang out socially with people from work, I just wanted to get out of there.

Being in a job that feels right for you, what's that like?

It's hard to put into words how different it feels! I wake up in the morning and I want to go to work. I want to get in there. Because I love it, a lot of my social group is work people. I enjoy being with and working with my colleagues now, we're similar personalities. And because I enjoy my job, I'm a more pleasant person! I stay late, I keep working until 8, 9, 10 in the evening. It doesn't feel like work, or a job. It's my passion, something I'm genuinely interested in. It's about energy too. In the sales role, I never had any energy, I was lethargic, wanted to be anywhere else except at work. Now I have a very positive energy and attitude. I just want to get things done.

What do you think you do that makes you really good at your job? What energizes you about it? What do you love the most?

You can't ignore the knowledge requirements of the job. My business unit is responsible for marketing 'licence apparel', official merchandise for football teams like Manchester United, Chelsea, Barcelona… you have to have a knowledge of the game. I've always loved using my knowledge (even in things outside of work like pub trivia quizzes!) and now I have to do that every day. In the sales role, I might have occasionally got into a conversation about how England performed in their last match or how good a player is, for example, but it would have been as an aside on a sales call, whereas in this role my knowledge is integral to everything. If I didn't have the knowledge I do and keep up with the game, I wouldn't be able to do my job well, and our marketing would have very little direction.

I work with the same people on a regular basis now and I like that. As I said at the start, it can take me a bit of time to warm up to people. In this role I've been able to establish deeper working relationships. I, my colleagues and our clients really understand each other and work really harmoniously. The sales role involved more flitting around to different people, I never felt I was truly working together with anyone.

My job is very creative. I come up with ideas. It's very visual. It's about design. Thinking about how we can tell a story in an interesting way. How we communicate stuff to people effectively. I really, really enjoy the creative brainstorming meetings I have with my colleagues. It's great to have ideas moments on my own too, when an idea pops into my head maybe when I'm driving or something, but I and some of my marketing colleagues formed weekly 'covert' meetings where we sit in a relaxed environment and just come up with ideas. It's great. Something always comes out of it.

I really enjoy working with my designers to come up with marketing content. I love it when something we created a few weeks or months ago comes through for real – when a catalogue, or a landing page on our website, or a marketing email has an impact – I get a real sense of satisfaction. The visual design, the headlines, the copy are all rewarding to me. Putting something out there in the world and seeing people's reaction to it. I still work with my social media guy, I love the instant response to my work. In sales it never felt like there was a project with a concrete or satisfying result. When I won an account in a sales role, I used to feel it was just more work to manage that account! I find it hard to be motivated by a number, even though I have to hit numbers in my current role, it's more about whether I'm being creative. Am I doing things that other people love or appreciate? Maybe my dream job might be something with a more subjective result to it, maybe something truly artistic...

There are organizational and planning elements that I enjoy too – like for a 12-month campaign. I'm good at those things in this role because I'm interested in what I'm doing.

The only part of the job that doesn't come naturally to me is the analysis, but because I enjoy so much of the job I'm willing to work at it. Numbers have never been my strong point, but I'm happy to try hard in this role... analysis may be out of my comfort zone, but I look at things more holistically now.

Looking back over your life, were there any early signs that seem to make sense now? Were there things you loved doing, or did people say things about you?

I think it comes back to the creative element and the story telling. I think my proudest moment at primary school was when I wrote a story; we had a little creative writing project to do, and I think I was the only person who had to go on to a second piece of paper! My mum glued some coloured pieces of paper together for me so it was like a really long scroll. The story was called 'The Magic Carpet'. My headmaster read it out in assembly because they liked it so much. Looking back now, the project-based work, the creative element and the sense of satisfaction at someone's subjective appreciation of what I'd done, rather than getting a maths question right, were maybe all indicative of what I'd go on to enjoy. I always hated maths. I never really liked things where there was a right or wrong answer, I liked to be able to talk my way into a good answer. I liked essay-based tests, where I could argue a point and creatively persuade. I never liked subjects that were black and white, I always preferred shades of grey.

What do you think is important for you and others about being in work you love?

Work is a huge part of your life, so you may as well do something you love or at least that comes naturally to you. Why would you go through life spending 60–70 per cent of that life not enjoying your work and struggling?

Also, most work means that you're being paid to do a task or project, and if you don't enjoy it, there's probably never any satisfaction of completing something. I think that human beings need a sense that what they're doing is worthwhile, and whether you are religious or not, life for most people has to have some sort of meaning. Maybe many people derive that meaning from their family, but for me without direct family of my own, work takes on that sense of purpose in my life and defines for me whether I'm a success.

How does your experience affect how you recruit/treat/coach your employees?

My experience has certainly impacted the way I've hired people. At interview, the first thing I ask is, 'What is it about this role you'd enjoy, and what excites you about it?' Obviously people need to have the necessary tools and skills to do a job, but I want the people who work for me to come to work with the same sense of satisfaction that I do. In coaching too, for example, I went out for lunch just the other day with a designer I work with who I'd noticed was a bit demotivated, and tried to help him to understand which parts of the job he enjoys and doesn't enjoy. I can use that information to help my people, put more on their plate that they'd like to be doing and maybe give the things they don't enjoy to others who might… so I can assign things in a more 'people intelligent' way. As our company grows and changes, and new projects develop, I want to know the strengths and weaknesses of my people, because I think that would make me a good manager.

What advice would you give to other employers about people being in a role that's right for them?

I think it's really hard for employers. I probably said all the right things at my interview for the sales role. I'm sure I sounded like the perfect person for the job! I know there are questions you can ask that might get beneath what the person wants to project in their effort to get a particular job. And I try to do that; when I was interviewing for my replacement for the social media manager role, I spent about five or ten minutes just chatting with the candidates about football, trying to gauge their passion for the game, their comfort with talking about it. I tried to get them to communicate about it too, because if they couldn't share their opinions about the game, then they probably wouldn't have been be a good fit. And it doesn't stop with the hire. There has to be regular follow up with how the person is doing. That's what wasn't there for me. I could have spent another year of my life helping the company achieve its goals if I'd been moved into an area that better suited my needs. I cost my company money because I wasn't hitting my targets, I was just a 'warm body'. And, without blowing my own trumpet too much [laughs], they missed out on a year of my awesome marketing ideas… so multiply that across the whole organization of 700 people, if I wasn't alone in my situation, the impact could be significant. So there's real financial cost and missed opportunity cost. And people also leave. They get tired of being stuck in a role and move to companies where they feel there are more growth opportunities, somewhere bigger or where they think there's more flexibility. So, being willing to talk to your employees about their strengths can prevent financial losses (due to poorly performing staff and unnecessary staff turnover), and stops you missing out on people that could be making you money and doing well for you in other roles. Your people are the biggest asset you have so you have to make the most of them. All your other resources mean very little without your people.

What advice would you give your younger self about your career?

If I could go back, and I was at that fork in the road at the start of my career where one job was better financially for me but wasn't a good fit, and the other was a better fit but wasn't so good financially, I would take the latter. Ultimately, my decision to focus on my more immediate needs didn't really pay off, and probably ended up costing me a lot more money. It's tough because there were mitigating circumstances for me with my need for health insurance, but I could have started with more of an open mind and a belief in my ability to turn the initial opportunity into something more long term. Instead, I took the sales job, knowing it wasn't really suited to me, but I thought it would 'tide me over' until I could find something else. But the negative impact was far greater than I ever imagined. I totally underestimated how it would make me feel. I've learned from that experience and going forward I wouldn't ever make that mistake again. I've seen how being in the wrong (or right) job can affect everything in your life.

What's it been like to talk about this with me?

It's been good. It's helpful to stop and think about myself. Though your past is always there in your subconscious informing you, there are some things that you haven't actually thought about for a long time, like my 'magic carpet' story! Talking about everything crystallizes things and makes me realize that

I'm not that much of a different person than I was when I was seven or eight… it gives me confidence that I'm doing the right thing!

David Reebok: from Trader to Business Owner/CEO

David is in his late thirties. He loves to have a goal and work hard to achieve it. He was 'laser-focused' in achieving his goal to become a city trader, and was able to use his natural analytical abilities in that role for 18 years to be an 'above average performer', but not the best. Though he thrived in the more analytical trades, he is not a risk taker, preferring to be 'in control'. He is a team player and felt himself to be a 'one-man-band' within the trading group. David also values learning, progression and helping people and eventually he felt that these aspects were not being fulfilled in his work. By then he had taken over running the business, and felt that a corporate role was more his 'calling'. He decided he wanted to build a meaningful business of his own. As CEO of a crowd funding platform for early-stage businesses, David now has an end goal that he sees as meaningful, he is able to 'help people' and he is learning 'all the time'. His analytical strengths, hard-work ethic and goal-driven nature help him to set company strategy and achieve success in an exciting, innovative, team environment. He feels that he is a 'happier and nicer person', now that he has 'something meaningful' to do.

What are you like as a person?

I'm pretty driven and not afraid of hard work. I am very analytical. I'm a team player and like others to be happy. I'm not a cut-throat businessman. I love having an end goal. I have run a few marathons. Having a goal and working hard to achieve it appeals to me.

My family and close friends will tell you that I am the person who will drop everything to help others. I've got a close group of friends and I have always been their port of call if they need help. The friend who was my best man at my wedding said in his speech that everyone values my opinion and advice. I'm also a fun and lively person on a night out!

Tell me about your career before you became a business owner

I started A levels but stopped doing them and got a job. Then I realized I was ticking along without a particular goal. I decided I wanted to go into the

City and become a dealer. I had watched a TV programme called *Capital City* – everyone in it looked smart, cool and had money and success. So I decided to go and get a degree and go into the City. I was very analytical about the decision and laser-focused on what I wanted and what I had to do to get it. I worked hard to achieve it. I used my student grant to pay for courses that would differentiate me when I was applying for jobs. I did my trading exam the day after I finished university and started work as a trader in the financial futures exchange. I was unusual. Most people do the exam a year after finishing university. I was a trader for 18 years. I was good as a trader but I don't think it was what I was best at. I was an above average performer and was always in the top 50 per cent. The thing I got a buzz out of was the more analytical trades. I wasn't great at risk taking. I need to be in control and if I could analyse something it gave me more control over what I was doing. I have never considered myself a lucky person – you can take the luck out of things by being analytical. That's what I liked. I overthink everything. I also liked the camaraderie. We were a relatively small company so there was a good team mentality. I also loved the money. I liked the fact my pay was based on my performance. If I made a lot of money I liked the fact that it was my performance that had made that happen. It felt like good, honest reward. I am not money-driven, though – for me it's about reward for a good job. If I had been more cut-throat I'd have made a lot more.

One thing I didn't like about trading was the fact that you were a one-man band within a group. Some people looked after themselves and not the team. I'd rather be tied together in a team.

How did you make the transition into running a business?

The company was then bought and me and another colleague took over the running of the UK operation.

When I took over running the business it was tough to get used to a more corporate role but I felt it was more my calling. And my wife backed me all the way which was really important to me. When I was in the City earning big money I heard about people who had built businesses and I was envious. I wanted to build something meaningful. I like learning and when I was trading I was basically doing the same thing at age 35 as I did when I was 22. There was no learning or progression. There is a big difference between being a trader and leading a business.

In 2011/12 I took the tough decision to step away from the company I was running and do something myself. I had invested in the company that I am now running. It's a professional-facing crowd funding platform.

We facilitate investment in early stage businesses. It's all about innovation via investment. It's exciting.

Doing work that feels right for you, what's that like?

I'm immeasurably happier than I would have been. The door is always open to go back to trading but the thought of it feels horrible. I'm learning so much more now. And I'm challenging myself in different ways. Out of 18 years in the City I was only learning for two of those. Now I am learning all the time. It's exciting. Running a business, there are more things to achieve and be good at than making money every day.

I also like to help people. That's why I had to take myself away from working too closely with the entrepreneurs I was helping because if we hadn't raised enough money I would top the rest up myself!

In 2011 we were at the bottom of a big recession. I'll always remember I went to Shoreditch and walked into a cool space with guys dressed in jeans. I sat in a meeting with a guy who seemed to have no fear of not having money and he told me it was the most exciting place in the world. I found it incredibly exciting and I thought it had a good chance of being meaningful.

I've got an end goal that is meaningful and I have a clear strategy of what I need to do. It's working towards that goal that's exciting.

The only thing I miss is the lack of financial security, which is weird as in other senses I thrive on lack of security.

I want to be in work that I love because I want to feel happy really. I'm a happier and nicer person now that I have something meaningful to do.

Looking back over your life, were there any early signs that seem to make sense now? Were there things you loved doing, or did people say things about you?

I was always a hard worker and entrepreneurial. When I was a kid I took on three paper rounds and got others to do them and took a commission. I bought and sold stationery at school at a profit. I had lots of jobs too – hard work didn't bother me.

What advice would you give your younger self about your career?

I'd say have the confidence to move jobs more quickly. I had opportunities but it was probably lack of confidence that stopped me. I think with a bit more confidence I would have naturally moved towards things that suited me better.

What advice would you give to other employers about people being in a role that's right for them?

The thing is, if you find the right thing for someone they will perform multiple times more efficiently. If they are happier they will be so much better at what they do and the place will be a happier place. If people could get help when they are young to find out what kind of work would be right for them the world would be a better place.

What's it been like to talk with me about this?

It's been great. Interesting. It's not often you take time to reflect like this.

Strateas Scotis: from Physiotherapist to Assistant Coffee Shop Manager (Costa)

Strati is 24. He was 'born into hospitality,' as his father owned and ran a busy café under the Parthenon in Athens, and he was always surrounded by people as he had four siblings; he speaks of having the 'need' to be surrounded by people 90 per cent of the time. The one-to-one nature of his job as a physiotherapist did not offer the possibility to make joyful social interactions with his older clients who were often in pain and sad or grumpy. Strati felt frustrated that the rules of this job did not allow him to give real value to his clients, he felt he was cheating them, and, as his story about caring for an old man in Southampton illustrates, he believes in value and justice when it comes to accepting pay for his work. He believes in working hard and loves to earn good money for his work, but only when the circumstances seem fair.

Strati loves to feel comfortable in his working environment, as if at 'home', to know exactly where everything is and what to do; that relaxes him and frees him to focus on his customers. Strati becomes especially energized when talking about interacting with his regular coffee-shop customers, people who come back 'for him', how he feels they are his guests, and how he wants to make them smile, share a joke with them… to 'make their day'. He is a very caring person, saying, 'If you saw someone on his own in the corner of your room, obviously the first thing you would do is go over and talk to him…' The fact that he uses the word 'obviously' here is a clue to his natural instinct to act to make people feel happier. These interactions with strangers who become his regulars (in large part because of his caring, friendly hospitality) make him feel great about himself, give him 'loads of energy', and are his greatest reward in his role at Costa: 'I just can't wait every day to see specific people coming in, make them a coffee, make jokes with them, make them laugh and smile… it makes my mood really… My customers aren't just customers, I feel them like my own people…'

What are you like as a person, and what are your interests outside of work?

I'm Greek and it probably explains a lot. I'm really into culture. I love travelling, reading, theatre, arts… everything. Holiday for me isn't about being by a pool, it's all about the sightseeing and going to museums. I'm into music, I used to work as a singer. I'm a very positive person (but I can be really grumpy too!), and I'm adventurous and full of energy, I have to do something all the time, like taking five hours to clean the house just because I'm bored… I do that! I'm sociable and outgoing, but sometimes I just need to be alone with my books and don't want anyone to disturb me. If I want to do something, I'll do it and I don't care what people say… I'm very stubborn.

Tell me about your career, before you started working in hospitality

I was born and raised in our family business. My dad used to own a café/restaurant. It was a very successful one. It was literally underneath the Parthenon in Athens. My mum used to take me there, so I used to spend many hours of my life sitting at a table there playing, so I was always part of that business. But at school I was into sports and I started in table tennis when I was 4. I got into the national team of Greece and then I was in the 2004 Olympics (I didn't do very well, but I was there!). Growing up, all I wanted was to become a professional player and I was doing really well, but I had an injury which forced me to stop playing… so at age 18 I had to change my plans for the future. I trained as a physiotherapist, not because I liked the idea, but because my coach from the team thought it would be a good thing for me to do, as it was a rising profession that could keep me close to my sport and team. And my parents liked the idea, so I did it. I enjoyed studying it and got my Bachelor with very high grades. But when I started actually doing it in my first paid job (I was 20 then), it was not what I expected. I hated myself for doing it! I was in a very small gym with basic machines and I had to work with very old people who had injuries or back pain, and I had to show them what to do to improve their movement or strengthen their muscles. I know I did a good job for those people, but for me, just standing there, giving them orders about what to do, being paid loads of money for doing it, it just felt wrong. I felt that really anyone could do what I was doing, just showing them a simple, obvious exercise. These people were in need, in pain, and I felt I was doing something that anybody could tell them. I felt like I was taking advantage of them. It's not that physiotherapy is wrong, but in some countries (and it was so in Athens), you're not allowed to touch the patients so all you can do is show them what to do. I hated it. The other part of the physio's job is massage, and I loved that part, actually using touch to make people feel better. I still do that part now, I have my own massage bed. But at the time, you didn't really have a choice, and I didn't have the opportunity to do massage in my job. So, then I tried to follow my other big passion, singing, to be a professional singer. It was great, but the money is not good and I supported myself by working in a florist and in a small supermarket as a cashier. At that point I decided to come to the UK.

What was it like being a square peg in a round hole?

When I was working as a physiotherapist, I had to drag myself into work every day. It didn't feel nice. I was dealing with sick people, people in pain, and they could be grumpy. Even though my job in Costa is probably more stressful than the physio job (you're dealing with a massive queue of people not just one person at a time, for example), working as a physio drained me more than working in Costa. It really drained me. Yes you can try to joke with the physio clients, but you never know how they are going to take it. I never felt good about myself, or rewarded, when I went home at the end of the day.

[There follows an aside that came up when Strati was answering this question. I am including it because I think it demonstrates his caring nature and offers an interesting insight into his character. It also shows that he can feel fulfilment in a caring role in the 'health service' if there is opportunity for real connection with the 'client', as opposed to the physio job, where that opportunity for human connection seemed to him to be missing.]

I forgot to mention that when I was working at the station café, I also worked as a carer for an old man who lived near to the station. All I had to do was call in after my shift, make him a cup of tea and give him his dinner, give him his medicine, put him to bed and lock the door. I was doing that for three years and I have to say that that was rewarding. Many times I refused to accept payment, even though it was a job, because it just felt wrong. This man, he had no family, all he had was two people going in, one in the morning to give him his breakfast and lunch, and me. He was a very clever man, he used to be a science Professor at Solent University, he'd had a very interesting life. He was really open with me, told me stories about his life, his travels to Asia, Latin America… I felt like he was like a grandfather to me after three years, he taught me many things, and every time after I left his house I felt really good because I'd done something really good for a really good man. When he passed away, I refused to take my pay because he had become my friend, it didn't feel right to take money from a friend. When an old person who is about to die wants you to be part of their life, that felt really good to me. Those kinds of rewards, they're more important than money.

How did you make the transition into hospitality?

When I arrived in the UK, I got a job in a coffee shop in Southampton at the central railway station. I started as a waiter and got promoted twice in one year. It felt like home and I can say that I did a good job. I knew exactly what I was doing, I was born into hospitality, I didn't need the training, I loved that I had lots of regular customers and I knew exactly what the drink was, what they were going to order, if they were going to pay cash or card. I just had this relationship with the customers. I knew them. Even though I was struggling, working loads of hours on the minimum wage, I didn't want to leave. I felt secure and comfortable in the environment. My manager was lovely and helped me with many things in my life, and when she left and I felt the new manager was lazy – I can't deal with lazy people because it seems unfair. I applied for Costa and now I'm working as the Assistant Manager there.

Being in a job that feels right for you, what's that like?

Well first of all the salary is great. Anyone who says money isn't important is lying! Costa is a very good brand and having that on my CV is very good for me. And the way the company operates means that I can get promoted, maybe become manager or even higher than a manager. They take the staff from the bottom right through to the top – I really like that. Then the job, I really like being in hospitality. I like serving people. I like having a chat with people, trying to make their day, having a joke with them. I like having regular customers, I look forward to them coming in. I like socializing with the customers, people you don't really know, but you feel you do know them. To have relationships with people who come back in especially to see you, ask about you and chat with you, it's rewarding, it makes you feel good. There are some issues with the job, my colleagues are much younger than me, so I find it quite difficult to build friendships with them, but the parts of the job I like mean I will keep doing it.

What do you think you do that makes you really good at your job? What energizes you about it? What do you love the most?

Even if I didn't like the job, I'd do it well because I'd put the effort in, it's my job and I want to do it right. But, to be honest, I don't think you can do something really well if you don't like it. Like when I was a physio, I did a good job but I wasn't excellent at it, I didn't want to be excellent, because deep down I didn't care about it. In the shop [Costa] I put my smile on, even if it's a difficult day, have a chat with my customers, with my colleagues, try and make a child laugh or smile at me, and the reason I'm trying to be good at it is because I like it. There's been many times when I've gone into work a bit moody, or there's a challenge with a colleague like someone's called in sick, and someone chats with me or gives me a smile back, or I see my regulars coming in, and it gives me loads of energy. I know I keep saying that, but having those people that I know, even though I don't really know them, and actually, I don't really want to know them outside work – sometimes they ask me to do something outside of work, but I don't really want to because I just want them to be the part of my job that actually makes me feel good... it's not the same if one of my best friends comes in to the coffee shop, I would be happy to see them, but it wouldn't give me the same energy or attitude, it wouldn't make me so happy as a 'stranger' that I have a chat with. I just can't wait every day to see specific people coming in, make them a coffee, make jokes with them, make them laugh and smile... it makes my mood really. It's the most important thing. I don't know what makes me really good at connecting with my customers, but I know I feel really comfortable in the environment, I spend more hours there than in my house, it feels like being home, I feel really confident and I know exactly what I have to do, I know everything in there. So, when I see people coming in it's like I welcome them into my environment, like they are my guests and I have to make sure that everything is alright for them – as if you were having a party in your home. If you saw someone on his own in the corner of your room, obviously the first thing you would do is go over and talk to him, make sure he is OK, try and make him a bit happier, introduce him to some other people, see how his day was, make him more comfortable… and it's what I do. My favourite part of the day is when it's my turn to go and make sure the tables are clean. I mean, you don't just go and clear the tables, you chat to the people, ask them how is their day, how was the coffee, how was their food… it's just like having a party and you are taking care of your guests. My customers aren't just customers, I feel them like my own people now. I want to go and talk to them.

Looking back over your life, were there any early signs that seem to make sense now? Were there things you loved doing, or did people say things about you?

I think that one of the reasons I'm so sociable and I'm open with people, is that I have two brothers and two sisters. I was born and raised in a house with seven people living there all the time. I think it's more like a need for me to be with people and chat with people, rather than it just happening [due to circumstance]. I mean, since I moved to the UK, I've lived with my best friend (since we were very young in Greece together), but I feel lonely. I have loads of friends, I've always got people around me… but it's not a house with seven people in it! It feels wrong! I've always had people to talk to. Of course we all have moments when we want to be on our own, but in general, 90 per cent of the day, I want to have loads of people around me. It makes me happy and makes me feel 'not lonely'!

What do you think is important for you and others about being in work you love?

Well looking back at the physio job, I don't think any one of those clients would come back to ask for me! I did a good job, but I never went the extra mile. I did the job I had to do and when the hours were up, I left. In Costa you could say that the job is make the drink, take the money, off they go… but I try not to do that, I do go the extra mile, go out there, chat to them, take something extra to them — I had a couple the other day, they are regulars and the woman told me it was their 30th wedding anniversary; I got a cake, put cream on the top, made a heart with chocolate sprinkles and took it to them and wished them happy anniversary. They are a part of my daily routine and I like doing stuff to make them happy, I want to make them happy. I like it! I know they will come back and ask about me if they don't see me, or they will ask me how is my family in Greece because they know I'm Greek, or how was my last trip to Spain because they know I went to Spain. Because I like my job, I go the extra mile, and that affects my customers because they will come back for me. Not for the coffee or for Costa, but they will come back for me.

How does your experience affect how you recruit/treat/coach your employees? And what advice would you give to other employers about people being in a role that's right for them?

When I recruit people – I get loads of CVs every day, and actually I'm interviewing tomorrow – I don't really care about the CV, I just call them all in for an interview in one day. I chat to each person for 10 minutes and I try to see if they have the things that really matter in hospitality: being smiley, being kind, being a nice person in general. Knowing how to make coffees and how to serve coffees, I don't really care about, because you can teach that. You can't teach them to be nice or to be good people to be around, or to have a good mood or aura in general. Anyone can work in Costa as long as they are kind, smiley and have a good aura. I think it should be the same in any job, although obviously you can't be an architect if you haven't been trained as an architect, but if you love to dance, you can dance, and you may never have been formally taught to dance. In many jobs it's the attitude that's really, really important.

What advice would you give your younger self about your career?

Be more confident and don't give up. Especially after my injury, when I was a teenager, I couldn't imagine myself doing anything else other than table tennis. I was so desperate but actually everything just worked out, and now I'm more positive about my future than ever. So, just be patient, and positive.

What's it been like to talk about this with me?

I enjoyed it! Many of those questions I've never thought about before. I found out stuff about myself. It is a bit like psychology isn't it? I feel like I've just had a session [laughs]!

Lynne Stainer: from Accident Claims Negotiator/Manager to Florist (own business)

Lynne is 52. Until the age of 42 when she was offered redundancy, she worked as an Insurance Claims Consultant for a large multi-national insurer, where she had always envisaged she would have the 'job for life' that was the goal of many of the baby-boomer generation. She loved the variety in her work, the investigative research, and the relationships she built with her clients and teams, and felt that she had a lot to offer right up until the time she left the insurance industry. She didn't feel like a square peg in a round hole because she enjoyed aspects of her job. But, she became increasingly frustrated by company restructuring and policies that fragmented the 'cradle to grave' method of managing claims and the 'investigation through to result' process that she believed in and enjoyed; in the end, the environment she found herself in did not allow her to sufficiently play to her strengths and compromised her values. Lynne has an innate desire to put good into the world, and she felt the compensation culture around insurance to be wrong. As a florist, she is able to see her projects through from start to finish, enjoys the varied nature of her work, the relationships she builds with her brides to develop their wedding schemes, and the fact that she creates beautiful designs from nature, which she loves. Most importantly, she is now able to use her strengths of being able to visualize things and convey her ideas to others so that they can imagine them too. Floristry lets her play to these strengths *and* to her creativity and ability to know what looks right. Lynne now knows that she is putting goodness into the wedding days of her brides, feels valued for who she really is, and is fulfilled and happy in a job she truly loves.

What are you like as a person, and what are your interests outside of work?

I'm very down to earth and straightforward. People would describe me as quite calm and easy going. It takes a lot to wind me up! I love dancing and anything to do with nature… walking and gardening. I'm a really honest person, I'll always tell the truth or speak up, even though I'm naturally diplomatic. I'm sensitive and intuitive, I instinctively know when something is wrong or something is right. I'm a logical and very analytical person. And I've got quite a low boredom threshold, I like variety.

Tell me about your career, before you started working in floristry

When I was at school, if you were in any way academic you'd be directed towards a more academic kind of career. Anything vocational wasn't explored in any shape or form. A 'job for life' was the goal. I had an interest in the law so I went on to do law and economics at A level. My parents weren't very supportive of a university education, so I needed to find work at 18. I worked in a bank for a year, but it was just process after process, there was no room for thought, it wasn't challenging... quite boring. So I moved into insurance claims and worked for the same large multi-national insurer for the next 23 years.

For a long time the job was interesting and I liked the variety. I did all local authority claims, no matter what the class of business (motor, landlord and tenant, employer liability, land charges, building control... you name it, I did it). I became a 'team leader' and had my own selection of clients. At that time, relationship with the client was very important and I liked that, making sure my clients were happy, visiting them to keep them informed, and investigating and negotiating claims. It was a very wide-ranging job, which I liked, and it included training new team members.

Then the organization was taken over. I was given the opportunity of a big promotion, which I went for, and by that time I was the most senior or 'technical' – meaning my ability to investigate and negotiate a claim – person in our office, responsible for claims of £250,000 and upwards and for the technical claims handling standards of all claims handlers in the office (over 100 people). This training element was a huge part of my role and I had a team of other senior claims negotiators to help me with it.

Under the new system, all claims of over £25,000 were handled by my team from cradle to grave (a methodology I believed in), but below that, all claims were split into different processes handled by different teams. These teams had all been set different objectives or key performance indicators. Team managers were picked primarily for their soft or people skills, rather than for their claims knowledge or experience. Some team managers and members had claims knowledge to varying degrees, but as time went on de-skilling became inevitable as people left and new, often less experienced, people came in. The underlying belief was that technical claims people lacked soft or people skills and that good claims knowledge was not always necessary to be a good team manager. The problem was, however, that without good claims knowledge it wasn't always possible to understand the implications of the decisions being made or the objectives being set. It was my job to strengthen and improve claims knowledge throughout the whole office, but the whole set up was having the opposite effect – it was very frustrating for me. To compound this, teams were often set key performance indicators that were in conflict with the goals of other teams and/or that compromised their ability to handle claims to a good standard. The de-skilling resulted in high levels of claims leakage (claims were costing a lot more than they should) and poor customer satisfaction. The set-up often put good claims handling into direct conflict with other management objectives, often with expensive results. Trying to put right what was going wrong was often a thankless and soul-destroying task. This was the final phase of my career in insurance.

What was it like being a square peg in a round hole?

I don't think I ever consciously felt like a square peg in a round hole. I think I had a tremendous amount to offer in my career, even at the end. But, [the management] saw what they wanted to see and there was much more to me that they ignored. I needed my managers to listen to me. I had ideas and was open to ideas but they took the view that if you were a 'technical consultant' you'd been around a long time, and would be closed to new ideas. I felt strongly that the stereotype they had in their minds didn't apply to me.

Also, I've since learned that to feel happy in my career, I have to feel that I'm doing some good. And the truth is that a compensation culture actually does nobody any good at all. You see greed, victim mentality, self-pity, pure fraud... all in attempt to get more money. People don't see how harmful that is to themselves. If people focus on their symptoms and how bad they feel, psychologically they accept that as the truth and they become far more injured or in pain than they need to be. It does absolutely nobody any good whatsoever. I think at the end of my career in insurance, the need to do good probably began to be more important to me. I was starting to rebel, I was feeling old, tired and cynical, and I wanted a change.

The only part of the job I enjoyed by then was training others, because I felt I was doing some good there, but otherwise I wasn't getting any personal satisfaction, there was no buzz. I was stressed. I'm a very sensitive person so people's comments and the political games would affect me; it was hard for me not to speak out. I would have to say something if I thought what was being suggested was a bad idea (even though I was known for my diplomacy), but my suggestions were often dismissed, so it made me feel misunderstood, wrongly criticized, feel 'What's the point?', even though I'm not like that, so I kept going anyway. I felt almost insulted by some of the games being played. I felt I was fighting a very hard battle, and doing it on a daily basis. The right thing to do in the end was to walk away.

How did you make the transition to floristry?

Throughout the whole country, the insurance industry was shrinking, and a decision was made to close the office I worked in and we were all served with redundancy notices. There were opportunities to move to a different office, and I was told that the experience I had was more or less unheard of. I would have been quite attractive on the open market. But the opportunities in the south of England had decreased and I didn't love the job enough to want to move north or to London or anywhere else.

I had compulsory careers counselling, and there were a couple of defining moments in that for me. The counsellor asked, 'You've got about 23 years of your working life left, is this how you want to spend them?' It was a real wake up call. There was a realization deep down inside that this was my *life* we were talking about. There was no going back from that moment. Then it was about deciding what to do next, and that was a long and painful process for me, because if you're 42 and you've spent 23 years in a culture where validation has always come from outside (in performance reviews, appraisals and so on), you don't actually really know yourself. I'd accepted other people's view of me, and it was always in a work-related context.

So, I was given Richard Bolles' book *What Color is Your Parachute?* to work through, and two of the exercises in there, in particular, were responsible for the changes in my life.

First, I was asked to come up with five of my life's greatest achievements, with the criteria that I had to have enjoyed and have been proud of each one. I can't tell you how much I cried over this exercise, because I could think of absolutely nothing. It took me about two weeks to come up with anything, and when I did I realized that the things had nothing to do with insurance at all.

The other thing, from the book, was that you had to come up with one truth about yourself, that no matter what anyone says or what happens, it's unshakeable, you never deviate from this truth. And, the thing I came up with was that, visually, I know what works. I know what looks right and what doesn't, and nobody will ever change my mind on that. My problem was understanding what that could ever possibly have to do with a job in insurance or the corporate world.

So, coming back to the greatest achievements. At one time in my career, as a team-building exercise, I and my team had the chance to do a challenge together. It was to design and create a garden for a special-needs school. I love gardening and nature. We built a sensory garden that would also teach the children about life, with the changing seasons. Even the Hampshire landscape architect who visited said it was amazing. They gave me a 'thank you book', it makes me cry just thinking about it… pupils, teachers, saying how much they loved the garden. It was the first time I'd felt truly appreciated in more than 20 years.

Next I had to think about why I'd enjoyed my great achievements, and I saw that I loved to see a project from beginning to end, that I'd enjoyed investigative research, talking to people on a one-to-one, finding out their ideas, adding in my own research to see what could fit, and then the end result. I asked people for ideas for possible careers and perhaps the closest we came up with was landscape gardening, but it still didn't feel quite right. Then one day on a plane to Argentina for a needed break, my friend said to me, 'What about floristry?' It was a light bulb moment. I instinctively knew it was right. Based on all the work I'd done up to that point, it logically made sense to me. Everything clicked into place.

Being in a job that feels right for you, what's that like?

I work alone now, I have my own business doing bespoke wedding and event flowers. Ninety-nine per cent of my work is weddings. I work with the bride… her input is more important than mine, her preferences, I'm adding the finishing professional touch, but also adding in my ideas, to create the look that she wants. We have a consultation together, and in about two hours we'll have the complete scheme planned… bouquet, button holes, table centres, church flowers. I'm different to other florists in that all my work is bespoke. I love that no design is ever really repeated because everybody is different, and I think that is how it should be.

I like the constant change in my work, the short-term projects. I've done all kinds of venues from ferries to Highclere Castle, contemporary boutique hotels, rustic barns… and I love that variety. It's great! I do a wedding one week and then I'm on to the next. New ideas, new people, new colours, new flowers, different style, different venue… I feel energized. I love it that people say to me, 'It was fantastic coming to see you because of all the ideas!' At the end of my career in insurance, people thought that all my ideas were rooted in the past… the complete opposite to how I now see I really am.

At the end of a wedding day, it feels amazing. To be honest it takes me a bit of time to 'come down'. It actually generates energy, which gives you confidence to perhaps try some new or different things, it's like an ever increasing circle. I've got more adventurous as I've gone on.

Working with nature is very therapeutic for me too. There's nothing more healing than nature, you've got to respect nature and work with it, its variations... to transform something natural and create something beautiful, it's an incredible feeling. The only thing I ever get stressed about is when I've got to be somewhere with flowers and I get stuck in a traffic jam!

I feel happy and fulfilled now and completely at peace with who I am and what I do — not something I ever felt before in my life. I no longer dread being asked what I do for a living — claims negotiators are right up there with tax inspectors in the popularity stakes!

What do you think you do that makes you really good at your job? What energizes you about it? What do you love the most?

I love everything about my job now! I love it when a bride gets excited, the moment when she can see it all. I see that little spark of excitement in her eyes and she's like, 'Oh my God, that's going to look amazing!' I love that moment. Not everyone can visualize things, but I can, so it's my job to show where I'm coming from and convey my ideas back to the bride. And I have to get to know the bride, know her tastes... and maybe they don't really know their floral style at all, so I have to do a little bit of digging to get there. That's interesting and challenging for me! I'll be aiming to reflect the bride rather than me, but the designs will look like they've been made by someone who knows what they're doing, and that's why they've chosen me.

Then there's the moment of creation. When you design something, the initial idea is a little bit loose, you have an overall effect that you want to achieve. You start with an idea in the back of your mind, but it hasn't come to life, it starts to live when you begin to make it. And it almost has a personality of its own then, because you've combined the essence of the bride, nature and a little bit of yourself. I love that.

I'm good at what I do because I can visualize things, and also because of my attention to detail (the same thing that made me good at managing insurance claims!). And because of my ability to listen, my ability to hear other people's ideas... people are infinitely interesting to me. Because I'm very sensitive, if a bride isn't happy with an idea, I'm going to know it. And I'm not afraid to say something about it, but I'm diplomatic, so if I see a hesitation, I'll check with her and she'll be honest with me because I'm open and relaxed about it. I'm not in any way fixed in my ideas, I can go with the moment.

On the day, it can be stressful for the bride, but I am calm and reassuring, and I know I help make their day perfect. One of them even nominated me for a wedding industry award. I get so many lovely emails, and people come a long way to see me because my work is so different. They know they are getting something unique that reflects them. When I see the look of joy on a bride's face, it's lovely, it's just perfect.

Looking back over your life, were there any early signs that seem to make sense now? Were there things you loved doing, or did people say things about you?

When I told my mum that I was going to do floristry, she said, 'Did you know that when you were four, you could name every single flower in the garden?' Apparently, I used to follow her around the garden endlessly asking 'Tissit?' (the nearest I could get to 'What is it?')!

I'm told I always had an exceptional eye for detail and especially colour. I was very particular about my clothes, from a very early age – the colours and styles had to go together. Actually, this whole thread runs through almost my entire family in their various professions, and they also all loved plants and gardens and were keen gardeners. So I think I have genetics to thank for a lot! Funnily enough though, I wasn't considered good at art at school, I was never able to draw, it was by far my worst subject. I do remember one pottery class, though, I made a dinosaur, I can still see it now and I loved it. Whatever I was making, it had to be beautiful! It didn't have to be 'pretty' but it had to have something special about it.

I always preferred to listen and think about what was being said than to talk, so had the reputation for being quiet. Yet, an early teacher told my parents 'she may not say a lot but make absolutely no mistake, it is all going in' – an early sign of my need to think and analyse everything, so I can make my own mind up.

On the caring [doing good for others] side, I am told I took great care of my mother when she was pregnant with my sister. I was just three but always remembered a plain biscuit helped morning sickness, so as soon as I saw any sign of her feeling unwell, off I would trot to get her a biscuit. I used to love looking after my sister when she was born, too.

What do you think is important for you and others about being in work you love?

I think it changes your life in ways that you can't even begin to possibly imagine. If you're in work that you love, you'll be surrounded by this positive energy and that will have an effect on everyone you come into contact with and every experience that you will ever have. It will improve all your relationships, and even the way that you think. There's nothing that it won't touch.

What advice would you give to other employers about people being in a role that's right for them?

I think that if organizations could be a bit more relaxed about who does what duty, if they could look at the positions they have and allow people to play to their strengths, they could build world-beating teams. People have different natural abilities and strengths, but in big corporations, you often end up with people struggling to succeed in certain parts of their role, while the person sitting next to them might have been born to do the job, but is not given the chance. Why not have more flexibility in terms of who does what, and see if you can actually create something amazing?

If an organization looks for a broad range of competencies and insists everyone has them, they are in danger of heading towards mediocrity. I believe the best teams, those that really are capable of exceptional results, will be made of people who excel at a narrower range of skills individually; but, with the right blend of individuals all playing to their individual strengths yet working together, there is little limit to what they could achieve. You wouldn't turn down Lionel Messi as a team member because he wasn't much good in goal! If you've got the chance to recruit a 'flare player' with a strength you really need for a particular job, don't ignore them because they don't match the 'norm' you have traditionally gone for. Have more of an open mind.

What advice would you give your younger self about your career?

I would encourage her to try and get to know herself a little bit better and do the things she loves. I wouldn't have wanted to be without the experiences I had, but I think it's best if the head and heart are in agreement about a career. I think the heart can't always be happy if the head takes control. There was a bit of head and heart conflict when I started out in floristry because I know that to start your own business you need to have experience in the business you want to be in and I didn't, and I was deeply unhappy about that, even though my heart was telling me to go for it. It's why I worked part time first and slowly built things up, as I felt more comfortable with that. Ultimately, though, I'd say, if you want to be happy, take your head into account, but don't ignore your heart, and don't waste a life doing something you don't believe in or that makes you unhappy

What's it been like to talk about this with me?

It's been fine, it's been lovely. Hard in places because some of it is a long time ago and it's tough to be so open and honest about some things, but I have been. It's been quite moving, hasn't it? Talking about it, I feel that I don't regret any of my experiences and I feel very lucky to have found what I have.

Reference

Bolles, R (2013) *What Color is Your Parachute? A practical manual for job-hunters and career-changers*, Ten Speed Press, Berkeley, CA

FURTHER READING

Books

Boniwell, I (2006) *Positive Psychology in a Nutshell: A balanced introduction to the science of optimal functioning*, Personal Well-Being Centre, London

Buckingham, M and Clifton, DO (2001) *Now Discover Your Strengths*, The Free Press, New York

Buckingham, M and Coffman, C (1999) *First Break All The Rules*, Simon and Schuster Business Books, London

Clifton, DO and Nelson, P (1996) *Soar with Your Strengths*, Bantam Doubleday Dell Publishing Group, New York

Coffman, C and Gonzalez-Molina, G (2002) *Follow This Path: How the world's greatest organizations drive growth by unleashing human potential*, Warner Books Inc, New York

Cooperrider, DL and Whitney D (2005) *Appreciative Inquiry: A positive revolution in change*, Berrett Koehler Publishers, Inc., San Francisco, CA

Csikszentmihalyi, M (2002) *Flow: The classic work on how to achieve happiness*, Random House Group, London

Drucker, P (2006) *The Effective Executive*, revised edition, HarperBusiness, New York

Grenville-Cleave, B (2012) *Introducing Practical Psychology: A practical guide*, Icon Books Ltd, London

Linley, A (2008) *Average to A+: Realising strengths in yourself and others*, CAPP Press, UK

Linley, PA and Joseph, S (eds) (2004) *Positive Psychology in Practice*, Wiley, New Jersey

Roarty, M and Toogood, K (2014) *The Strengths-Focused Guide to Leadership*, FT Publishing International, London

Seligman, M (2003) *Authentic Happiness: Using the new positive psychology to realise your potential for lasting fulfilment*, Nicholas Brealey, Boston, MA

Articles

Ancona, D, Malone, TW, Orlikowski, WJ and Senge, P (2007) In praise of the incomplete leader, *Harvard Business Review*, 85 (2), pp 92–100

Baumeister, RF, Bratslavsky, E, Finkenauer, C, Vohs, KD (2001) Bad is stronger than good, *Review of General Psychology*, 5, pp 323–70

Brim, B and Asplund, J (2009) Driving engagement by focusing on strengths, Gallup. Available from: businessjournal.gallup.com/content/124214/Driving-Engagement-Focusing-Strengths.aspx (accessed 10 December 2015)

Buckingham, M (2005) What great managers do, *Harvard Business Review*. Available from: https://hbr.org/2005/03/what-great-managers-do (accessed 10 December 2015)

Corporate Leadership Council (2002) *Building the High-Performance Workforce*, Corporate Leadership Council, Washington DC

Fleming, JH, Coffman, C and Harter, JK (2005) Manage your human sigma *Harvard Business Review*. Available from: https://hbr.org/2005/07/manage-your-human-sigma (accessed 10 December 2015)

Goffee, R and Jones, G (2013) Creating the best workplace on earth, *Harvard Business Review*. Available from: https://hbr.org/2013/05/creating-the-best-workplace-on-earth (accessed 10 December 2015)

Larsen, TA, Smith, NK and Cacioppo, JT (1998) Negative information weighs more heavily on the brain: The negativity bias in evaluative categorizations, *Journal of Personality and Social Psychology*, 75 (4), pp 887–900

Sorenson, S (2013) How employee engagement drives growth, *Gallup Business Journal*, 20 June. Available from: www.gallup.com/businessjournal/163130/employee-engagement-drives-growth.aspx (accessed 10 December 2015)

Tucker, L (1999) Connections between neuroscience and the theory of multiple intelligences: Implications for education, *Biology*, 202. Available from: serendip.brynmawr.edu/bb/neuro/neuro99/web3/Tucker.html (accessed 13 November 2015)

Reports

Future of Work Research Consortium (2015) *The Gen Z Survey*, Future of Work Research Consortium (FoW), London

North, D (2013) *Welcome to the Strengths Revolution: An in-depth study into the benefits of strengths-based recruitment*, Engaging Minds, London

INDEX

Note: page numbers in *italic* indicate figures or tables